Science Education for Gifted Learners

Why are the brightest students increasingly turning away from the sciences?

How can science teaching offer differentiated learning experiences suitable for even the most exceptional students?

In today's technological society schools have an obligation to develop and challenge all learners, yet it has become clear that in science many of the most able students are not being stretched.

Science Education for Gifted Learners examines official recommendations and gives practical advice on how to use the most effective strategies in today's classroom. Science teachers reading this book will be equipped to encourage and support their most able pupils, as the contributors explore the wider debates about the provision for learners who are labelled 'gifted' and 'exceptionally able'.

This accessible yet authoritative text addresses key issues such as:

- What we mean by gifted and able children
- What to do about the gifted children that slip through the net
- Providing challenging science teaching through modelling and talk
- 'Multiple exceptionality' – high ability scientists with learning difficulties
- Students whose exceptional abilities are focused on limited aspects of the subject
- Identifying gifted students without excluding those with latent abilities.

This invaluable companion reiterates the principles of good science teaching which can help teachers ensure that *all* their students are engaged and challenged.

Keith S. Taber is a senior lecturer in science education at the University of Cambridge.

D0302354

Science Education for Gifted Learners

Edited by
Keith S. Taber

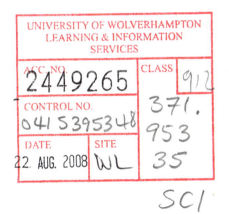
 Routledge
Taylor & Francis Group

LONDON AND NEW YORK

First published 2007
by Routledge
2 Park Square, Milton Park, Abingdon, Oxon, OX14 4RN

Simultaneously published in the USA and Canada
by Routledge
270 Madison Ave, New York, NY 10016

Routledge is an imprint of the Taylor & Francis Group, an informa business

© 2007 Keith S. Taber for selection and editorial matter; individual
chapters, the contributors

Typeset in Sabon by Florence Production Ltd, Stoodleigh, Devon
Printed and bound in Great Britain by Antony Rowe Ltd, Chippenham, Wiltshire

British Library Cataloguing in Publication Data
A catalogue record for this book is available from the British Library

Library of Congress Cataloging in Publication Data
Taber, Keith
  Science education for gifted learners/Keith S. Taber
       p. cm.
    Includes bibliographical references and index
  1. Science–Study and teaching.   2. Gifted children–Identification.
  3. Gifted children–Education.   I. Title
  Q181.T215 2007
  507.1–dc22   2007002175

ISBN10: 0–415–39533–X (hbk)
ISBN10: 0–415–39534–8 (pbk)
ISBN10: 0–203–96204–4 (ebk)

ISBN13: 978–0–415–39533–5 (hbk)
ISBN13: 978–0–415–39534–2 (pbk)
ISBN13: 978–0–203–96204–6 (ebk)

Contents

Figures

Tables

Contributors

Steve Alsop is Associate Professor and Associate Dean, Faculty of Education (coordinating research and continuing professional development) at York University, Canada. He taught science in secondary and primary schools in the UK before moving into teacher education and research. Previously, Steve coordinated the Centre for Learning and Research in Science Education at Roehampton University, where he currently holds the position of Senior Honorary Research Fellow. Steve's research interests are within three broad themes: science education and effect; teacher education; and education for sustainability. He has published widely and his recent books include *Analysing Exemplary Science Teaching* (Open University Press) and *Beyond Cartesian Dualism: Encountering Affect in the Teaching and Learning of Science* (Kluwer Press).

Richard K. Coll holds a Ph.D. in Chemistry from the University of Canterbury and an Ed.D. in Science Education from Curtin University. He is Associate Professor of Science Education at the University of Waikato. His research interests are concerned with scientific literacy and the use of analogies and mental models in science teaching.

Vivien Corrie is currently Assistant Principal at Linton Village College, Cambridgeshire, as Director of Teaching and Learning. She has been teaching science at secondary level for ten years. While she was Head of Science at this high performing school, Vivien developed the teaching and learning of thinking skills as a key strategy within the department for engaging and motivating able learners, as well as raising pupil attainment at all levels.

John K. Gilbert is currently Professor Emeritus of Education at the University of Reading, and Editor-in-Chief of the International Journal of Science Education. He took a B.Sc. (Leicester), a D.Phil. (Sussex), and a Postgraduate Certificate in Education (London), all in chemistry. He then taught chemistry in secondary (high) schools before moving into science education research at both school and university level. His early work on students' 'alternative conceptions'/'misconceptions' has evolved into that on models and modelling in both formal and informal science education. In 2001, he was the recipient of the award for 'Distinguished Contributions to Science Education through Research' from the USA-based National Association for Research in Science Teaching.

Andrew Grevatt is an Advanced Skills Teacher in Science at Uckfield Community Technology College, East Sussex. He is a member of the Cams Hill Science Consortium. In his ninth year of teaching secondary science, Andrew is currently studying for a part-time Professional Doctorate in Education at the University of Sussex. Andrew's research interests are in progression and literacy in science and teachers as researchers.

Vanessa Kind is Course Leader for the Postgraduate Certificate in Education (school-based) and Postgraduate Certificate in the Practice of Education in the School of Education at the University of Durham. Prior to her appointment at Durham Vanessa was head teacher of an international primary-middle school in Trondheim, Norway, having previously taught in further and secondary education, and been Lecturer in Science Education at the Institute of Education, University of London. Vanessa's research interests centre on post-16 science education, context-based science education, the development of science teachers' subject knowledge and pedagogical content knowledge and teachers' continuing professional development.

Ralph Levinson is the Course Leader for the MA in Science Education at the University of London's Institute of Education. He taught science for twelve years in London comprehensive schools. His interests include the teaching of controversial and socio-scientific issues; the development of pedagogical content knowledge in pre-service science teachers; citizenship and science; arts and science; and the public understanding of science.

Matthew Newberry teaches at Cams Hill School, Fareham, Hampshire, and coordinates the Cams Hill Science Consortium. The consortium was formed in 2000, and is a partnership between Cams Hill School, science teachers at over 30 primary and secondary schools, the University of Reading and Science Advisors from Hampshire and West Sussex LEAs. Matthew was previously a member of the Advisory service in Hampshire.

Maria Helena Pedrosa de Jesus holds a Master's degree and a Ph.D. in Science Education from the University of East Anglia, and is currently Associate Professor at the Department of Didactics and Educational Technology, University of Aveiro, Portugal. Her main research interests are classroom based, both in higher and secondary education, looking at how questions promote active learning, critical thinking and the understanding of students' learning processes in science. Questions are also used for mentor training to promote critical reflection and professional development. She has been director of a Master's level course for those supporting trainee teachers for the last eleven years and she teaches on courses for intending and in-service teachers at Master's and undergraduate levels.

Fran Riga has taught science and mathematics (among other subjects), in South Africa, in an American international school in Greece, and in England. She is currently undertaking part-time doctoral research into student learning in astronomy, and is a part-time research assistant in the Faculty of Education at the University of Cambridge.

Phil Scott is Professor of Science Education and Head of Postgraduate Taught Courses at the University of Leeds, where he is also Director of the Centre for Studies in Science and Mathematics Education. His key interests are in physics and science education; teaching and learning science concepts in high schools; and the role of language in the acquisition of science concepts. He works with the White Rose University Consortium Science National and Regional Learning Centres. He has previously been Head of Physics, Head of Science and a senior teacher in West Yorkshire comprehensive schools.

Keith S. Taber is Senior Lecturer in Science Education at the University of Cambridge, and he is the Programme Manager for the part-time Ph.D. degree in Education. He previously taught science (mainly chemistry and physics) in schools and further education. He has been a Teacher Fellow of the Royal Society of Chemistry. He is the physics education tutor for the Postgraduate Certificate in Education, and teaches on the M.Phil in Educational Research. He supervises graduate students exploring aspects of teaching and learning in science. His own research has particularly concerned aspects of conceptual learning, progression and integration in science.

Mike Watts is Chair in Education and leads Education at Brunel University. He is responsible for developing teaching, research and consultancy in the School of Sport and Education. He teaches on postgraduate programmes with a special interest in enhancing learning and teaching. He researches classroom-based research projects in both formal and informal educational settings, evaluating the effects of policy and curriculum innovations on learning outcomes. He has conducted major studies of classroom inter-actions. His recent work looks at ways in which a learner's own questions can be used as a basis for enquiry-based teaching, ways in which feelings and emotions shape learning, and ways in which classroom technologies can be used to enhance learning processes. He is a passionate supporter of motorbikes and Welsh rugby.

Alan West is an experienced science teacher with wide knowledge of business education links gleaned through development and implementation of the National CREST Awards over a fourteen year period. His company,

Exscitec, provides enrichment opportunities on behalf of HEIs and education authorities to schools as a provider of STEM outreach activities for students of all ages; much of this work is with gifted and talented cohorts.

Carrie Winstanley is Principal Lecturer in Education at Roehampton University. She works with undergraduate and postgraduate students teaching a range of education courses, including general social psychology, philosophy of education, museum and gallery education and more specific work concerning children with different educational needs (particularly high ability and learning difficulties). She is interested in the ethics of provision for the able and critical evaluation of pedagogy for highly able children and empirical and theoretical research into 'gifted education'. With a decade of teaching experience in a range of schools, she is keen to keep up practice by running workshops and activities with highly able children.

Preface

This book is primarily intended to support teachers and schools in developing science provision to meet the needs of the most able students. The book derives from a series of seminars sponsored by the University of Cambridge's Faculty of Education on the theme of 'Meeting the Needs of the Most Able in Science', and most of the chapters derive from the Cambridge seminars.

> Consistently high-quality provision for gifted and talented pupils, for example in secondary schools, remains the exception rather than the rule.
> Bell 2004: 4

The impetus behind the seminars, and this book, was a belief (reinforced by the remark above of the Chief Inspector of Schools), that many of the secondary students who are most capable in science are not being sufficiently challenged, and so are failing to find the subject fascinating and exciting enough to want to continue to study science beyond the school leaving age. Of course, some students are keen to continue to study science (because or, or despite, their school science experiences), and some aspire to careers such as medicine or veterinary science where college-level study of science subjects is a pre-requisite. Yet, whereas science subjects may have at one time been widely considered (rightly or wrongly) to be especially suitable choices for the most able, this is no longer the case.

> You sort of research, and I find it quite interesting researching and again finding how things work and finding why they happened, and linking them between different . . . like interpretations, and other things, and at the moment we're linking it all together, so yeah, that's quite interesting.

It is not just that biology, chemistry and physics have to compete with 'new' fashionable college subjects such as business and finance, psychology or computer studies. Many students' experiences of the secondary curriculum suggest to them that intellectual stimulation is to be found elsewhere, in subjects such as history where there is time to critically explore issues and develop ideas about why things happen. In the humanities subjects students are challenged to be analytical, to evaluate evidence, to find a synthesis among disparate sources and ideas. I have used the quote above, from a 14-year-old in a top science set in a comprehensive school, in presentations to science teachers. This able student was explaining to me why he hoped to continue his study of history when he finished secondary school. The irony, of course, is that this is how science teachers might hope their able students perceive science!

As the 'Meeting the Needs of the Most Able' seminar series was based in Cambridge, and therefore attended by teachers, trainee teachers and researchers working in England, the English science curriculum and government policy provided the backdrop for the seminar series, and provides a context for many of the chapters in this book. That is not to suggest that we feel that the experience of gifted science students in England is atypical. Gifted students should be challenged and extended *whatever* the educational context – and the advice and ideas in this book are largely applicable regardless of the specifics of the local curriculum or school system. However as most (not all) of the authors are working in the English system, it is this context in which many of the examples discussed in the book are grounded. In particular, a concern about the amount of 'content' in the English National Curriculum for Science, and the consequences of this for classroom practice, was a key factor in initiating the seminar series. Much of the demand here is in terms of the quantity of material to be tackled, and certainly not the depth of understanding expected. Indeed, some of the representations of the science offered in the official curriculum do not encourage too much critical engagement.

When teachers are under pressure to 'cover' a syllabus and 'get results', and when they even suspect that students who appreciate the nuances and complexities of topics may be penalised in examinations (as the student who understands at a high level may not produce the 'stock' response assigned marks in the examiner's marking scheme), then the temptation to 'teach to the test' and encourage rote learning is strong. In England, teachers and schools tend to be judged in terms of the proportion of candidates able to achieve modest examination results. (The main published measure of a school's effectiveness is the percentage of students attaining five or more passes at grade C or above at the school leaving age – students attaining higher grades or passing more subjects provide no premium.) In such a climate, the need to challenge those expected to easily get the top grades may not be the highest priority.

Some readers will recognise these issues, and share the view that too often the standard school science fare does not really challenge the most able to develop their scientific thinking, their understanding of fundamental concepts, and their appreciation of science as a cultural activity and powerful knowledge-developing system.

Other readers may have more pragmatic reasons for referring to this book. In recent years the UK government (in common with others around the world) has recognised that the most able students are often not being fully developed in many schools, and has drawn attention to the issue, first in the inner cities, and now throughout the school system. New government policy has highlighted the issue of the education of the most able, what the UK government labels the 'gifted and talented', as something that schools *must* address and respond to. Schools are being asked to identify their most able students as *gifted* (in relation to academic subjects) and/or *talented* (in relation to creative subjects and sporting prowess), and to have policies in place to show the 'special needs' of this group are being taken into account in the planning and teaching of classes.

Head teachers and their management teams, governors, educational authority advisors, parents and official school inspectors, are among the interested parties who will be expecting to see evidence that the science department is identifying students 'gifted' in the subject, and providing them with appropriate science education. This book should prove very valuable to heads of science and science teachers looking for advice on how to meet the needs of their most able students.

This book offers a range of perspectives on how to make learning science more engaging and challenging for those students who are currently finding it lacks relevance or intellectual stimulation. The authors who have been invited to contribute to this volume are all known to hold expertise in some aspect of education of significance to teachers concerned about science provision for their most able students. Some of these experts have a particular interest in the education of the most able. Others are more concerned with approaches to making science education more relevant, more interesting and more challenging for all students: but approaches that have particular value in teaching the most able. Collectively they offer a vision of science education for gifted students.

Keith S. Taber, Cambridge, August 2006

Acknowledgements

This book derives from the Able Pupils Experiencing Challenging Science (APECS) Project, a collaborative project between the Universities of Cambridge, Reading and Roehampton (see www.educ.cam.ac.uk/apecs/).

This project was supported by the University of Cambridge Faculty of Education's Research and Development Fund, through the 'Meeting the Needs of the Most Able in Science' seminar series.

The editor is grateful for the comments and suggestions of four anonymous referees, who commented on the original book proposal for the publishers.

Fran Riga's careful reading and checking of the complete manuscript was very much appreciated.

Chapter 1

Science education for gifted learners?

Keith S. Taber

This book is about *science education for gifted learners*. Such a title implies that:

- We can identify groups of students that we might consider 'gifted'.
- Some particular brand or type of science education is best suited for these specific learners.

Neither of these assumptions would be universally shared. Therefore it is important to establish, at the outset, the understanding of some key issues that has informed the book. In this introductory chapter, therefore, I explore the intellectual landscape into which the later chapters will be located, each contributing something to the scenery. To do this, I address a number of core questions relating to the notion of 'science education for gifted and able learners':

- How valid is the notion of 'gifted learners'?
- How is the term 'gifted' used in this book?
- Why should we *expect* gifted learners to have 'special needs' in science?
- How can teachers identify gifted learners in science?
- What kind of science education meets the need of gifted learners of science?

These are 'big' questions, and this chapter will introduce the main issues and arguments, and establish a framework for reading the other, more detailed, contributions in this book. The last question, in particular, is explored in various forms throughout the book.

How valid is the notion of gifted learners?

The term 'gifted' (along with similar descriptors, such as 'exceptionally able') is commonly used in educational discourse, and along with related labels such as 'intelligent' and 'creative', tends to be well understood *in general terms* without there being a clear consensus of what *exactly* is being defined. Most teachers, and others working in education, would have a vague idea of what to expect of a gifted learner, without their necessarily being any detailed agreement between different users of the term (Maltby 1984).

It seems that there are at least three problematic aspects to the notion of a gifted learner in science:

- How gifted is gifted?
- How broad is the 'gift'?
- How fixed is the 'gift'?

There are no definitive answers to these questions: rather our answers depend on our *choice* of definition for the term.

How gifted is gifted?

Commonly, students are assigned to groupings such as gifted and able in terms of their ranking within a cohort. So, UK government policy (as of 2006) on 'gifted and talented' students refers to the *top* 5–10% of students:

> All schools are required to identify a gifted and talented pupil cohort comprising 5–10% of pupils in each relevant year group. These are pupils who achieve, or who have the ability to achieve, at a level significantly in advance of the average for their year group in their school.
>
> DfES 2004a: 25

Under this policy the 5–10% includes three groups of students: those with ability in one of the 'academic' subjects (the 'gifted'); those with talent in art, music, PE, sport or creative arts (the 'talented'); and those with 'all-round' ability (the gifted *and* talented!).

Collectively, the gifted and the talented (and the gifted *and* talented) are also referred to as 'the able' in some UK government documentation (DfES 2002a), where the label 'exceptionally able' is used for *the most able 1%* of the cohort *nationally*:

> This group includes a very few outstandingly able pupils, such as the boy aged seven who could write the caesium/water reaction balanced symbol equation and another of a similar age who described fusion in terms of the mass and atomic numbers of hydrogen and helium.
>
> DfES 2003: 4

Although this example is taken from a 2003 government initiative, it is reminiscent of work on gifted learners undertaken in the 1960s (before a focus on gifted learners became unfashionable). Fisher described how a group of gifted primary pupils (*c.* 10 year-olds) with an interest in science were able to discuss the gas laws:

> This desire to take an active part in discussion has led more recently to a consideration of the factors which affect the pressure of a gas, being treated in a semi-formal manner, and here was a powerful demonstration of the advanced ability to separate variables and exclude variables in the investigation of relationships. Preconceptions were dealt with in a more immediate manner and progress was very rapid; this topic involves mathematical concepts.
>
> Fisher 1969: 131

Definitions of 'gifted' etc. are clearly arbitrary to some extent, so – for example – one research study into giftedness used the term 'gifted' for the top 10% of the sample, 'highly gifted' for the top 5%, and finally, 'extremely gifted' for the top 2% (Heller 1996). Clearly, any definition that *implies* an objective scientific measure of giftedness, in terms of percentiles, is based on the assumption that students can be ranked along a single dimension. An obvious dimension to use here is 'intelligence', although that is itself a highly contested concept. Nonetheless, it is not unusual for giftedness to be defined in terms of attaining a certain cut-off on an IQ (intelligence quotient) test: e.g. the 3–4% of students having a measured IQ score of 130 (Montgomery 2003a).

There are well-established, and reliable, ways of measuring IQ that may make such an approach seem relatively attractive (see Chapter 3). However, reliability does not imply validity – just because IQ scores can be approximately reproduced on re-testing, that does not mean that IQ is a good indicator of what we might find it helpful to mean by giftedness. Indeed there are significant doubts about the IQ construct (e.g. Gould 1992).

How broad is the 'gift'?

It is generally recognised that IQ scores tend to correlate well with academic attainment, but there are major problems with using IQ as a means for identifying the gifted. It is likely that this correlation is largely an artefact of traditional notions of what academic study is about: that the types of items on IQ tests tend to test verbal and logical abilities that have traditionally been central to academic study and assessment (Gardner 1993), but may relate to a narrow definition of intelligence (cf. Sternberg *et al.* 2000). Although such a correlation offers some ability to predict academic success for students across much of the range of scores, it may have little to say about the exceptional abilities that gifted students can show (see for example Chapter 4 and Chapter 6).

One problem is that, if we are interested in exceptional individuals, their exceptionality may go beyond the abilities needed to do well on IQ tests.

Stepanek argues that: 'as the concept of intelligence becomes more fluid and multidimensional, the concept of giftedness also evolves' (1999: 6). For example, being gifted in science could be considered to be as much about being 'creative' as intelligent. Heller (1996) uses a multidimensional concept of giftedness (the 'Munich model', p. 44), where giftedness comprises:

- intelligence (intellect)
- creativity
- social competence
- musical ability
- psychomotor ability/practical intelligence.

According to Heller's research these five areas make up *independent* domains of giftedness, and few students are gifted in several of these distinct domains.

Sternberg (1993: 6–9) has proposed a 'pentagonal implicit theory' of giftedness, suggesting that a person has to meet five criteria to be judged as gifted:

- the excellence criterion (extremely good at something relative to peer group);
- the rarity criterion (showing a high level of an attribute that is rare among peers);
- the productivity criterion (the dimension of excellence must potentially lead to productivity);
- the demonstrability criterion (demonstrable through one or more valid tests); and
- the value criterion (the dimension of excellence must be a valued one in the society judging the person as gifted).

In Sternberg's model, giftedness is defined in terms of exceptional ability (relative to the rest of the population) that can be clearly demonstrated, and is able to lead to some tangible outcome. However, Sternberg sees 'giftedness' as relative in another sense as well: that we should only recognise giftedness in areas that are culturally valued (be that sprinting, taking free kicks in soccer, rapping, or building up profitable businesses). Sternberg's model resembles Gardner's (1997) analysis of what allows an individual such as Mozart or Virginia Wolf to be extraordinary enough to be judged a genius – that the individual may have exceptional talents, which relate to an existing domain of human activity (composing music, writing novels, etc.), and are recognised by those other individuals who at that time make up the 'field'. (For example, in Chapter 2, Gilbert and Newberry discuss Nobel Laureates – scientists receiving the ultimate recognition from their peers.)

One advantage of Sternberg's model is that he does not define giftedness in vague terms such as 'academic ability'. So using Sternberg's approach, *we may choose to* consider a student as gifted in terms of their ability to build circuits, visualise molecular structures, undertake accurate and precise titrations, develop scientific analogies, interpret complex graphical information, draw accurate scientific diagrams, mentally obtain order-of-magnitude mathematical solutions, or indeed *any* of the myriad skills that are valued in learning science.

This is important, as most science teachers are aware that the most able learners are not always exceptionally strong 'across the board' even within science, or within an individual science discipline such as chemistry. Ignoring this point can lead to both putting too much pressure on the nominated gifted students (see, for example, Chapter 4) in areas where they are not especially strong, and also ignoring the potential of other learners to work at very high levels on certain types of tasks.

How fixed is the gift?

One of the associations of the term 'gifted' is that it may seem to imply something innate: there at birth and giving the potential for achieving at exceptional levels. It is undoubtedly the case that an individual's genetic make-up has a significant influence on their manifested strengths, and on the ease with which they are likely to develop different skills and abilities. It is also true that any potential has to be relative to particular environmental conditions.

So, for Sternberg giftedness implies a potential that should lead to exceptional achievement *without* exceptional support: i.e. to meet his five criteria of giftedness 'with a minimal amount of practice or without good environmental support' (Sternberg 1993: 18). Other commentators take a different view, and consider 'giftedness' may derive from experience as much as genetics.

Stepanek argues that 'if intelligence is not static and can be learned, then giftedness can also be developed' (Stepanek 1999: 6). Allowing for under-achievers and the masking effects of learning difficulties (see Chapter 3), would mean setting the cut-off for identifying gifted learners at a much lower percentile. Montgomery (2003a) suggests that some *potentially* gifted pupils are found among those with IQ scores of 110–115, so that all students in the top 20% should be considered as possible candidates.

The danger of labelling learners

These considerations suggest that in looking to meet the needs of 'gifted' and 'able' students we should be wary of the potential effect of labelling students in schools. If we decide that, say, 5% of the students in a school are gifted in science, then we are signifying that the vast majority have not been endowed with such gifts. This majority will *not therefore be expected* to demonstrate exceptional ability, and are not considered suitable to be considered for 'gifted provision'. This is important, as teacher and learner expectations are known to be very significant factors in subsequent attainment (e.g. Rosenthal and Jacobson, 1970), so it is important that such expectations are carefully informed. Yet, the discussion of giftedness above suggests that identifying a group of students as 'the gifted science learners' in a school is not straightforward. Particular identification criteria may well disadvantage groups such as girls (see Chapter 4) or students from cultural minorities (see Chapter 5).

So identifying gifted learners through standard test scores is clearly an oversimplistic approach. Even assuming that such tests are reliable, they only show attainment of students under the current regime. If some learners are better suited to different, more challenging, curriculum demands then we cannot assume they are always those who score highest on the current standard assessments. Also, science is not a unitary activity: the most creative may not recall the most facts; those who can plan experiments or write accurate observational descriptions are not always the same individuals who excel in calculations.

Many students in schools are already recognised as having special needs which impede their progress: they may have specific learning difficulties (dyslexia), attention deficit problems, partial deafness, or any of a host of conditions and problems that could readily mask their exceptional potential in science (see Chapter 3). Some of the most talented scientists even suffer from behavioural traits found on the autism spectrum (e.g. Sacks 1995; see also Chapter 4).

A related concern is the implication that it is *students* who are able or gifted, whilst others are not. This reinforces an implicit view that gifts or abilities are fixed at birth, or at least by school age, and need to be recognised, but could not otherwise be nurtured. Clearly, children do show different levels of attainment from their earliest schooldays, and it is generally the case that current academic attainment is a good indicator of future progress – at least in the 'academic' context: 'high test-scores or marks in school are not a reliable indicator of adult careers, except for those who continue in a similar path, such as teachers and academics' (Freeman 1998: 7). We would certainly not see this as justifying any model where people are labelled as being of some fixed ability without the potential to develop (Hart *et al.* 2004). Even if Einstein's lack of achievements at school is often exaggerated, there is little doubt that one of the greatest scientific minds in human history was very unlikely to have been identified as a gifted student (Pais 1982).

Education is about trying to help people reach their potential, and it seems likely that very few of us ever reach our potential to the extent that no further educational experience is indicated! This clearly does not mean that all students can be moved into the top 5% if given enough support, whatever testing regime we instigate. However, we should be wary of any system that at one point in time identifies gifted or able students who will be exclusively able to learn from some special educational approaches or provision, whilst excluding other students as *permanently* unable to benefit.

Educators still have a lot to learn about the educational provision that will be optimal in developing students so that they can make the most progress in their scientific skills and understanding (see Chapter 16). All students, whatever their current levels of attainment, have 'gifts', have abilities, have propensities, have potential to attain more. It is not unreasonable to believe that a better designed science curriculum, more effective at matching demand to a student's immediate potential for development, could produce many more learners attaining at levels we *currently* consider exceptional.

Who are the gifted in science?

Despite the genuine caveats discussed above (that the term 'gifted' is used in different ways; that learners may be gifted in some aspects of science and not others; that the distinction between the gifted and other learners is a permeable one) it is clearly useful that a book about science for the gifted should suggest how we might define gifted learners in the context of school science.

The suggestion here is that we should consider as gifted learners in science those students who, given appropriate support, are able to either:

- achieve *exceptionally* high levels of attainment in all or some aspects of the normal curriculum demands in school science (for example: completing substantial sets of numerical problems quickly and with very few or no errors; speedily obtaining full and highly precise sets of results in school practical work; producing highly detailed and accurate accounts of science topics at the level presented in the curriculum); or
- undertake some science-related tasks at a level of demand well above that required at that curricular stage (for example: apply complex algebra not expected at school level; demonstrate the ability to use sophisticated models not normally met in school science; synthesise and relate apparently disparate areas of science without prompting, etc.).

If we consider the term 'able learners' to apply to those students capable of meeting current curriculum demands to a high level in science – the students who will be in 'top sets' and will attain the top grades in school leaving examinations – then we would usually expect gifted students to be a subset of our able learners.

However, as gifted students may have particular abilities and aptitudes rather than an even profile of strengths, it is quite possible that under this definition some gifted science learners may *not* be among those generally considered able. The implication here is that able learners are self-evident in most classrooms (they are by definition the ones doing well in science!), but *the gifted learners may not always be so obvious*. The gifted learners are capable of the exceptional, but may only be exceptional when given the right opportunities and encouragement.

The special needs of gifted learners in science

This definition of gifted learners in science implies that these individuals have special needs. The basis for making this claim is a view of what education is about – helping people achieve their potential. If gifted learners are those able to attain exceptional levels of achievement on current curriculum requirements, or with the potential for achievements that go beyond what is required in school science, then current provision does not provide them with the basis for achieving what they are capable of, and so developing new skills and abilities.

Vygotsky's notion of the 'zone of proximal development' (ZPD) is useful here. According to Vygotsky (1978), educational assessment should be less about what an individual can currently achieve unaided, than what is currently just 'out of reach' without help. According to this view, working within current capability (in the present 'zone of actual development', ZAD) may increase accuracy or speed (or confidence), and is sometimes useful, but does little to help the learner attain *new* capabilities. Genuine development takes place in the ZPD, and the skilled teacher provides suitable support ('scaffolding') to challenge the learner to move beyond their current capabilities. The principle is that attaining new skills and abilities with suitable support enables subsequent attainment with less (and eventually no) support. At this point what was previously just out of reach is now part of what can be achieved unaided within an extended ZAD, whilst the ZPD has enlarged to include what was previously well beyond reach.

If learners are to show what they are capable of, then they need to be challenged to work outside their ZAP and within their ZPD a significant amount of the time. Students *able* to achieve at exceptional levels in school science, or able to meet demands beyond those experienced in the classroom, are seldom working in the ZPD, and will not be developed further.

Not only are these learners not being developed, but they are also in danger of being bored. Gifted learners in science may 'be easily bored by over-repetition of basic ideas but enjoy challenges and problem-solving' (DfES 2003: 15). Most *able* students may well be satisfied in meeting the current demands made of them, but it is unlikely that students capable of performing at exceptionally high levels are really feeling fully challenged by their work in science. Gifted learners 'are dissatisfied with over-generalised explanations and inadequate detail' in their science classes (DfES 2003: 15). The highest achievers spend extended periods of time familiarising themselves with the nuances of a field (e.g. Gardner 1997), and such level of engagement is essential if gifted learners are to experience an authentic 'cognitive apprenticeship' (Hennessy 1993) in science (see Chapter 2).

Csikszentmihalyi (1988) has explored the nature of the 'flow' experience, where engagement in a task leads to a level of concentration and satisfaction that enables much to be achieved apparently 'effortlessly'. In such a state, learners become oblivious to the passage of time, and other environmental conditions, and totally absorbed in the task. It is doubtful that gifted learners often experience such a state in response to standard curricular demands. No wonder that the gifted may 'be critical or appear disinterested and can display unacceptable behaviour' (DfES 2003: 15). Clearly as educators, we have a responsibility to develop the affective response to science (see Chapter 4): and we do a disservice when we bore the most able learners.

All students have an entitlement to be challenged at a level where they can succeed and make progress. Many learners at school level experience limited success in science. Our *able* learners succeed, although it is likely that the *range* of challenge in school science is restrictive, even when the *level* is well matched. Our *gifted* students may feel very little challenge in school science, and may look for that challenge in other subjects, or – failing that – become disaffected with school completely.

How can teachers identify gifted learners in science?

If we are to identify the gifted in science, then we need an approach that identifies them in terms of their aptitude for learning from more demanding science instruction, and not just their high scores on existing tests. A number of characteristics of able learners in science have been suggested (Stepanek 1999; Gilbert 2002; KS3NS 2003a; see also Chapter 2). These characteristics may be considered to form a number of clusters. The first of these concerns *scientific curiosity* (see Box 1.1, cf. Chapter 2, Chapter 4).

A second cluster relates to their *cognitive abilities* (see Box 1.2, and also Chapter 6).

A third cluster of claimed characteristics concerns the student's *meta-cognitive* abilities (see Box 1.3, and also Chapter 6).

Finally, it has also been suggested that some gifted science learners will take on roles, and exercise effective leadership in group work (see Chapter 14).

As our choice of definition of gifted learners in science encompasses students who undertake some science-related tasks at a level of demand well above that required at that curricular level, it is important to be aware that we would not expect those we would consider gifted as having *all* these characteristics (especially when giftedness coexists with learning diffi-culties, see Chapter 3). Lists such as those should be seen as useful indicators when looking to identify gifted learners. Classroom teachers need to also be able to work with (all) their students to ask the fundamental question: *is the current curriculum provision really challenging and developing these learners?*

Box 1.1 Gifted science learners show curiosity

It has been suggested that gifted science learners:
- have hobbies where they collect and compile data or scientific artefacts;
- may be interested in collecting, sorting, and classifying objects;
- have strong curiosity about objects and environments;
- show high interest in investigating scientific phenomena;
- have a tendency to make observations and ask questions;
- may be inquisitive and want to seek explanations for the things and events they observe, often asking many questions, especially 'Why?';
- may have an interest in the derivation (roots) of science terms;
- may demonstrate intense interest in one particular area of science to the exclusion of other topics;
- want to quantify experimental results by counting, weighing or otherwise measuring.

What kind of science education meets the need of gifted learners of science?

> Provision [for the gifted] should include extension in depth and enrichment in breadth: extension through additional support and challenge, and enrichment through opportunities in the classroom and outside school.
>
> (DfES 2002a)

Provision for the gifted could include *accelerated* learning – 'giving students school work that is in keeping with their abilities, without regard to age or grade' (NDE 1997: 56) and/or *enrichment* ('the provision of in-depth multidisciplinary exploration of content beyond that provided in the regular curriculum' (NDE 1997: 32). Sternberg (1993) argues that the type of provision that is appropriate depends upon what we value:

> If we value rapid learning, then acceleration makes sense. If we believe that what matters is the depth or care students take probing into what they learn, enrichment will be preferable. If both are prized, a combination might be best.
>
> Sternberg 1993: 15

In these terms, enrichment might often be the better option for developing gifted learners who we hope will find science a source of fascination and intellectual satisfaction.

Box 1.2 Gifted science learners demonstrate high-level cognitive ability

Gifted learners in science are said to:
- readily learn novel ideas;
- recognise and use formal scientific conventions;
- have a more extensive scientific vocabulary than their peers when explaining things and events;
- have quick and extensive understanding of concepts, such as reliability and validity, when drawing conclusions from evidence;
- relate novel ideas to familiar ideas;
- make connections rapidly between facts and concepts they have learned, and make connections between scientific concepts and observed phenomena;
- move beyond the information given, and move ideas from the context in which they have been learnt to an unfamiliar context;
- quickly understand models and theories in new situations and use these to explain phenomena;
- have the capacity to leap ahead or jump steps in an argument and detect flaws in reasoning of others, and rapidly perceive the direction of an investigation and anticipate outcomes;
- produce models, and mathematically model;
- generate creative and valid explanations;
- be willing and able to think abstractly at an earlier age than usual;
- be prepared to live with uncertainty;
- be willing to hypothesise, manipulate variables fairly and make predictions;
- identify patterns in data where the links are not obvious;
- suggest a variety of alternative strategies for testing predictions or gathering evidence.

Box 1.3 Gifted science learners show metacognitive maturity

Gifted science learners are said to:
- be able to sustain an interest;
- show good powers of concentration;
- reflect on their own thinking and learning;
- form overviews of sectors of a subject;
- excel and persevere at their own choice of activity and produce high quality work;
- want a greater depth of understanding.

Within mixed-ability groups, it may also be possible to consider the *differentiation of roles* among learners (to complement differentiation approaches based upon different tasks, different levels of teacher support, or expecting different levels of outcome). This brings us to the very real issues of (1) whether gifted and able students should be separated from their (currently) less able peers; and (2) whether appropriate science education for the most able is something *other* than just very good science education. In the UK, setting in science has become the norm, especially in the upper secondary school, even though it is recognised that mobility between sets is often difficult, so that setting often seems to 'set' a limit on what a student may eventually achieve in school science. In some schools, setting also leads to unproductive ('difficult') classes where students *currently* showing limited attainment may include more capable students, due to disinterest or disaffection, and where much of the teacher's attention is focused on class-room management issues.

There is research suggesting that when mixed-ability teaching uses appropriate differentiation strategies it can be *at least as effective* as setting (Boaler 1997). Yet, such approaches require skills that not all science teachers feel confident that they possess, and legislate against some less intensive modes of lesson planning (see Chapter 6). A review of research on ability grouping reports that at secondary level: 'Ability grouping in sets or streams has been found to have no overall effect on achievement, compared with mixed ability grouping; advantages for high ability pupils have been found where advanced curriculum materials have been used' (Harlen and Malcolm 1999: 53).

The UK policy on provision for gifted students requires that their programme 'must be distinct and discernibly different from that followed by pupils who are not part of the cohort', whilst 'recognising that distinctiveness and difference can be achieved through effective use of differentiation in all settings'. The policy reminds teachers that differentiation is always an issue, 'but needs to be particularly effective when the range of abilities is wide' (DfES 2004a: 28).

> It is certainly the case that the most able students benefit from the opportunity to work with others operating at a similar level, and this beneficial experience may be difficult if they are dispersed in many different classes. However, these students can also benefit greatly from taking on leadership roles in groups, and from providing peer tutoring for other learners: cooperative learning, if handled properly by a skillful teacher, enhances the learning of high-ability students.
>
> NDE 1997: 80

Perhaps the ideal allows the most able students to spend some time working in inclusive classes, but having some opportunities to work with peers having comparable strengths. One possible way of doing this is by 'target grouping

– the formation of groups to tackle specific issues or projects for a relatively short period' (DfES 2002a). It is also possible to consider enrichment opportunities outside the normal school day, such as programmes providing optional science sessions where keen and able students can undertake activities designed to challenge them intellectually (see Chapters 14 and 15), or through summer schools, schemes to develop students' creativity and Olympiads and science fairs (see Chapter 13). Another rather specific form of enrichment is that of providing gifted learners with mentors – 'experts in a field who may assist a student with his or her understanding in that area' (NDE 1997: 85).

Whatever the organisation of teaching, it is important that the nature of the learning that is promoted meets the needs of gifted learners, and so the challenge is matched to what they are capable of. A number of principles of good practice in this area have been proposed (NDE 1997; VanTassel-Baska 1998; Stepanek 1999).

Focus on concepts

Teaching for the gifted should have significant and 'deep' content, with an emphasis on learning and understanding concepts (rather than memorising facts), and opportunities to engage in conceptual exploration in depth and over time (see Chapter 2).

Focus on enquiry

Effective learning for the gifted may often be organised around an enquiry approach with students taking the role of active investigators, investigating real problems and situations (see Chapter 13, and also Chapter 11).

Higher-level thinking

Teaching for gifted students in science should emphasise questions that enable the learner to analyse, synthesise (for example, providing opportunities for interdisciplinary connections) or evaluate information (see Chapter 6), and should model authentic scientific thinking (e.g. see Chapter 2).

Metacognition and self-regulation

Teaching should encourage gifted learners to use and develop their metacognitive abilities (see Chapter 6). Teachers can help learners develop towards self-regulation by looking to offer a choice of tasks and activities (see Chapters 5 and 12), providing opportunities for self-directed activities (see Chapter 14), and letting students take the lead in setting agendas (see Chapter 9).

Product and audience

Gifted learners can be set tasks producing authentic products; and set tasks exploring genuine problems – where their findings can be reported to a genuinely interested audience (see Chapters 4, 9 and 15 for examples).

Variety and pacing

It has also been suggested that it is particularly important to use a variety of teaching strategies when working with gifted students (e.g. see Chapters 10 and 11), and there may be distinct requirements in terms of organising curriculum time (see Chapter 2). A rapid pace is sometimes recommended for introducing new material to gifted learners, and any time 'saved' should be used instead to offer more opportunity later for reflection on, and integration of, learning.

Science education for gifted learners

In this book we try to offer the best advice that is available, drawing upon our actual experiences of working with gifted learners of science, both within mainstream curriculum contexts, and in special programmes. More research is certainly needed, to find exactly what is possible in 'typical' classroom contexts (see Chapter 16). Our concern is that learners should be challenged to achieve more, but in conditions where they are suitably supported within appropriate learning environments, so that their potential may be realised without risk to their confidence, interest and self-belief.

Learning environments need to offer stimulating and relevant contexts (see Chapter 11); and offer support for learners to take responsibilities for learning and for initiating dialogic exchanges with teachers (see Chapters 8 and 9). Such learning environments will allow the gifted learners to thrive, and – we suspect – may well facilitiate many more learners to (at least on certain occasions, in certain contexts) demonstrate *exceptionally* high levels of attainment, and the ability to undertake some science-related tasks at levels of demand well above that usually expected.

Chapter 2

The characteristics of the gifted and exceptionally able in science

John K. Gilbert and Matthew Newberry

As suggested in Chapter 1, it is much easier to talk about gifted learners in science than to agree on exactly who might be gifted, and how we should recognise them. In this chapter, John Gilbert and Matthew Newberry consider what enabled Nobel Laureates (as archetypical gifted scientists) to develop their exceptional intellects, and in particular the development of scientific 'intuition', and how this might inform provision for the gifted in science education.

Problems of identification

Who are the 'gifted and exceptionally able in science'? The UK government defines them as being the 5% to 10% highest achievers (here in science) within each and every state school. By implication this is irrespective of the social and cultural backgrounds of the students (QCA 2006). There are several problems with this view. First, there is no firm evidence from longitudinal studies that 'giftedness in science' (or in anything else) – meaning that such a person is imaginative and creative – is a fixed personal characteristic. Second, there is no evidence, one way or the other, that 'giftedness in science' (assuming that it *is* a personal characteristic) is evenly spread throughout the whole population (or indeed evenly spread out through different sectors of society). It is entirely possible that social reasons could dictate that particular schools may acquire a disproportionately high or low share of such students. Third, the development or realisation of giftedness requires access to expert teachers, high quality resources and suitable experiences, which are not evenly spread across schools. Poor opportunities may hinder the recognition and/or the development of giftedness. Last, and perhaps most important, since the 1990s, the school assessment regime in England has become heavily focused upon the published comparative 'league tables of schools' headline figures of the numbers of students achieving target grades at different stages. These figures are being used to identify targets for future grade attainment and to focus financial and practical support for schools. Having to recognise the more modest achievements of the many does not adequately evaluate the knowledge and skills that gifted science students might be expected to display. Doing well at school may well just be a case of being diligent and hardworking. This focus is hindering the identification of gifted students. The qualities shown by higher achieving students, however valuable, are often insufficient evidence with which to identify giftedness.

With the recent UK government focus upon the 'Every Child Matters' agenda, teachers are being encouraged to change their pedagogy to target and support gifted and talented students. However, over recent years science teachers have had very little practical experience in identifying these students, let alone altering and adapting their pedagogy to address their learning needs. If we wish to identify the characteristics of giftedness in science the authors believe that it is helpful to turn to that group whom the community of scientists deem to be *primus inter pares* – the Nobel Laureates in the sciences.

An unequivocal demonstration of giftedness in science: the Nobel Laureates

Each year the Nobel Prize in each of physics, chemistry, physiology or medicine, is awarded to one or more distinguished scientists. Marton, Fensham and Chailkin analysed the transcripts of the round-table discussions that constituted the Swedish television programmes 'Science and Man' *[sic]* for the years 1970–86. The collective of laureates expressed the view, in fourteen of those years, that *intuition* had played a significant part in their work (Marton, Fenshamand Chailkin 1994).

The word 'intuition' was used by the laureates in three distinct ways:

- Intuition as the process of getting the idea at which you arrive. It has to do with moving along a path from a starting point towards something as yet unknown. Moving along this path involves asking the right questions, producing answers to those questions, selecting which one has the greatest potential, judging the relevance of different pieces of information.
- Intuition as a non-logical feeling for the significance of an idea. It has to do with a feeling of certitude about the value of a conclusion, reached without a consciousness of the steps involved. There is an artistic sense to this experience, an exercise of taste, a feeling of the correctness in what has been done.
- Intuition as a personal capability. It has to do with the exercise of established mental skills, whether they be inherited or developed.

The Nobel Laureates had all probably been subjected to a 'transmission of knowledge' school science curriculum, as is still the predominant pedagogical style today. Yet they survived intellectually, not only being able to exercise scientific intuition at the highest level but also being able to recognise this capability in themselves. How did this come about? Had they the good fortune to be taught science by a highly knowledgeable, skilled and inspirational teacher? If so, they were lucky, for, as we know from our own experiences at school, truly inspirational teachers are sadly all too rare. (In Chapter 4, Steve Alsop refers to research showing that very few of a sample of successful scientists cited school as a major influence on their choice to enter science.)

The introduction and continued focus upon 'league tables' of public examination results in England has unfortunately had the effect of standardising pedagogy and ensuring that much teaching is 'to the test'. Given the importance of the league tables most schools ensure that their 'best' teachers are given key target groups of Year 6 or Year 9 SATS borderline pupils, the C/D borderline at GCSE and the E/F borderline at A Level. Regrettably these two factors tend to mean that the 'gifted and talented' are all too often left to their own devices. Inevitably, many become bored and decide to take science no further (Gilbert 2006).

Societies will want to develop and foster 'giftedness in science' because of the vital role that cutting-edge science plays in the creation and development of novel technologies and hence in the future success of the nation's economy. As we have argued earlier, there is no evidence to suggest that giftedness in science is a fixed personal characteristic and that, as the limited resources of our best and most inspirational teachers are being encouraged to focus upon improving the achievement of the middle ability students, then the true potential of the most able and gifted students is not being realised. We suggest that, rather than relying completely on the results of tests that are not valid for this purpose, a better way forward would be to base the school science curriculum *for all pupils* on what is known about how giftedness is exercised. Those students who react most positively to such a curriculum will therefore be encouraged and supported to demonstrate their giftedness throughout their school careers rather than being identified from test results taken at certain stages. What, then, are the principal features of giftedness in science that could be explicitly nurtured?

Education to support the identification of giftedness in science

Forty-two of the seventy-two laureates in the Marton *et al.* analysis were unable to comment on *how* they had developed scientific intuition. The others felt that it was based on knowledge of the particular subject of their research, acquired through and used in extensive experience of that subject. There does then seem to be a need for students who are, or may become, gifted in science to focus on phenomena that will sustain their attention over a period of time. In this way they will acquire a breadth of information about, and experience of, such phenomena. In doing so, they will acquire an emergent understanding of the nature of science (see Chapter 14). An understanding of the nature of science will provide an overview (or meta-commentary) on what is being done in specific instances and will shape the evaluation of the significance of those instances. It will also be associated with the development of those skills that can be conjectured as underlying the exercise of intuition: the use of analogies, the production of visualisations. In doing so, students will acquire and/or display those intrinsic qualities associated with giftedness, namely a deep and abiding interest in science. They will also acquire those extrinsic qualities associated with giftedness, namely the ability to produce high-quality scientific output through collaboration with others. These requirements pose severe challenges to nature, style and delivery of science education, as are discussed next.

Education in the conduct of scientific enquiry

Developing an understanding of the nature of science

Anybody who is in any way gifted in science must be on the way to a grasp of the philosophical nature of science. However, science is a very diverse activity, conducted in situations where direct intervention into natural systems is possible, for example in an exploration of the consequences for behaviour of altering genes, to where it is quite impossible, for example in an exploration of the formation of galaxies. This means that no one fixed method for conducting scientific enquiries or agreeing on knowledge as scientific can exist. However, a series of general philosophical principles for the conduct of science have been identified (Rutherford and Ahlgren 1990; Matthews 1994). These are that science is broadly based upon:

- **Realism.** There is a material world that is independent of human experiences and knowledge.
- **Fallibilism.** Although humans can come to have knowledge of the world, that knowledge is imperfect and may be changed.
- **Durability.** Although scientific knowledge is fallible, existing knowledge is only gradually modified or abandoned.
- **Anti-methodism.** There is no one correct way of conducting a scientific enquiry.
- **Demarcationism.** It is possible to separate scientific endeavours from non-scientific endeavours, mainly in terms of a willingness to change explanations in the light of empirical evidence. This boundary does shift over time e.g. the submission of acupuncture to scientific enquiry.
- **Predictability.** Successful scientific theories should not only provide explanations for existing empirical observations, but should also enable the successful prediction of other possible observations to be made.
- **Objectivity.** As far as it is humanly possible, what is perceived during science should be free from prejudice or bias.

- **Moderate externalism.** Although every effort must be made to make science as objective as possible, what phenomena are to be investigated are subject to debate and hence to the operation of personal, social, or national, interests.

How is an emergent understanding of the nature of science manifest? The Qualifications and Curriculum Authority (QCA) has advocated multiple criteria to be used to identify students who are 'gifted and talented in science' (QCA 2006). Whilst retaining the original wording, all of these have been grouped in the sections below. As they are all concerned with observable behaviours in students, our ascription of meaning to each criterion carries a variable level of inference. Those criteria concerned with the nature of science are:

Pupils who are gifted in science are likely to:
- enjoy researching obscure facts and applying scientific theories, ideas and models when explaining a range of phenomena;
- ask many questions, suggesting that they are willing to hypothesise and speculate;
- think logically, providing plausible explanations for phenomena (they may be methodical in their thinking but not in their recording);
- put forward objective arguments, using combinations of evidence and creative ideas, and question other people's conclusions (including their teachers'!);
- understand the concepts of reliability and validity when drawing conclusions from evidence.

Although these criteria are worthwhile pointers to attitudes and actions that are a precursor to an understanding of the 'nature of science', they are not explicitly linked to the principles listed above. As will be shown later, this can be done.

The operation of analogy

It has been argued that all invention and discovery take place by the use of analogy: the less familiar is described in terms of the more familiar (Lakoff and Johnson 1980). The general case for an analogy is 'A is like B'. That is, some elements of A ('the target'), which is understood less well, are considered as being like some elements of B ('the source'), which is better understood. The elements may either be the entities of which it is composed, the relationships between those entities, or both of these (Gentner 1983). For example, in a crystalline ionic solid, the entities are the ions of which it consists and the relationships are the mutual electrostatic interactions taking place.

Valuable though it is, analogical thinking can go astray. Thus, where entities and relationships in A and B are alike, the 'strength' of that similarity may vary widely. More importantly, entities or relationships in B may be incorrectly identified as having a similarity to those in A (Hesse 1966). Studies have shown that young children have considerable difficulty in learning the rules that govern the use of analogies (Goswami 1992). Although there seem to have been few studies of this problem in respect of older school-age students and adults, it is highly likely that the problem persists. If the successful use of analogy by the gifted is a vital part of their learning about the nature of science, it is necessary that we make sure that all students understand both how analogies work and the strengths and weaknesses of using them as a tool to describe, explain and improve understanding of scientific phenomena. This will create the conditions in which giftedness can be fostered and developed rather than identified. Again, as will be discussed later, this can be done.

The exercise of visualisation

There are two standard definitions of the verb 'visualise': 'make visible to the eye' and 'form a mental image' (Pearsall 1999). Expanding on these, the first definition refers to the systematic and focused display of information in the form of tables, diagrams and graphs (Tufte 2001), whilst the second refers to the reception and processing of information in the brain leading to the production of a mental image (Reisberg 1997). Both of these meanings play a part in the exercise of intuition. It is thus important that all able students are given opportunities within the science curriculum to become 'metacognitive in visualisation' or 'metavisual', that is, they can exercise the skills of visualisation in all scientific (and other) contexts (Gilbert 2005b). They must be able to apply all the conventions that govern the ways in which external representations are produced. They need to be able to learn how to produce mental images of the greatest validity to those external representations and be able to manipulate (reflect, rotate, invert) these. Most importantly of all, they must be able to interconvert external and internal representations. Explicitly teaching these skills to all able students will provide opportunities for giftedness to develop and emerge through learning science. How all this can be done is sketched later.

The skills that underlie intuition

The nearest that QCA (2006) comes to addressing intuition may be inferred from the observations that:

> Pupils who are gifted in science are likely to:
> - be imaginative;
> - use different strategies for finding things out (practical and intellectual) – they may be able to miss out steps when reasoning the answers to problems;

- consider alternative suggestions and strategies for investigations;
- analyse data or observations and spot patterns easily;
- make connections quickly between facts and concepts they have learned, using more extensive vocabulary than their peers;
- think abstractly at an earlier age than usual and understand models and use modeling to explain ideas and observations. For example KS3 pupils may be willing to adapt and apply abstract scientific models in order to form a scientific explanation of a phenomenon; KS4 pupils may be able to use higher-order mathematical skills such as proportionality, ratio and equilibrium with some abstract ideas when offering explanations;
- show intense interest in one particular area of science (such as astrophysics), to the exclusion of other topics.

Some of these attributes involve the use of analogy: the pupils have to think of one thing as being like some other thing and to forge links between facts that have no overt relationship. Others of them involve the use of visualisation: internal representations have to be created and expressed as external representations and vice versa.

The development of intrinsic qualities as a learner

There are three main intrinsic personal qualities that a gifted learner of science has to develop. First, the ability to apply intellectual rigour to a topic of interest such that a personally satisfactory conclusion is reached. Second, the capacities to identify phenomena of particular interest. Third, the ability to provide an appropriate explanation of what has been found out. How might these qualities be developed?

The development of intellectual rigour

The quality of intellectual rigour is difficult to support. We live in an age when public models of the time span of concentration are very short e.g. the 'sound bite' approach to most political interviews, the frequency of scene change in many TV programmes, the format and structure of computer games. Even internet sites are set up in a fragmented format, with continuity and depth of argument difficult to find. Within our schools, modular course structures, topic-based learning, the universal adoption of a structure for the school timetable based on a sequence of regularly changing approximately 1-hour time slots, the use of the 'three-part lesson', and the implicit valuation of passive learning that these support, all conspire to reinforce these aspects of the media. Moreover, there seems to be a strong element of anti-intellectualism in British public life. Thus any student who shows sustained interest in school in anything intellectual is not only likely to be mocked by her/his peers, but also is often encouraged by her/his parents to spend their time on 'more healthy' social activities, for example sport. Different communities and socio-economic groups are likely to have very differing attitudes towards science and the value of studying scientific courses at further and/or higher education. Parental and family support for gifted and talented science students varies widely depending upon a multitude of factors. The factors include: the family's current and past socio-economic backgrounds, their cultural expectations, religious background, available role models to highlight potential career pathways, employment opportunities within the locality. Even within an individual town, the different schools serve very different catchment areas which reflect these different factors. We would disagree with the blanket approach of identifying the top 5 – 10% in every school as being gifted and talented; not only are the numbers of gifted and talented students likely to be very different in different establishments, but the methodologies and pedagogies to support identification and nurturing of the gifted scientists needs to be very different in different types of schools. These are social realities and must be counterbalanced if giftedness in science is to be realised.

Rigour can best be supported by sustained encouragement of it by parents and teachers separately and, most importantly, by a partnership between the two. To take just one example, in a general evening 'Year 9 Science Study Workshop' at Cams Hill School, parents and their children were encouraged to work together to form scientific explanations of everyday phenomena and to take an interest in science in the news. As part of this activity each family were provided with a CD of experiences and resources, which they could then use at home to support learning. Parent participants in this shared learning activity commented that:

> The 'kitchen sink science' [activity] is the only thing that I have seen which has made me aware of the increased thinking needed in science. It's a good, quick, tool to use either independently or together.

> I think it ['kitchen sink science'] will captivate the kids' imaginations and bring science alive. My daughter will use the CD on our computer and we will play the family games [provided].

> Excellent explanations.

> A very different way of learning.

If a rigourous address to themes of interest is to be shown by able students, how can this be demonstrated? In the opinion of QCA (2006):

> Pupils who are gifted in science are likely to:
> - read widely, particularly science and science fiction;
> - have scientific hobbies and/or be members of scientific clubs and societies;

- be extremely interested in finding out more about themselves and the things around them;
- be able to sustain their interest and go beyond an obvious answer to underlying mechanisms and greater depth;
- be inquisitive about how things work and why things happen (they may be dissatisfied with simplified explanations and insufficient detail);
- decide quickly how to investigate fairly and manipulate variables;
- strive for maximum accuracy in measurements of all sorts, and take pleasure, for example, from reading gauges as accurately as possible (sometimes beyond the accuracy of the instrument);
- be easily bored by over-repetition of basic ideas;
- enjoy challenges and problem-solving, while often being self-critical;
- be self-motivated, willing to put in extra time (but they may approach undemanding work casually and carelessly).

Although these criteria do draw welcome attention to the issue of where interest comes from and to motivational (and hence demotivational) issues (see Chapter 4), the emphasis is too heavily weighted towards laboratory practical work. As we will see next, a broader view is needed.

A useful place to look for 'sources for the development of interest in science' is the experience of the Nobel Laureates.

Nobel Laureates: cases of having become very interested in a scientific phenomenon

As part of the annual interview of the Nobel Laureates, they were invariably asked 'how did you become interested in science?' An analysis of the eleven interviews that could be accessed in respect of the thirty-five awards for Chemistry between 1990 and 2005 found five factors to be mentioned (Nobel 2005):

- The influence of a very good teacher (three responses):

It probably goes back to a teacher in junior high school – who was very challenging and got me interested.

R. Grubbs 2005

- Access to experimental toys (two responses):

I have always been curious about things – working with my hands – when I was about 8 years old my brother gave me a chemistry set – it channelled my interests.

R. Schrock 2005

- Access to books and magazines (three responses):

My father was an electrical engineer – when I was about 8 – my parents bought the 'Book of Knowledge' and I read it all the time. My father subscribed to 'Popular Mechanics' – I was exposed to science and technology from the beginning.

J. Fenn 2002

- Self-teaching (one response):

My family had no scientific interests – my father was a shopkeeper – as a child I became extremely interested in mathematics – I spent much of my time from 12 years onwards teaching myself mathematics.

J. Pople 1998

- Practical work (one response):

My father was a balloon maker – when I was 14 or 15 I would work in the factory – I did everything – it was a good education – after 12 or 13 I was learning on my own.

H. Kroto 1996

How do these sources of interest map on to all the criteria for giftedness in science?

- Self-teaching. This source of interest was the most evident in the QCA list. Thus: 'researching obscure facts', 'interested in finding things out', 'being self-motivated', 'thinking logically', 'making connections between facts and concepts', 'thinking abstractly', 'able to sustain interest', 'be inquisitive', 'enjoys challenges', 'is self-motivated'.
- Practical work. This also has a high profile in the QCA list. Thus 'applying scientific theories', 'understanding the concepts of reliability and validity', 'using different strategies for finding things out', 'considering alternative suggestions', 'analysing data', being able to investigate fairly', 'strives for maximum accuracy'.
- Access to books and magazines. This was briefly recognised: 'shows interest in particular areas of science', 'reads widely'.
- Good teacher. This source too was only briefly recognised in the QCA list: 'asks many questions', 'puts forward objective arguments', 'easily bored by repetition'.
- Experimental toys. This source may, or may not, be in the QCA list: 'be imaginative', 'has scientific hobbies'.

The QCA list places great reliance on 'practical work' and 'self-teaching'. However, what the opportunity sample of Nobel Laureates also shows is the high value that should be attached to the support provided by aspects of family life. The best that we can hope to do is, when a student who has the potential to become 'gifted in science' is identified, to ensure that the family is drawn centrally into a network of support that is developed.

The capacity to provide explanations

In the world of education, an explanation may be defined as the answer produced to a question asked (Gilbert *et al.* 1998). A typology of explanations has been proposed:

- Intentional explanations: These answer the questions 'why is this phenomenon of interest?' and 'why is this enquiry being carried out?' In order to motivate engagement in the question, this type of explanation should be provided to students at the outset of the enquiry.
- Descriptive explanations: These answer the questions 'how can we name and/or classify this phenomenon?' and 'how does this phenomenon behave?' This is the simplest form of explanation.
- Interpretational explanations: These answer the question 'of what is this phenomenon composed?' Having described how a phenomenon behaves, an interpretational explanation describes the nature of the entities of which it is thought to be composed.
- Causal explanations: These answer the question 'why does the pheno-menon behave as it does?' A causal explanation uses an interpretational explanation to describe the causes of the effects that are manifest in its behaviour.
- Predictive explanations: These answer the questions 'how will this phenomenon behave in other circumstances?' and 'if the predicted behaviour is observed, why is this so?' (Gilbert *et al.* 1998). The highest form of explanation in science, a predictive explanation uses a causal explanation to suggest what the interpretational explanation might suggest the behaviour of the phenomenon might be in different condi-tions. Empirical confirmation or disconfirmation of a predictive explana-tion is a key element of scientific methodology.

Visualisation, both external and internal, is involved in all the forms of explanation. Analogy plays a key role in the first major step, that of providing an interpretational explanation.

The experience of teachers in the Cams Hill Science Consortium (see Chapter 15) suggests that much of school science consists of many descriptive explanations, some interpretational and causal explanations, and few if any intentional and predictive explanations. Students who are 'gifted in science' will want far more intentional explanations, as justification for their emergent sustained engagement in specific phenomena, and predictive explanations, for these are the trigger for rigourous work. Most importantly, those who are gifted in science will seek out explanations that are more powerful, that is those which are capable of supporting more insightful predictions and which have greater scope in that they can be applied to a wider range of phenomena (Gilbert *et al.* 1998; see also Chapter 12).

Development of the extrinsic qualities as a learner

From the analysis of the quotes given earlier, one characteristic of Nobel Laureates seems to be that their science education benefited greatly from access to resources that provoked intuition. Those resources could have been people who were expert in the teaching of some field of science, or books and other printed resources developed by such people, or access to experiences that gave them opportunities to exercise multiple skills, or, best of all, combinations of all three. It is widely accepted as a general principle of education that all learning is *situated* (Greeno 1998), that is it is bounded by the physical and intellectual context in which it took place. Those individuals who subsequently showed excellence in their scientific thinking had been able to enter into an *apprenticeship in thinking* (Rogoff 1990) from a person, resource, or through an experience. That is, they were shown how to produce explanations for phenomena of increasing quality and power. Taking the broadest interpretation of an educationally productive context, situations which allow for the most effective learning are those which, after Greeno (1998):

- Permit the learner and the resource to be seen as a 'community of learners'. There is substantial equality of power in the relationship, such that both parties can be seen as co-constructing knowledge, rather than the resource merely transmitting knowledge to the learner.
- Require the maximum interaction between the learner and the resource. This means that there is the greatest range of opportunities for both parties to pose questions, produce possible explanations, and debate the relative worth of these.
- Encourage the transfer of learning to other situations. The quality of any explanations produced is tested by exploring their value in producing an analogical set of explanations for a phenomenon that is apparently very different from the one in which initial learning took place.
- Provide tasks of high quality, those that require the construction of explanations of wide applicability, that generate radical predictive explanations that are empirically substantiated.

Effective learning in such situations requires that the student who is 'gifted in science' has or develops the capability to interact productively with others, including the teacher. Because of the poor quality of the experiences often had by many such students and the fact that the curriculum is interpreted as a series of facts and concepts to 'learn by heart', these skills are often badly underdeveloped. What is called for is provision for genuinely *personalised learning*, such that their needs are met to the greatest extent (DfES 2004b).

The provision of education for the gifted and talented in science

An appropriate science education for this group of students will involve the provision of suitable tasks, a suitable classroom environment, an emphasis on the nature of science, on the explicit use of analogy and of visualisation. Those students who respond fully to such a provision are more likely to be shown to be 'gifted in science' in the long run. Taking each of these in turn:

The provision of suitable tasks

What kinds of things may be of personal interest to gifted science students such that suitable tasks can be generated in consultation with their teachers? Topics that provide a personal challenge, that are found fascinating, that have relevance either in their personal lives (e.g. stem cell technology, organ transplantation) or which deal with existential issues (e.g. environment pollution, the possibility of life elsewhere in the cosmos), have been suggested by students (Osborne and Collins 2000). This is to give a somewhat more student-centred interpretation of the views of Millar and Osborne: 'Scientific knowledge can best be presented in the curriculum as a number of key 'explanatory' stories . . . [and] should introduce young people to a number of important ideas-about-science'(Millar and Osborne 2000). How might these topics be focused on? Although many will involve laboratory practical work, some will involve the use of the internet to identify contemporary facts and trends, and others the use of case studies from the history and philosophy of science. The element of challenge can be included by making interesting topics take the form of problems to be solved. In a typology of 'problem types' (see Table 2.1), the higher numbered problem types present the greatest challenge (Johnstone 1993; Mbajiorgu and Reid 2006). In the highest level of problem type, the student seeks an explanatory answer to a question that she/he has devised in conjunction with the resource (typically, a teacher), decides on the enquiry method to be used, and evaluates the range of incomplete, often contradictory, data obtained.

The address to these latter problem types corresponds closely to the notion of 'open work' (Simon and Jones 1992). Giftedness might be identified by seeing how far through this typology a given student can progress with suitable support: the truly 'gifted in science' will be able to tackle successfully problems of a 'high level' type at an unexpectedly early age.

Table 2.1 A typology of 'problem types' From Mbajiorgu and Reid (2006), after Johnstone (1993)

Type	Data	Method	Goals	Skills bonus
1	Given	Familiar	Given	Recall of algorithms.
2	Given	Unfamiliar	Given	Looking for parallels to known methods.
3	Incomplete	Familiar	Given	Analysis of problem to decide what further data are required. Data seeking.
4	Incomplete	Unfamiliar	Given	Weighing up possible methods and then deciding on data required.
5	Given	Familiar	Open	Decision making about appropriate goals. Exploration of knowledge networks.
6	Given	Unfamiliar	Open	Decisions about goals and choices of appropriate methods. Exploration of knowledge and technique networks.
7	Incomplete	Familiar	Open	Once goals have been specified by the student the data are seen to be incomplete.
8	Incomplete	Unfamiliar	Open	Suggestion of goal and methods to get there; consequent need for additional data. All of the above skills.

The availability of time in which to address such problems is a major stumbling block. Although allocations of time longer than the usual 1-hour blocks do seem necessary, it is equally important that a sequence of such blocks, probably associated with periods of entirely private study, be available. Given the constraints of our somewhat 'Victorian factory-like' school timetable model used within secondary schools in the UK, such time may only be available in out-of-school hours. This suggests a more creative use of 'homework' is required. All too often homework consists of repetitive or reinforcing tasks set for ease of moderation and marking by the teacher. Homework tasks designed to support students achieving 'gifted and talented' status in science might consist of a novel problem, decided upon in conjunction with the teacher, addressed using a range of resources, over a period of several weeks or months.

The provision of suitable support in the classroom

It is extraordinary that only one criterion suggested by QCA (2006) seemed to be related to the interaction of the teacher and scientifically gifted student in the classroom. Thus: 'Pupils who are gifted in science are likely to:

• enjoy talking to the teacher about new information or ideas.'

For a teacher to provide effective support for such a student, that person will need to possess high levels of 'subject knowledge' (the specific facts and general principles of the subjects being investigated) and of 'pedagogic content knowledge' (the ability to transform the abstract ideas of science into an intelligible form) (Shulman 1987). Perhaps even more importantly, the teacher will have to be sufficiently self-confident to be able to accept a greater equity in terms of power and authority than is usual. This will be allied to the view taken of the nature of education: seeing it as the 'co-construction of knowledge' will lead to a much more constructive classroom environment for the 'gifted scientist' than will the view of it as 'the transmission of established knowledge'. There is clearly a need for sustained investment to support the professional development of science teachers within UK state secondary schools so as to offer training, guidance and materials to enable and embed these changes in pedagogy and teacher–pupil interactions within the classroom.

Education in the nature of science

The National Curriculum (Science) for England states that:

> Science stimulates and excites pupils' curiosity about phenomena and events in the world around them. It also satisfies this curiosity with knowledge. Because science links direct experience with ideas, it can engage learners at all levels. Scientific method is about developing and evaluating explanations through experimental evidence and modelling. This is a spur to critical and creative thought. Through science, pupils understand how major scientific ideas contribute to technological change – impacting on industry, business and medicine and improving the quality of life. Pupils recognise the cultural significance of science and trace its worldwide development. They learn to question and discuss science-based issues that may affect their own lives, the direction of society and the future of the world.
>
> DfEE 1999: 15

The clear implication is that *all* students learn about the 'nature of science'. The QCA criteria for recognising the 'able and talented in science' use many elements of this quotation, suggesting that only this group will acquire such knowledge and expertise. So one would expect the student who is gifted in science to have a much-better-than-average grasp of these principles and to be interested in them. These principles can be developed either explicitly by instruction and/or by the practice of enquiry followed by a reflection on the processes involved and their attainment tested for (Abd-El-Khalick and Lederman 2000). Such an approach should be explicitly taken for the 'gifted in science'.

However, if the criteria for the nature of science (Rutherford and Ahlgren 1990), given earlier in this paper, are cross-referred to the criteria for the 'gifted in science' (QCA 2006), the following pattern emerges:

- realism: not addressed;
- fallibilism: addressed through 'applying models', 'being imaginative', 'thinking abstractly';
- durability: addressed through 'making connections of known concepts';
- anti-methodism: addressed through 'using a variety of strategies in an enquiry';
- demarcationism: not addressed;
- predictability: addressed through 'asking questions and hypothesising', 'constructing explanations', 'questioning existing explanations';
- objectivity: addressed through 'analysing data' and 'enjoying challenges and problem-solving. Will often be self-critical';
- moderate externalism: addressed through 'researching obscure facts', 'showing intense interest in some phenomena'.

This analysis suggests that a much more comprehensive treatment of the nature of science is needed in respect of this particular group of students than might be inferred from the QCA advice (see also Chapter 14).

Education in the use of analogy

The 'Cognitive Abilities Test' (Strand 2003), given to many pupils shortly after they enter secondary school, is said to provide a stable measure of their reasoning skills under three headings, 'Verbal' (their use of words), 'Quantitative' (their use of numbers) and 'Non-verbal' (NV, their use of shapes or figures). The application of the NV reasoning test may be of use in identifying students who have a high level of competence in analogy use and who are therefore likely to be able to show scientific intuition in suitable circumstances. The NV component is said to show the ability to:

> recognise similarities, analogies and patterns in unfamiliar designs . . . the mental abilities required to complete these tests demonstrate how pupils understand and assimilate new information . . . [they have] good predictive ability i.e. they are relatively good predictors of future academic attainment.
>
> NFER 2006

Treagust *et al.* developed an approach to teaching the nature of analogy for use by science teachers (Treagust *et al.* 1998). In summary, it consisted of:

- identifying the concept to be taught;
- drawing on teachers' experience to identify a suitable source for the analogy;
- discussing the ways that the source is like the target;

- discussing the ways that the source is unlike the target;
- deciding on an analogy to be used in teaching
(the 'teaching model' – Gilbert *et al.* 2000).

There seems no obvious reason why this approach should not be used explicitly with pupils. An emergent theme of many different action research case studies conducted by teachers within the Cams Hill Science Consortium in secondary schools across Hampshire and West Sussex over the last 5 years is that explicitly teaching students the skills of using models and, more importantly, modelling (see Chapter 7), within a sequence of lessons has been shown to significantly improve understanding and engagement with abstract phenomena such as balancing equations, the biochemical pathways in photosynthesis, the action of enzymes etc.

Education in visualisation

How can we provide opportunities to develop the skills of visualisation? A range of techniques has been identified for developing the capacity to produce external visualisations (Gilbert 2005b). A pragmatic approach is to be explicit about the stages involved as external representations are produced (Hearnshaw 1994). A more broad ranging approach that has yet to be put into practice is the systematic development of 'visual literacy skills' (Christopherson 1997). Internal visualisation has been taught with the use of stereodiagrams, teaching cues and the systematic introduction to 'reflection, rotation, and inversion' (Tuckey and Selvaratnam 1993). Both aspects can be brought together in the systematic teaching of the skills of modelling (Justi and Gilbert 2002).

How can we evaluate the attainment of metavisual capability? There are several tests available for the ability to form mental images. The ability to mentally manipulate spatial forms can be tested with the 'Purdue Visualization of Rotation' test (Bodner and McMillen 1986), while the ability to identify and retain a visual pattern in the presence of distractions can be identified with the 'Find-a-Shape Puzzle' test (Pribyl and Bodner 1987). There is a clear need to draw these together into one composite, user-friendly, test.

Conclusion

If we wish to identify pupils who are 'gifted in science', then, to repeat what was written earlier, one way is to provide them with suitable stimuli and see how they react. The key to the whole enterprise must be to seek the *active engagement* of pupils in work that they find interesting. This will involve the teacher in planning for pupil creativity, in sharing the learning agenda with the pupils, in addressing themes in modern science through debate and, most importantly of all, engaging in an effective learning partnership involving teachers, students and parents.

Chapter 3

Gifted science learners with special educational needs

Carrie Winstanley

It is clear from Chapters 1 and 2 that the identification of the gifted in science is far from straightforward. In this chapter, Carrie Winstanley explores a further complicating factor: many learners who have potential for exceptional performance in science may also have special educational needs that can mask that potential. Teachers of science need to be aware that some students capable of very creative levels of work will underachieve in normal class settings – a source of frustration for teacher and student – unless their potential is recognised and appropriate support allows them to actualise that potential.

This chapter is concerned primarily with the highly able pupils who have a significant discrepancy between their potential and their performance. This statement is deceptively simple (see, for example, Ziegler and Raul 2000). Each aspect of it is contended as concepts of high ability, potential and performance are all complex and contested (Ziegler and Heller 2000: 6). The first part of the chapter deals with the sticky concept of giftedness, and later sections consider various specific learning difficulties and disabilities and the issue of underachievement.

The notion of 'giftedness'

The notion of giftedness is often woolly, sometimes confusing and almost always complex and controversial. This is evidenced by the complexities that arise in trying to define the target group for provision, let alone deciding what kind of support is best to offer. There are many myths surrounding the field of gifted education (as it is internationally known), and all of the following statements come from teachers and/or parents attending in-service or support sessions, concerned about helping the able pupil. They show the concerns and confusions of people working with able children:

- Gifted children don't need any help as they will do well without support.

- Giftedness is hereditary, so there's nothing we can do.
- Giftedness is environmental, so the parents are really the ones who should help.
- I have a boy in my class who has a high IQ but his learning problems cancel out his giftedness.
- There's no such thing as giftedness, there's just more or less hard working.
- Anyone who succeeds in school is gifted.
- No one has done research that proves anything about gifted children.
- All our pupils come from low-income families so none of them are gifted.
- How can you tell if they are gifted if they never actually do their class work or homework?
- I have some that are gifted and others at the other end of the spectrum who have dyslexia and AD/HD.

Some of the statements are vague and some reinforce or reflect stereotypes, such as the idea that gifted children are from wealthy backgrounds. In some extreme cases, in aiming for equity and to avoid elitism, children have been held back in order for them not to be too advantaged (see, for example, Feather 1989). Others demonstrate conceptual confusion, such as considering ability and learning problems to be part of a single dimension, therefore equating such difficulties with low ability. The criticism of the statements is not intended as an indictment of teachers or parents. There is no good reason to expect them to know about the latest research in the field. Indeed the scholarly literature is confusing and contradictory and there is no consensus about identification or provision, although key themes tend to recur. The statements demonstrate that wider dissemination of new ideas is needed, as well as more in-service teacher education. 'Without exception however, there is a need for training of teachers globally which in turn will prepare them to recognise and meet the needs of children from all cultures who exhibit gifted attributes' (Baldwin et al. 2000: 571).

The nature of high ability

Teachers and parents can be uncomfortable with the notion of gifted education due to the shadow that elitist practices of the past continues to cast on the field. Here, provision had been focused on a narrow band of children, identified using tools that allow only for an exclusive focus on traditionally measured intellectual ability, producing an elitist definition. With such methods, pupils already favoured by standard curriculum content continue to receive advantage and those who may be able, but have some other difficulty, are yet again denied the opportunity to demonstrate their strengths.

Gifted education is wrongly characterised by this outdated vignette though. Research and practices have moved on to become increasingly inclusive as children with disadvantage and difficulties are better understood. Methods of identification and ideas for provision lean heavily on the contemporary received view of intelligence and of ability and, as a result, ideas in this area are slowly changing. In the past, the focus has been on 'schoolhouse giftedness'.

> Schoolhouse giftedness might also be called test-taking or lesson-learning giftedness. It is the kind most easily measured by IQ or other cognitive ability tests, and for this reason it is the kind most often used for selecting students for entrance into special programs.
>
> Renzulli and Reis 2000: 369

Clearly, many pupils would not be identified as able when viewed through the schoolhouse giftedness lens. These limited criteria would result in likely failure of pupils with problems such as difficulties with presentation, sensory impairment, or a negative attitude to testing stemming from unconformity or an idiosyncratic approach to set tasks.

The notion of IQ is, in itself, open to question. Although still favoured by psychologists and recommended as a useful diagnostic guide to uncovering learning problems, when people talk of 'IQ' there is little understanding of the range of tests available and the complexity of analysing the data. For example, some Mensa tests (www.mensa.org.uk/mensa/joining.html) and those published in newspapers and on the internet, claim to allow people to assess their own IQ, but such verbal and non-verbal reasoning quizzes are far removed from the battery of components that go to make up a thorough and valid assessment of intellect and skills such as the WISC-R (Weschler Intelligence Scale – Revised) tests or CATs (cognitive abilities tests) (Benson 2003). Recognition of some of the limits of IQ coupled with a shift towards valuing different skills and capacities has resulted in more children being encouraged to express their less conventional abilities and others have been given more equitable opportunities to show how they learn using their own first language, for example, or an aid to overcome a problem.

Researchers, practitioners and policy makers have widened their definition of high ability, so expanding the pool of children in receipt of provision. Reviews of twenty-five years of research demonstrate this move.

> Whereas until fifteen or twenty years ago the field was dominated by one dimensional giftedness concepts and corresponding IQ measurements, a large majority of more recent models are based on multidimensional or multifactorial psychometric concepts of intelligence – e.g. Gardner's (1985) theory of multiple intelligences – or on approaches from information theory and cognitive psychology – e.g. Sternberg's (1985) triarchic intelligence model. Other models still include elements from

socialisation theories, e.g. Monks' (Monks *et al.* 1986) extended Renzulli model.

Heller and Schofield 2000: 123

These and other similar changes have benefited able children with difficulties who may not shine in academic subjects. Continuing research into psychosocial aspects of development and varying pedagogies has also helped show that less obviously able children can flourish in the right environment. This is partly through in-depth examinations of highly able children including some influential long-term studies (e.g. Heller and Schofield 2000; Freeman 2001; Gross 2004).

Such longitudinal work and case studies help to expose the failings of policy and practice whilst showing how children with difficulties can achieve with appropriate support. The sum of research demonstrates that ongoing studies are needed and that there is a clear precedent for having a range of conceptions of high ability:

> There is no ideal way to measure intelligence and therefore we must avoid the typical practice of believing that if we know a person's IQ score, we also know his or her intelligence. . . . we have cited these concerns to highlight the even larger problem of isolating a unitary definition of giftedness. At the very least, we will always have several conceptions (and therefore definitions) of giftedness.

Renzulli and Reis 2000: 369

It is also vital to remember that, however it is measured, aptitude is not the sole predictor of success. There is no guarantee that recognition of ability will ensure a pupil's success. The recognition is *likely* to be necessary, but is certainly not sufficient to avoid failure. Pupils' motivation, work ethic and the learning and home environments are also significant factors in success (see also Chapter 4). This is not a new or startling discovery and was noted clearly by the pioneer of the concept of hereditary intelligence, Francis Galton:

> By natural ability, I mean those qualities of intellect and disposition, which urge and qualify a man to perform acts that lead to reputation. I do not mean capacity without zeal, nor zeal without capacity, nor even a combination of both of them, without an adequate power of doing a great deal of very laborious work.

Galton 1869: 77

Even if his views were extreme and are now largely outdated, or at least tempered by our better understanding of people and society, this quotation shows that the field of gifted education has always understood that aptitude must be recognised so it can be fostered.

More recent conceptions of intelligence bring with them their own difficulties. Without clear scores and tests, there are blurred lines and a lack of cut-off points or clear distinctions between different levels of high ability. In terms of policy-making, this can be difficult. Where flexible, wide-ranging definitions and dynamic definitions are adopted, a revolving-door model is needed for provision, allowing pupils to be afforded the chance to demonstrate aptitudes even where there are only rare flashes of ability in the classroom context. Pupils are flexibly assigned to enrichment and extension tasks rather than tested, labelled and set fixed work. Of course, this is difficult to implement as there are practical implications, but it allows pupils to be identified in provision-led contexts where different skills and capacities can be expressed.

Checklists and guidelines for assessing children and trying to spot high ability are now ubiquitous but quality varies and usefulness can be limited by the problems that arise in trying to observe children whilst teaching a class. Sometimes different checklists can suggest contradictory qualities, such as these examples taken from the DfES website *Excellence in Cities*, and from Eyre (1997).

Able pupils are likely to:

Demonstrate unusual curiosity	Exhibit boredom
Finish work with ease and speed	Take extra time to complete tasks to a high standard
Have many friends	Be quite isolated
Contribute willingly in class	Refuse to comply with instructions
Be interested in a broad variety of topics	Only express interest in a narrow range of subjects
etc. . .	

One unusual schedule for assessing the able is the 'Nebraska Starry Night'. This highlights behaviours such as 'unusual ideas' and 'use of humour' rather than looking only for the typical factors of knowledge and general aptitude for a subject. Using such methods will help to create an inclusive notion of giftedness, which embraces heterogeneity, encompassing pupils who are potentially difficult to recognise and with diverse needs.

> the task of identification shifts from a search for the gifted few to assessment of the talent, strengths and aptitudes of all students, and to identification of high level talent potential among those who are especially precocious or advanced in their talent development. . . . it is becoming clear that relatively large numbers of youth demonstrate one or more potential talent strengths . . . which if identified and nurtured may lead to high level creative achievement in adulthood.
>
> Feldhusen and Jarwan 2000: 279

Table 3.1 The bright child and the gifted child (after George 1992)

Bright child	Gifted child
Is interested	Is highly curious
Answers the questions	Discusses in detail
Knows the answers	Asks the questions
Top set	Beyond the group
Grasps the meaning	Draws inferences
Is alert	Is keenly observant
Completes the work	Initiates projects
Has good ideas	Has unusual and silly ideas!
Enjoys school	Enjoys learning
Good memory	Good guesser
Is pleased with learning	Is highly critical
Is receptive	Is intense
Learns easily	Already knows
Enjoys straightforward sequential presentation	Thrives on complexity
Enjoys peers	Prefers adults or older pupils
Absorbs information	Manipulates information

Even if a wide range of ideas about giftedness is used, there is still a clear difference between the gifted student and the bright, capable and hard-working student. George (1992) has produced a provocative list of characteristics of bright and gifted children (Table 3.1). He shows how the bright child fits the conventional role of school pupil and proving less disruptive in school than the gifted child.

This list is not exhaustive or definitive but it does highlight some differences between children whom teachers tend to recommend for provision – 'bright children' – and those regularly referred to the Special Educational Needs Coordinator for some kind of investigation. These 'gifted children' can also be underachievers, frequently fitting the non-conventional high ability profile.

'Spiky scorers' and pupils with multiple exceptionalities

In the UK, the language used to describe children with high ability together with a difficulty or impairment is still rather new and unfamiliar. Throughout gifted education literature, the following phrases can be found: 'double exceptionality'/'doubly exceptional', 'dually exceptional', 'gifted handicapped' (Clark 1992, cited by Feldhusen and Jarwan 2000: 275), 'having multiple exceptionalities' and the popular shorthand of '2E'. In this chapter, I am using 'multiple exceptionalities' as this now seems to be the prevailing phrase and includes the widest group of pupils forming the following groups:

- high ability and mobility difficulties
- high ability and sensory impairments

- high ability and learning difficulties
- high ability and autism/Asperger's syndrome
- high ability and AD/HD
- high ability and social/behavioural difficulties
- high ability and cognitive impairment
- high ability and long-term chronic illness
- high ability and cultural disadvantage.

Since the concept and understanding of high ability is such a troublesome area, it is unsurprising to learn that research into the nature and needs of the dually exceptional is rather rare.

> Those who have tried to bridge the gifted/special gap over the years have had difficulty obtaining resources or research funding because the topic falls between two stools and could be regarded as too small a population to merit concern. Equally, from the intervention point of view, the most obvious sign of difficulty is the special need; the other, the giftedness, is regarded as a bonus but they can cancel each other out.
>
> Montgomery 2003b: 5

Some types of multiple exceptionality are more easily defined than others, but certain disabilities, syndromes and learning difficulties can be hard to pin down. Sensory impairments, for example, vary in their severity. Even among the community of people who have been advocating for such pupils for many years, there are sharp divides over questions of exact definitions and also of provision, such as the role of specialist schools in meeting children's needs.

'Learning difficulties' encompasses an enormous range of conditions and issues including dyslexia (a processing difficulty); dyspraxia (a spatial difficulty); aphasia (language difficulties) and dysgraphia (handwriting problems). These terms are frequently challenged and little clear consensus exists. Autism and Asperger's syndrome are well documented within the field of gifted education (see also Chapter 4), but understanding of the causes and issues remains sketchy and controversial. Both types of autism can lead to social and behavioural problems which in turn can exist as problems faced by pupils without these syndromes.

Perhaps the most controversial of the exceptionalities noted above is AD/HD (attention deficit hyperactivity disorder, which can in itself exist in a variety of combinations: ADD – attention deficit disorder; HD – hyperactivity disorder; AD/HD – attention deficit/hyperactivity disorder), partly because of the common treatment making use of stimulant drugs and partly due to scepticism concerning the existence of the condition. It may seem almost contradictory to include those with cognitive impairments in a book on gifted children; how can people with cognitive impairment be described as able? The work of pioneers such as Feuerstein (1980 and 1987, see Sharron 1987) has helped to show that children with global developmental delay can be helped to demonstrate remarkable achievements and abilities. Consider, for example, the talents and gifts of children with Down's Syndrome and Williams Syndrome. This latter group typically have cognitive impairment coupled with particular pockets of high ability, in some cases recorded as extraordinary. They tend to exhibit, for example, a proclivity for unusual words, very adept social and empathic behaviour, fluent speech and advanced musical ability and sensitivity. Children with Down's Syndrome are a heterogeneous group with widely varying abilities and strengths. As research deepens into the difficulties they face, improved pedagogies emerge and with the current strategy of inclusion, new opportunities have been created. Some students with Down's Syndrome have gone on to achieve Master's degrees. Pupils who suffer from long-term chronic illness (commonly asthma, epilepsy, sickle cell anaemia and diabetes) are liable to miss time at school, thereby affecting their academic performance. All of this makes defining people with multiple exceptionalities particularly complex.

The able population must be inclusive. Children with learning problems and disabilities must be allowed the opportunity to benefit from provision, as should children from disadvantaged backgrounds. Cultural disadvantage should be considered as part of dual or multiple exceptionality as such backgrounds are widely understood to affect performance and self-esteem, sometimes even serving as the cause of a learning or behavioural problem. No student's learning takes place in a vacuum and so context must also be taken into account. Some researchers consider this to be so important that it re-frames the way in which we perceive the notion of difficulty.

> Through a social constructivist lens, [however,] it is impossible to describe adequately any one person's actions without an adequate account of the contexts in which the actions take place' (McDermott, 1976, p. 106). From a *social constructivist perspective*, the student is not the problem (a *deficit perspective*), nor is the teacher the problem (*an ecological perspective*).
>
> As Freedman and Combs (1996) put it, 'the problem is the problem' (p. 47), and rather than being the problem, each person 'has a relationship with the problem' (p. 66). Therefore, the essential question in response to the appearance of learning difficulties is, 'What's going on here?' To respond effectively to such a question: 'it takes a complex system of interactions performed just in the right way, at the right time, on the stage we call school. And, as it turns out, this is precisely what is required to construct students as 'smart'.
>
> (Dudley-Marling 2004: 489 original emphasis).

As noted, shifting paradigms in psychology and sociology have given rise to newer ways of considering ability and Sternberg's notion of giftedness as developing expertise is one of the more popular of these ideas (2001). Other researchers have found that their definitions have been challenged through examining a wide range of people. Here, Morelock and Feldman (2000) are discussing the impact of research into prodigies, savants and people with Williams Syndrome:

> It has become clear that to understand giftedness and talent, we must seek more precise articulation of the relative roles of general cognitive ability and domain-specific intellective capacities as well as the interplay between them (Morelock and Feldman 1993). Special groups such as these show promise of providing this understanding.
>
> Morelock and Feldman 2000: 227

Some researchers refer to dyssynchronicity (e.g. Terraiser 1985; Montgomery 2003b: 2) and others distinguish sharply between those who have 'dual' and multiple exceptionalities. The full range of issues will tend to include the following:

> gifted children who also have disabilities, especially learning, developmental, and social-economic disabilities. Dual exceptionalities may include: autistic savant syndrome; developmental delays in speech, language and motor coordination; disruptive behaviour (including conduct and oppositional-defiant disorders); anxieties, and eating disorders (Moon and Hall, 1998). Gifted children may also have specific learning disorders (LD), and attention deficit/hyperactivity disorder (AD/HD) (Moon and Hall, 1998).
>
> Colangelo and Assouline 2000: 605

A simple definition would be that a child with multiple exceptionalities, in this context, would be highly able and also have some kind of difficulty that will be likely to affect their ability to effectively express their high ability. The common response of hard-pressed schools is to focus on remediating children's problems, rather than tackling their high ability with further challenge. Though entirely well meaning, this tactic is often counterproductive. More appropriate would be support that is also intellectually challenging.

Underachievement

Not every child with high ability and some kind of learning difficulty or disability will be an underachiever. However, the chances of children with multiple exceptionalities being unable to express their abilities are unsurprisingly greater than for children without such problems. Underachievement is a nebulous area for study and the gifted underachieving pupil has been a source of frustration for numerous teachers, leading to many research reports (notably work done in the 1970s by Kellmer-Pringle through to studies by Freeman, 1998 and Wallace, 2000). Freeman (1995) has differentiated between 'underachievers' and 'non-producers', considering underachievers to have low self-esteem and emotional distress with a barrier to their performance. Non-producers tend to be self confident, choosing not to conform, but can achieve highly when they are motivated. It is most likely that children with multiple exceptionalities fall into the first of these categories. Wallace suggests that children fall into three categories: coasters, who achieve reasonably but expend little effort; high fliers who achieve highly and work hard; and 'other categories' including those who are disruptive and/ or disaffected. Montgomery identified clear links between dual exceptionality and underachievement in early writings, but particularly clearly in her 2000 publication, *Able Underachievers*. She recommends that educational provision be targeted at a wide group of pupils in order not to miss those with learning problems that could affect the manifestation of their high ability. She echoes Kellmer-Pringle (1970) and Silverman (1989) who recommend allowing a ten-point drop in minimum level of attainment to get on to a programme for those with learning disabilities.

Colangelo and Assouline point out the differences and similarities between underachievers and children with multiple exceptionalities, and the importance of distinguishing between psychological difficulties and dual exceptionality. 'While the psychological issues have clearly been shown to play a role in underachievement, it is critical to note that not all underachievement behaviours have a psychological root' (Colangelo and Assouline 2000: 604). What is required is a shift in attitude to underachievement:

> Historically, underachieving gifted students in the classroom have been viewed as defective merchandise in need of repair. . . . Future research needs to move away from the 'fix the broken' mentality of working *on* students, to one of working *with* students to develop understanding and learning. . . . Alleviating tendencies leading to learner marginalisation and perceived underachievement is the goal.
>
> Schultz 2002: 204–5

Issues for teachers working with underachievers

Some underachieving able pupils are considered undeserving of resources because of their negative attitudes and difficult behaviour. Others are written off because of physical disability or sensory impairment. One project looking at children of high ability with sensory impairments showed that many people (teachers, researchers and lay people) had not considered such a combination could be valid, unless they had close personal contact with people with disabilities (Winstanley 2004). These (sometimes 'invisible') children may choose to stay out of the limelight, underperforming for one reason or another. Deliberately performing badly at school may seem a strange tactic, but many pupils do so for various reasons such as boredom and a dislike of school-work, particularly when the only reward for working hard is being given more of the same tasks.

My own research suggests that children whom teachers expected to perform averagely without any trouble, resorted to a battery of time-wasting techniques. They tended to make an explicit effort to live up (or down) to their teachers' expectations, even making deliberate errors in order to avoid being put into a work group that was given extra tasks. They made clear decisions about which tasks to complete and which to undertake painfully slowly, based on factors such as the follow-up choices available and the teacher's mood. They were adept at duping their overstretched teachers but were certainly not demonstrating their academic potential (Winstanley 2004). Children will deliberately fail tests to move into a lower set if they can be with friends, or escape from a particular teacher (Hallam and Ireson 2000).

Even when given exciting tasks and teacher attention, some able pupils will not apply themselves because of peer pressure and the school ethos. They are affected by their age and gender and whether their friendship group is in sympathy with the aims of schooling or not.

> Few children relish being called 'brain' or 'geek' or 'nerd'. Consequently one of the most favourite of strategies is for gifted students to deny their own giftedness, with the most gifted students being most likely to protest their giftedness (Swiatek, 1995). Many minority students who are gifted feel under additional social pressure to conform to student norms.
>
> Gallagher 2000: 683

When the child's cultural group holds values that do not match those of the school, deliberate non-compliance is assumed to be bad behaviour triggered by the pupil's lack of understanding rather than as a rational decision (Lee-Corbin and Denicolo 1998). Able children who behave in this way may well be overlooked and yet some may be defying convention for specific reasons including non-acceptance of the values being, as they see it, imposed by the school (Slack 2003). Such problems are more likely with able children from a lower socio-economic background, an ethnic or religious minority community and among children of Travelling people. Highly able children falling into these groups are unlikely to be receiving provision designed to meet their needs, partly for reasons of funding, partly through lack of understanding. Many of these bright pupils remain unidentified (Lee-Corbin and Denicolo 1998: 57–60).

As already reported, some children have learning difficulties or other issues that can mask exceptional ability. Teacher awareness of multiple exceptionality is the most potent tool for beginning to tackle the pupils' needs. With such knowledge, difficulties are less likely to be dismissed as laziness or petulance. Teachers should also be alerted to the well-developed abilities of some gifted pupils in compensating for learning difficulties and other problems for much of their school career, so achieving reasonably and not attracting attention. Awareness of such issues has increased and this can be seen in shifting attitudes to children who have trouble with spelling, who are no longer inevitably assumed to be non-academic. Montgomery (2000) vigorously points out that spelling problems do not mean lack of ability. Despite being a rather dated piece of research in some ways, Kellmer-Pringle's includes an interesting and valid observation that the majority of 'able misfits' were: 'just doing enough that he [sic] will not be bothered by the teacher. As a result he is often rated average or below average but without being considered a real failure' (Kellmer-Pringle 1970: 20).

The role of parents is also significant (Lee-Corbin and Denicolo 1998: 21–4) and studies reinforce common-sense intuition that parents' marital and relationship problems negatively affect school pupils' performance through changes in lifestyle and emotional stress. When an underachiever's grades start slipping this is often less visible than those identified as high achievers.

Success in science?

All areas of human endeavour have their intrinsic quirks, joys and difficulties. They have their own ardent advocates, their resident experts and their detractors. The relationship between the field in general and its role in the school curriculum varies considerably due to a combination of factors including the nature of the field, and the popularity of the subject is affected by its perception in broader society (White 2000; Slack 2003). Science is no exception, and despite attempts to re-brand the subject as accessible and relevant to all (see for example Chapters 10 and 11), it still remains off-putting to many students with its 'men in white coats' image of complexity and abstraction. (Compare this with the image of scientists that students aspire to: see Chapter 4.)

There is a dearth of empirical research into giftedness in specific disciplines, but myriad papers exist concerning many other aspects of high ability. Hundreds describe the difficulties inherent in defining high ability, but hardly any focus on high ability in science. One of the few papers suggests a link between children's development and that of high achieving professionals:

> There is [also] a need for longitudinal studies that relate the characteristics of young children and adolescents to those of eminent scientists; most studies of eminence in science examine the characteristics of eminent adults after they have achieved acclaim; we need to know more about their cognitive and affective traits as children.
>
> Pyryt 2000: 434

This may well be correct, but other studies are also needed concerning different types of pedagogy with reviews on those that best meet the needs of the multiply exceptional pupil who may find traditional teaching methods somehow inaccessible. Science is also an umbrella term for a range of disciplines (Kind and Taber 2005) and some pupils will have an interest in one and not another of these sub-divisions. Traditional hierarchies and difficulty-ratings between the various aspects of scientific endeavour need to be set aside if pupils with potential difficulties are to be encouraged to study the more abstract aspects of the subject.

For some pupils, a positive attitude to science grows from an easy facility to engage with scientific ideas and think about scientific questions without any prompting. Where such pupils also demonstrate the resilience and determination to follow these questions through, we may say that they have a propensity for science, or scientific thinking. The degree of this interest and the ease with which the pupil can adopt and adapt the conventions of discipline will determine how conclusively we can describe the propensity for scientific thinking as an aptitude. Having a very obvious aptitude for scientific thinking could be described as giftedness in science by some indicators, whereas others would be more focused on the production of work that demonstrates such abilities.

Harnessing this interest and allowing for a broad range of expressions of learning and understanding will help to ensure that an inclusive approach is taken to the teaching of science.

Chapter 4

The emotional lives of fledgling geniuses

Steve Alsop

There is a tendency to think of gifted learners purely in cognitive terms. However, education is about developing the whole person, and as science teachers we are concerned with students' attitudes to and experiences of our subject, as well as their attainment. In this chapter, Steve Alsop looks at the emotions and science learning – considering both the affective responses of those recognised as intellectually gifted in science, and whether teachers should be considering 'emotional' as well as intellectual giftedness in science.

Introduction: In search of the scientifically gifted

If asked to name a genius, a number of scientists spring to mind, perhaps Albert Einstein, Rachel Carson, Isaac Newton and Rosalind Franklin. Albert Einstein, it seems, resides someway in popular culture as *the* archetypical genius; a gifted individual with advanced cognitive abilities combined with a social ineptitude. Of course one should be extremely mindful of icons. The stereotypical image of Einstein, while grossly oversimplified, has the potential to inspire or for that matter repulse young learners: 'Do I have to be like Einstein to be successful in science?' The answer, of course, is an indefatigable 'no, you certainly do not'. Indeed, a wide range of curriculum resources are now available in schools which refreshingly broaden such stereotypes – championing a more equitable, and pluralistic image of scientists and technologists.

However, there is still a connection somewhere between the concept of a genius, a gifted mind, and the subject of science. A brain surgeon, a geneticist, a palaeontologist, a cosmologist, a quantum physicist are all considered as especially smart. After all some science *is* 'rocket science' to reverse the popular phrase, and science in schools and universities still carries the baggage of a difficult subject with some of its sub-disciplines more readily associated with conceptual acrobatics – quantum mechanics, genetics and organic chemistry and so on.

It is not my intention here to consider whether science is a more difficult subject than other subjects, whether scientists are indeed more gifted than other professionals. Such considerations, the reader will appreciate, are in many ways meaningless. Similarly the idea of degrees of giftedness within the field should be avoided. Was Albert Einstein more gifted than Isaac Newton? Was Rachel Carson more intelligent than Joseph Priesley or vice versa? How could you possibly judge this anyway?

Having accepted this, however, I find myself in the rather paradoxical position of writing about gifted children in school science. My nagging consciousness tells me that in many ways such intellectual distinctions make as little sense in schools as they do within the academy (see Chapter 1).

'Gifted' is now a widely used term in education. In Canada, for example, there are gifted streams in many elementary and secondary schools and 'giftedness' is a label of designation associated with access to specific additional funding in much the same way as other labels in Special Educational Needs. Gifted students are classified as 'Exceptional Students' and as such they are required to have an IEP (an Individualised Educational Plan – see OME 2004) and specialised educational provision. Some school boards offer an inclusive policy and gifted students are educated in the mainstream (with additional provision). Other school boards, more commonly, offer specialised programmes usually starting after grade 3 (in the form of a gifted stream). In Canada, a gifted child is usually in the top 2% of the school population as determined by psychometric scales, intelligence quotients (IQs). Some pupils have IQs as high as 200, where 100 is considered the population average. Psychometric tests vary, but such assessments are nearly always conducted in out-of-school contexts and have a particular familiar style, although it should be noted that they are becoming increasingly more sophisticated and now often combine a range of assessment techniques.

Defined in such a way, giftedness, of course, does not necessarily equate to increased ability in science per se. Concepts of 'high ability, potential and performance are complex and contested', as Carrie Winstanley notes in Chapter 3. Indeed, significant numbers of 'gifted' students experience difficulties in 'gifted streams' in more than one subject discipline. Those excelling in language are sometimes only average in mathematics and vice versa, and gifted children can perform badly in some school tests because of the nature of the tests (they can be quite different to IQ tests) as well as for a host of other reasons.

Yet many gifted students do show astonishing ability in science and mathematics. Indeed, some become the focus of wide spread media attention. In the UK, for example, in 2001, Dylan Cobb passed GCSEs (examinations designed to be taken at the end of compulsory school, age 16) in mathematics and information technology at grade B, at age 5 – the age when many children start their formal schooling. And perhaps the most famous British prodigy of them all is Ruth Lawrence, who went to Oxford University at age 12 (the youngest person to do so), graduated at age 13 (with a first class degree) and became a professor at Harvard at age 19. Dr Lawrence is now a professor at the Einstein Institute of Mathematics, in Jerusalem, Israel. (Details of Ruth's considerable career accomplishments are available in Wikipedia (http://en. wikipedia.org/wiki/Ruth_Lawrence) and on her personal website (www.ma. huji.ac.il/~ruthel/).)

Needless to say, such cases spawn extended debate on the advantages and disadvantages of accelerated study, as well as the intellectual and social purposes of education. In Dylan's and Ruth's cases, it is perhaps interesting to note that their advanced study was supported outside of traditional schooling. Indeed, in a publication entitled *Curious Minds: How a Child Becomes a Scientist* (Brockman 2005), twenty-seven famous scientists are interviewed about their childhood influences. Of the twenty-seven only four directly linked their choice of career directly to their experiences in school science. (See also the discussion of Nobel prize winners in sciences, in Chapter 2.)

Chapter overview

This chapter is about such learners, albeit with a particular focus: I am interested in the role of emotion in giftedness. This might cause a serious pause for thought because I am sure that no child has ever been identified as gifted (in any subject let alone science) based on their emotional abilities. But this in many ways is my point, in 'science' and in 'giftedness' emotions can be too easily overlooked. Indeed, I suggest that the popular image of a 'gifted child *scientist*' is in some ways 'doubly' archetypal: intellectually brilliant, with extremely high IQs, and yet emotionally and socially lost. Derogatory labels such as 'Nurd', 'Boffin', 'Geek' and 'Brainiac' conjure up images that seem somehow especially appropriate in the context of science, even more so than in other subject areas; I wonder why? Emotional absence it almost seems is a prerequisite for scientific brilliance: although, once more, one has to be chary of generalisations.

The following discussions unfold in three parts.

1   My starting point is that advanced conceptual ability can create particular emotional needs and these can be easily overlooked. Asynchronous conceptual ability might too readily be equated with concomitant emotional and social maturity. Gifted learners, like all learners, need emotional support and I explore this pedagogically by using the concept of emotional scaffolding.

2   I then turn my attention to explore the connection between giftedness and autism (Asperger's syndrome – see also Chapter 3). There is much debate about whether Einstein and Newton owe their scientific giftedness to this syndrome.

3   I conclude with a discussion of emotions and definitions of science and giftedness. Here, I explore the rise in attention to emotions in schooling and what it might mean to be emotionally gifted, as well as what it might mean, and what it should mean, emotionally to study science.

Throughout, I hope to offer some advice for colleagues as well as inviting reflections on what it means, or should mean, to be scientifically gifted. We kick off by highlighting some of the emotional demands of conceptual superiority.

Giftedness and emotions–in–science education

As teachers we have all experienced extremely bright students: students who are ahead in their scientific thinking, attain extraordinarily high percentages in examinations and seem to grasp concepts at the wink of an eye. Such children have asynchronous conceptual abilities; they are advanced for their years – in some cases operating at a level equivalent to pupils many years older.

There is no doubt that for these children, and all others for that matter, affect plays an axiomatic role in their learning. Some emotions such as joy, excitement, interest, enthusiasm, curiosity and hope, can act to enhance cognition, while others (such as fear, anxiety, boredom) might serve to deaden curiosity and insight. It is difficult to see the bored, anxious and disinterested engaging in anything, let alone the creative pedagogical activities outlined in other chapters of this text. Clearly, a success of pedagogical activities is the way in whch they nurture emotions conducive to learning, in addition to their more readily articulated conceptual aims.

In any learner, intricate thought processes and complex emotions are combined. Gifted children have conceptual, emotional and social needs as all children do because all children are an amalgam of different conceptual, emotional and social abilities (far more diverse than readily supported in our age of structured curriculum and chronologically delineated schooling).

Take 'Graham', he may have an IQ of 180, be aged 11 and solve university level science and mathematics questions, but like so many other children he might be nervous about starting secondary school, gets frustrated with his handwriting, enjoys collecting Pokemon cards, hopes to play football for Arsenal, and finds that his sister gets on his nerves. This description is a vignette derived from several case studies recorded in Moon (2004) and Delisle (1984). The combination of adult intellectual *and* childhood interests is very common in gifted students.

Teaching students like Graham poses a series of pedagogical demands. It might, in many ways, feel like teaching an undergraduate student from a child's point of view. The question is how can such a child be expected to fit into a science classroom designed for children with more synchronous abilities? The answer is likely to be with some difficultly, and with considerable emotional support. Too often, as the literature firmly asserts, academic students are held back in 'one-size-fits-all' approaches to instruction (see Howley *et al.* 1995) – or 'one-size-fits-few' as I now commonly refer to them.

A particular danger, of course, is that conceptual ability might be naturally equated with emotional and social autonomy. Children who are bright can easily be thought of as needing less instructional support because they pose fewer conceptual pedagogical demands. After all they are gifted, and so why can't they be self-sufficient? As Winner (2002) explores, there are many 'myths of giftedness' (see also Chapter 3) including:

1   That gifted children are better adjusted, more popular and happier than average children. The challenging reality is that more frequently, nearly the opposite is true.
2   That childhood is always more pleasurable and more fulfilling because of the joy from challenge and reward from work. Indeed, the reverse is often the case; for gifted children childhood can be more painful, more isolated and more stressful because they do not always fit in with their peers and can set overly unrealistic expectations.

It seems that advanced conceptual ability might actually have an emotional downside. The onslaught of increased abstract thinking can create emotional demands, as the following example with Jennie beautifully demonstrates:

> In Jennie's mind at the age of four, God could not possibly be a loving God if He would refuse Heaven to anyone. And the terrible realization of her own mortality could not be softened by her mother's reassurances, because 'Nobody knows for sure; children die sometimes.' In spite of her impressive capacity for abstract thought, Jennie was only four. Her emotional needs, like those of other four-year-olds, included a trust in the strength and reliability of her parents and the predictability of a secure world. However, her advanced cognitive capacities . . . left her emotionally defenceless in the face of her own reason.
>
> Silverman 1986: 25–6

It is difficult to understand the emotional implications of grappling with complex scientific ideas at a very young age. As Ralph Levinson discusses in Chapter 10, controversial scientific issues are an inescapable part of contemporary life, but what might they mean to a very young gifted child? The ability to reason about global warming, genetic engineering, nano-technology, avian flu and cancer at a young age requires comparative emotional and social maturity. Without this, such issues might tumble into overly pessimistic images of the future; traumatic images of global destruction combined with the potential loss of family and friends.

The literature on gifted learners makes frequent reference to widened emotional ranges and heightened intensities. Indeed, such fluctuations the authors suggest can make students appear contradictory, seeming to be at the same time mature and yet immature, arrogant and compassionate, aggressive and timid (see Delisle 1984; Moon 2004).

In the classroom, gifted learners can certainly stand out in conceptual terms and many will enjoy the attention and adulation of their peers. Although others you might imagine yearn to be unnoticed, to simply be 'normal' and 'average'. On occasions, semblances of self-assurance will mask deep feelings of insecurity; the concept of self, our own particular strengths and weaknesses, is something that we all grapple with throughout our lives. Most children, I believe, have a pretty good idea of their relative performance in compulsory education, although as teachers working with groups of mixed ability students we sometimes like to pretend otherwise.

Needless to say, for students labelled as 'gifted' the public nature of success and the fear of failure can be intense. Perhaps, it is little wonder that many underachieve. It is sometimes easier to underperform rather than suffer the social stigma of being extraordinary, the social exposure of being in some ways intellectually 'out of phase' with one's peers.

Scaffolding gifted learners' emotions

As successful teachers, we know that children (including gifted children) arrive at the laboratory door with a range of thoughts, a series of opinions, affinities, attitudes, expectations, desires and a host of social agendas. These, in combination with our teaching, the curriculum and the learning environment, shape their learning.

My work, for example, has been concerned with the ways that as science teachers we support learners' emotional needs (Alsop 2005a). To describe this, I have been using the familiar term 'scaffolding' that can be traced back to the writing of Vygotsky (1988). Scaffolding usually refers to the ways in which teachers help students to cognitively structure their learning experiences. In contrast, colleagues and I have been interested in teachers' actions which are aimed at nurturing emotions conducive to learning, and those which aim to lower emotions which are potentially hazardous to learning. Our reasoning here is that children will conceptually flourish in the right emotional and social environment – more often than not, we suggest, the barrier to learning is actually not conceptual ability but emotional orientation. Interested, motivated, curious, enthusiastic, self-assured learners will succeed in even the most complex topic areas.

In the context of gifted learners, case studies highlight instances of perfectionism, idealism and extreme self-criticism. Examples are provided of students driven to extraordinary levels of performance with intense sensitivity to failure and judging oneself by impossibly high standards (Delisle 1984). As Helena, a gifted 3rd-year university student (attending a large university in Canada, and having a grade point average of over 90%) raised in our recent conversation:

> All my friends are high achieving and I'm scared of falling behind them. I know that my averages are high but I can't ever really relax, I have such

high expectations of myself and spend so much time revising just to live up to my standards. I know these are high but getting 80% would be a failure for me. My parents tell me to relax, but I never do. I don't want to fall behind.

As teachers, we need to be sensitive to *perceptions* of underachievement. All children need emotional support, encouragement and praise. Such scaffolding serves to lower the frustration of failure and underachievement, and in the longer term can help alleviate the anxiety of falling behind.

The goals that learners set themselves have been the focus of much attention in psychology. Studies contrast students who focus on *performance goals* doing better for grades (and other extrinsic outcomes) with those who focus on learning and understanding for intrinsic benefits, *mastery goals*. While this distinction is rarely definitive, with students adopting aspects of these positions in different contexts, it has been suggested that students with a particular preference for performance or mastery orientations thrive in classrooms with these particular profiles. Science classrooms which use competitive grading systems and other ways for students to publicly display performance suit some students while having a detrimental effect on others. Such research suggests that mastery goals associate with the adoption of longer lasting deeper learning strategies (including metacognition) while performance goals link with the adoption of shorter term rote learning approaches to study.

Instructional approaches can influence the adoption of these goals: science activities which scaffold student choice and that are appropriately challenging and collaborative can nurture mastery goals, while those that enable easy comparisons and use overly competitive grading systems can scaffold performance goals (Rhee Bonney 2005).

In the case of some overcompetitive gifted learners, mastery orientated activities can offer a less competitive and potentially more supportive learning environment. Indeed experienced teachers of the gifted stream often draw on self-directed, more autonomous open-ended differentiated learning activities (Austin 1995). Project work and science fairs are very popular in which learners are required to research a topic, present a paper and make connections to everyday life. Gifted learners often enjoy this freedom and can 'run' with activities of this type. (Some writers have compared them to a cheetah, see Tolan's (2006) famous essay.) Shifting away from a performance orientation can reduce the anxieties and pressures associated with over-performance.

As you might expect many gifted pupils are curious, often expressed in their intense insistence on knowing *why* all the time (Delisle 1984). *Wanting* to know why is of course different to *asking* why and these children seem to be continuously seeking, chasing down, answers to increasingly abstract questions. They have a refreshing inner thirst, a desire, for knowledge and challenge. Successful teaching needs to be sensitive to these motivations. As Sue, an experienced teacher of the gifted in a large inner city secondary school in Canada, highlights:

> One of the most important things about teaching exceptional students is accepting their propensity for innovation. They thrive on the challenge of solving problems in different ways, which is really cool but sometimes difficult as a teacher to accept and understand. You may offer three clear steps to calculate molarity, atomic and molecular mass and they take one step and get the right answer.

A key here seems to be pedagogical approaches that scaffold creativity rather than impose conformity. A learner's interest, and their desire for knowledge, needs to be supported while providing a space for self-expression and innovation. There are many ways of answering questions and sometimes a challenge is finding a new one. There is actually some evidence that gifted students find multiple-choice assessments difficult because of their closed nature – they see ways in which multiple selections might be justified (see Austin 1995).

Of course, children have particular interests and instruction is likely to be more successful if an effort is made to foster constructive emotions by relating subject matter with something familiar, interesting and relevant to them. Finding a subject that pupils have positive confident feelings about and using this as a context to explore science is a good approach. For example, I watched a science teacher use children's toys to explore motion (rather than using ticker timers). In this instance, the approach was successful because it explored concepts of motion within the context of familiarity and playfulness (toys). In another lesson a teacher selected to use the context of a 'mystery' to make data analysis more enticing. In both these cases the context is selected not because of conceptual reasons (in both cases the context did not structure the concepts), but because of emotional reasons to increase task value – making a subject more interesting by explicitly associating it with something of interest (a particular approach to emotional scaffolding). This is just one approach to 'emotional scaffolding' (see Roseik 2003; Alsop et. al. 2006a), one of the ways of scaffolding learners' emotions in science education (Alsop 2005b).

Children are successful more often if they approach a task/subject with the belief that they will succeed. (Psychologists explore this with the term 'self-efficacy'.) As science tasks require students to evoke higher order thinking and integrate a variety of new skills, students can perceive these tasks as extending beyond their present capabilities, and as a consequence even gifted students can feel a sense of failure before actually starting. In this instance, conceptual scaffolding, breaking the task down into a series of more manageable components and helping students to see a task in terms of a number of manageable subtasks has been shown in the longer and shorter term to increase self-efficacy (see Schunk 1989).

A fear of failure (exacerbated by perfectionism) can easily result in disenchantment and underachievement. In a given context, gifted children are likely to have different levels of self-efficacy and practice needs to be sensitive to this. Moreover, much research highlights a gender dimension to self-efficacy; adolescent girls often underestimate their abilities while boys can overestimate theirs, especially in traditionally male-dominated fields such as science and mathematics. This disparity that has been found to be more pronounced following puberty (see Eccles and Wigfield 1995).

Emotions, giftedness and Asperger's syndrome

Giftedness has become associated with a specific category of Special Educational Needs, classic autism and Asperger's syndrome (see also Chapter 3). Intriguingly during the 2006 Cambridge Spotlight on Science Festival, Professor Simon Baron-Cohen stressed the link between autism and increased systemising. Systemising, a basis of science, is the *drive* to understand how systems works and to be able to predict them.

There is much contemporary discussion about whether Einstein and Newton (as well as a number of other famous historical figures) might have been autistic. Professor Baron-Cohen and Ioan James both suggest that Einstein's and Newton's personalities were consistent with Asperger's syndrome (Baron-Cohen 2003) – manifesting themselves in intense pre-occupation with a particular topic combined with a social uneasiness; that familiar mix of intellectual brilliance and social/emotional ineptitude.

It is reported, for example, that both Einstein and Newton displayed intense interest in specific limited areas, and they both had trouble relating appropriately in social situations. On occasions they became so preoccupied with their work that they did not eat. Newton had few friends, was often bad tempered and barely spoke. If nobody attended his lecture, he still lectured to an empty room. He suffered a nervous breakdown at age fifty, preceded by periods of depression and paranoia (Baron-Cohen 2003). The first words that Einstein ever spoke (at age four) were 'the soup is cold' and in later years he juxtaposed his sense of social justice and social responsibility with his lack of interpersonal needs comparing himself to 'a lone traveller' (AIP 2004).

Such assertions remain controversial and will continue to be contested. Needless to say, geniuses can experience social difficulties without being autistic and while some high functioning autistics might exhibit intellectual giftedness in science, it does not mean that all gifted eccentric children are autistic. Neither does it imply that to be successful in science you need to display periods of social ineptness.

In more general terms while it is clearly impossible to question the brilliance of Newton and Einstein, it is clearly myopic to limit discussion of 'genius' to just two individuals. There are many other brilliant, gifted scientists who are extraordinarily socially and emotionally astute.

However, I am sure that there are many gifted child scientists who remain unnoticed simply because they are socially and emotionally compliant. Like many aspects of Special Educational Needs, children who are disruptive and eccentric tend to attract undue attention leading to special provision (Howley *et al.* 1995). This in part explains why so many boys, rather than girls, occupy the gifted stream – a source of wide spread concern (Pendarvis and Howley 1995; Moon 2004). Another failing of the process of the identification of the gifted is also the chronic under-representation of minority ethnics and economically disadvantaged students (Moon 2004). At the very least this suggests a reconsideration of the processes of identification and definitions of giftedness are urgently required.

Emotionally gifted learners in science: whatever next?

Of late, emotions have experienced a type of resurgence in education. Starting with Thorndike's analysis of 'social intelligence' and Howard Gardner's (Gardner 1993) highly influential text on multiple intelligences, intelligence is now considered in broader terms and encompasses intra-personal and interpersonal features. Emotional intelligence as a concept has gained wide spread appeal and psychological measures of EI (emotional intelligence) and EQ (emotional quotient) are widely available (see Beasley 1987 and Bar-On 1997). You might wish to test yourself.

EI gained considerable popularity in Daniel Goleman's (Goleman 1996) best selling book. On its cover it boldly advertises the way in which it 'redefines what it means to be smart'. An emotionally smart person is offered as somebody who maintains optimism in the face of obstacles, has the ability to motivate oneself and persist in the face of frustration; to control impulse and delay gratification; to regulate one's moods and keep distress from swamping the ability to think; to empathise and to hope. The text provides reference to a number of curriculum materials designed to nurture emotional development. Matthews (2006) has thoughtfully incorporated these concepts into science education.

EI and EQ have raised discussion of the role of emotions in schools and this is clearly a good thing. But IQs, EI and EQs and all other definitions of giftedness carry particular social and political agendas and to identify giftedness in any manifestation, of course, runs the risk of imposing particular values and beliefs. They are not neutral and favour some students more than others. Crucial questions here are 'which values?', and most importantly '*whose* values count?'

A particular critique of emotional intelligence, for example, is the way in which it focuses largely on 'controlling emotions'; an emotionally intelligent student is portrayed as a compliant labile student, a student who learns to control their emotional outbursts. Here, I have much sympathy with Boler's

(1999: 80) critique in which she unfavourably compares EI to 'social control and pastoral power through self-policing' – the process of making disenfranchised learners compliant and passive.

In my work, I have become intrigued by the emotions *of* science education – how our practices as science teachers promote or suppress different types of emotions. These interests are driven by two questions: (1) What might it mean emotionally to be a school scientist? and (2) What *should* it mean? Such questions might also be considered of giftedness; what might it mean emotionally to be a gifted scientist? And what should it mean?

In a collaborative study with science teachers, colleagues and I have been mapping the emotional contours of normal school laboratory life to better understand not only these contours but also how they are established and reinforced by our teaching. Our study, for instance, has compared learning in laboratories (grade 7 and 8, at ages 11 and 12) with learning at an earlier age in integrated classrooms (grade 6, ages 9/10).

Our video data shows children in grade 6 (age 9/10) being introduced to science in an integrated setting by engaging in open-ended play in atmospheres of emotional joviality. In contrast, in the science laboratory groups of grade 7 and 8 elementary students are recorded learning safety rules and of the dangers of not following instructions carefully enough (see Alsop *et al.* 2006a, 2006b). Of course, the physical settings of the laboratory and the classroom are very different. Safety is a critical issue, more especially in the lab. But might our situated practices be creating certain emotional (as well as behavioural) norms and rules?

Our data suggest that this is the case. Science in our grade 6 classrooms was introduced to be about *play*. In contrast, in the laboratory setting science was linked to *experimentation*. These terms, we suggest, can mean quite different things both pedagogically and emotionally. Through adherence to the concept of play, we found our primary teachers placed a greater importance on ownership, curiosity and outward expressions of joy in science. Children are recorded joking and laughing in free flowing self controlled activities. In contrast in the laboratory, experimentation was much more externally controlled by the teacher: a serious endeavour in which outward expressions of enjoyment, expressions of self, were more often than not reprimanded as misconduct (see Alsop *et al.* 2006a). Indeed, we have excerpts of data in which grade 8 children are being reprimanded for 'playing' (seen as messing about), while an almost identical act in grade 6 is being encouraged by the teacher as a good example of investigative science. For our teachers, at least, we suggest that grade 6 science and grade 7/8 science mean different things emotionally.

Of course, different teachers teach in very different ways and it is impossible to generalise from case studies. Our examples, however, raise some interesting questions. Through our evolving actions as science teachers might we be creating emotional norms to what it means to study science? Are we presenting an image of science as devoiced from self?

If so, we are fascinated by how this culture might be serving to attract some learners while repulsing others. A clutch of questions now seem to emerge. What values and whose values are supported by our current practices? Might emotionally connected gifted learners find the culture of laboratory science education alienating? Might emotionally unconnected gifted learners find it a more comfortable place to study? How can we make science education a place emotionally appealing to all learners?

At a time in which interest in science among secondary school children (in particular) is alarmingly declining (see Osborne *et al.* 2003; Nieswandt 2005), what would happen if we placed emotions at the centre of secondary (as well as primary) science education? Would a more evocative science education connect more children with our subject? Such questions at this moment are wide open and they form the focus of our ongoing work (see Alsop *et al.* 2006a).

In more general terms – moving beyond the stereotype – what *should* it mean emotionally to be successful in science, to be a gifted scientist? In a recent study, for instance, we asked a large group of science students (aged ten to thirteen) to draw a picture of themselves as the scientist that *they* would like to be in the future (see Figure 4.1).

There is a long history in science education of pupils drawing pictures of scientists and this consistently results in stereotypical images of white unkempt madmen in white coats surrounded by noxious substances (e.g. Sjoberg 2002) – I am sure that you are familiar with this image.

The vast majority of our pictures, however, cast a very different image. These students depicted themselves in traditional costumes (lab coats) but within the context of *care* – caring for animals, finding cures for cancer and saving the planet (see Figure 4.1). I was left wondering whether there is a tension between the stereotypical dispassionate image that students hold of scientists and the compassionate image of the scientist that *they* aspire to be?

In more general terms, in our practice, what image of a scientist are we, or should we be projecting? Might Rachel Carson, for example, a scientist who openly placed emotions at the centre of her practice, be held up as a genius because of the role she placed *on* emotions in her practice (a 'feeling-for-the-organism', see Carson (2002), and writers who have explored the notion of feminist science, e.g. Keller 1983; Harding 1991)? Or should we continue to be fascinated by iconic geniuses that reinforce the uneasy relationship between scientific brilliance and social and emotional finesse and thereby perpetuate the intellectual–emotional divide (see Alsop 2005a)?

In terms of gifted students, what type of future scientific geniuses should we be identifying and nurturing in our classrooms now and why?

Conclusions

My hope is that discussions in this chapter offer some useful advice for practitioners with exceptional students, as well as raise some important

Figure 4.1 The scientists students would like to become

questions of the role of emotions in giftedness in science education (and in science). My greatest fear is that discussion of 'gifted' can become reduced to the oversimplified story of individuals. We need to understand the ways in which our practices might evolve to support and enhance exceptional learners as well as how the social and institutional traditions of our subject might be changed to make it more inclusive. We need to be ever vigilant of our practices and how they might inadvertently be serving to exclude learners. Definitions and mechanisms of identification of the gifted which exclude girls, ethnic minorities and economically disadvantaged students clearly need to change.

In the end perhaps the most important question in discussions of giftedness is the purpose and nature of identification. We need to remember that exceptionality is culturally and contextually embedded in all human activity and, with this in mind, move beyond the stereotype and strive toward an education which values all children and seeks to help them realise their fullest potential in science. Through our practices, all children need to be able to see themselves conceptually and *emotionally* as part of science.

Chapter 5

Opportunities for gifted science provision in the context of a learner-centred national curriculum

Richard K. Coll

One of the themes that echoes through a number of chapters in the book is that a prescribed curriculum may constrain opportunities for providing suitably challenging and engaging work for the most able. This is certainly a common perception of the English National Curriculum (the setting of a number of contributions). In this chapter, Richard Coll offers an account of a rather different context – the New Zealand science curriculum, well known for being influenced by 'constructivist' pedagogic assumptions. However, as Richard points out, an enabling curriculum regime does not necessarily lead to the needs of gifted learners being met.

Introduction

This chapter explores how teachers may make use of curriculum flexibility to develop effective gifted education within science classes. It draws upon the New Zealand (NZ) experience, where provision for the gifted is considered to be uneven, but is a focus of interest. The New Zealand context offers particular opportunities because there is considerable potential for flexibility in the science curriculum (and other curricula). This chapter explores the situation, and offers suggestions for how best teachers might build on these opportunities. The concern about provision for the gifted in New Zealand schools has had a difficult gestation for a variety of reasons, and these are briefly described. A particular feature of the New Zealand context is provision of gifted and other education for the Māori (i.e. people self-identifying culturally as indigenous New Zealanders), and this has had a significant influence in informing both the principles of gifted education policy and the nature of the science curriculum. In terms of the former, there has been much concern with keeping an inclusive understanding of 'giftedness' in New Zealand schools. The curriculum has more flexibility than in some other countries (such as in the UK) and may be considered to be student-centred in nature. Indeed, the science curriculum has been described as 'constructivist' by commentators (including some who see this as an unfortunate development). This constructivist-based curriculum evolved in response to issues related to New Zealand's economic status at the time. The outcome was a curriculum statement that allows – indeed encourages – local input into the curriculum in order to meet the needs of the learners attending that school. In principle this allows flexibility which could help schools provide for their gifted learners in science, however these may be conceptualised and identified. In practice research shows that schools are using this flexibility to a differing, often limited extent. Provision for the gifted has also been the subject of research in New Zealand,where it has been found that there are some examples of good practice, but that there are seen to be barriers to implementing best practice, and that the approaches used offer both advantages and disadvantages. In science, some examples of practice are described. The final section of this chapter will draw upon the lesson of such research as exists into gifted provision, and science curriculum practice in New Zealand to offer ideas on how schools can draw upon the potential flexibility of a student-centred curriculum to meet the needs of their gifted learners in science.

New Zealand educational reforms

In the 1970s New Zealand fell upon economic hardship, because of the so-called 'oil-shocks' (when the cost of importing fuel increased substantially) and Britain joining the European Economic Community (changing its trading patterns). A new government came to power with a mandate for economic, social and educational change. A key feature of education reform was the role science and technology (and thereby science and technology education) must play in New Zealand's economic well-being (Beattie 1986; Picot 1988; Crocombe 1991).

The education reforms were enacted through a centre-periphery model (McGee 1997) with the first step being devolution of school administration (Lange 1988). This involved the dissolution of the department of education, education boards and school committees and replacement with an autonomous Ministry of Education (MoE), Education Review Office (ERO), and a community-based Board of Trustees (BoT) for each school. It became the BoT's job to govern the school, to set policies into place, to manage the annual budget within MoE guidelines, and to oversee staffing. Some felt that too much emphasis was placed on social and cultural matters (Shuker 1990; Matthews 1995).

The New Zealand school education system changed from a somewhat fragmented national curriculum to a more coherent structure for learners from Year 1 through to Year 13 (Bell *et al.* 1995; Matthews 1995). Curriculum and administrative reviews carried out from 1984 to 1987 resulted in the formulation of the *National Education Guidelines* containing the *National Education Goals* which specified the Ministry's overall objectives, the *National Administration Guidelines*, which specified the administrative framework necessary to achieve these objectives, and the *New Zealand Curriculum Framework* (MoE 1993a, 1993c), which set the scene for school-based curriculum development and implementation. The *National Education Guidelines* and *New Zealand Curriculum Framework* detail the elements deemed fundamental to teaching and learning in New Zealand schools (Box 5.1).

Curriculum documents incorporating essential skills were subsequently developed for each of the learning areas for Year 1 to Year 13, and national curriculum statements were developed for science, physics, chemistry, biology, and technology for Year 11 to Year 13. The science curriculum, like other curricula, comprised *achievement aims* and *achievement objectives* with specific content to be selected by schools (MoE 1993b). In addition to providing content prescriptions, the subject curricula were linked to the aims and objectives and essential skills expressed in the *National Education Guidelines*, the *New Zealand Curriculum Framework* (MoE 1996a, 1996b, 1996c, 1996d). For example, the school curriculum was expected to incorporate generic skills such as communication and literacy skills provided in the *New Zealand Curriculum Framework* as well as appropriate content.

External summative examinations were deemed incompatible with a learner-centred education system, and replaced by the National Certificate of Educational Achievement (NCEA) (Hume 2003). NCEA is criterion-based, but how the students meet the criteria can be decided by the school (subject to external moderation) with considerable flexibility in the choice of assessment activities. Assessment is a mixture of internal and external assessment and students are awarded one of, 'not achieved', 'achieved', 'achieved with merit', and 'achieved with excellence'.

Box 5.1 Prescribed NZ curriculum elements

Essential learning areas	Essential skills
Language and Languages, Mathematics, Science, Technology, Social Sciences, the Arts, Health and Physical Well-Being	Communication Skills, Numeracy Skills, Information Skills, Problem-Solving Skills, Self Management and Competitive Skills, Social and Cooperative Skills, Physical Skills, and Work and Study Skills

A learner–centred, constructivist–based curriculum?

A key philosophy underpinning the New Zealand curriculum documents was a shift from an exclusive science-for-some content-driven teaching approach, towards a more inclusive, science-for-all, learner-centred approach. Programme development is school-based, and each school is required to develop its own teaching approach with school performance in meeting curriculum needs evaluated by ERO. Content choice is thus flexible and more interactive activities and pedagogies are routinely employed (Hume 2003; Hume and Coll 2005). For example Milne (2004a) describes a teaching approach in which a primary science teacher allowed her students significant input into their learning activities – in this case designing a stand or hanger for a photo. The flexibility of the curriculum allowed the teacher to choose a topic of interest to the students, and to give them free rein to design the object using their choice of materials, to take into account the final use of the object and consider the aesthetics of their product. Other topics popular in New Zealand schools include environmental projects (Barker 2003) and science enquiry activities that form part of science fairs (RSNZ 2005) and Olympiads (Fletcher 1995).

The new curriculum documents are thus seemingly learner-centred in nature, although the curriculum developers themselves were somewhat reluctant to label them 'constructivist' (Bell *et al.* 1995). If the authors of New Zealand's curriculum reforms and documents did not see them as constructivist in nature, then many others did. The result of this was a rather heated, media-driven, debate (see e.g. Matthews 1995 and references therein). This debate has substantially dissipated and there is no great evidence that the curriculum damaged, or indeed improved, New Zealand students' learning (see Mitchell *et al.* 1993). Insofar as international monitoring evaluation exercises are concerned, New Zealand's performance in mathematics and science is above the international mean at Year 9 and about the mean at Year 5. It is one of six countries to report a significant improvement in mathematics achievement at Year 5, and one of nine countries to report a significant improvement in science achievement in the eight years from 1994 to 2002 (based on TIMSS data, see MoE 2004a, 2004b). Likewise for PISA (the Programme for International Student Assessment) the New Zealand student means placed New Zealand within the group of second highest performing countries for each subject area (MoE 2003). New Zealand had a wide distribution of achievement scores in each of the assessment areas, and the achievement of New Zealand students did not change significantly between the 2000 and 2003 PISA assessments in reading, mathematics or science (MoE 2003).

Overview of New Zealand education for the gifted

Up until the 1970s very little was done about education for the gifted in New Zealand (Mitchell and Mitchell 1985; Marland 1987; McApline and Moltzen 1996). There were a few advocates such as Parkin (1948) (see Moltzen 1996b, 2004) and there were calls for 'gifted' to be interpreted liberally (Hill 1977; Mitchell and Singh 1987; Bevan-Brown 1996, 2004; McAlpine 1996a, 1996b; 2004; Moltzen 1996a; Moltzen and Easter 2000). There was some recognition that New Zealand was lagging behind in provision for the gifted, attributed to what Moltzen (2004) terms a 'conforming notion' of egalitarianism in New Zealand society.

After the 1950s New Zealand, like other Western countries, became somewhat alarmed by Eastern European advances in technology in the so-called Sputnik era. As a consequence there was increased interest in gifted education, but this was based on enrichment in normal classrooms (O'Halloran *et al.* 1955).

The 1980s, as noted above, brought about many changes to the administration of education; specifically, the decentralisation of school administration. As also noted above, the intention was that schools, now more autonomous, could cater for all children with whatever special needs they might have (Mitchell and Drewery 1985; Pickens *et al.* 1992). Education for the gifted was overseen by school inspectors, but only as part of their general duties and there was brief mention of education for the gifted in a number of departmental documents (e.g. DoE 1972), but this was perceived as a 'difficulty' to which schools should respond somehow (Marris 1984; Thompson 1984; Moltzen 1992a, 1992b).

There was some evidence of schools using their new autonomy to provide for the education needs of the gifted in the 1990s with a number of schools implementing programmes for the gifted (Pickens *et al.* 1992; Moltzen 1996b, 2004). In cases in which schools did make provision for education of the gifted, acceleration (see Chapter 1) was deemed the best strategy (Moltzen 1995, 1996c), and this along with enrichment was the main approach, but there was little beyond-the-classroom enrichment (Moltzen 1996c). The late 1990s generally were characterised by greater appreciation of the importance of catering for diversity in New Zealand classrooms, including the gifted (ERO 1998; Moltzen 1998). There is little doubt this was facilitated by the reforms that preceded this era, particularly the devolution of school management and curriculum development.

After years of official neglect, 1997 saw the establishment of an education advisory board on gifted education, somewhat 'out of the blue' (Moltzen 1996b; Moltzen 2001a, 2001b). This board recommended a national policy and handbook (subsequently distributed to all schools in 2000) to help schools and specific teachers cope with education for the gifted. However, education for the gifted was still seen as 'desirable', rather than required (MoE

2000), but a need for teacher professional development was reiterated, and six special advisors were appointed by the MoE.

In 2002, at the behest of a working party, the government released a national policy on provision of education for gifted children and for the first time there was clear identification in the *National Administration Guidelines* of gifted and talented students as a group that require both identification and provision. From Term 1, 2005 it became mandatory for all state and state-integrated schools to demonstrate how they are meeting the needs of their gifted and talented learners (among others with special needs). A new funding pool for education programmes was established and targeted at gifted and talented learners, additional advisors and a national coordinator for education for the gifted were established, as was professional development for education professionals other than teachers and pre-service training in gifted education. A handbook for parents was produced (aimed at helping them identify and cope with their gifted children), and some ICT-based (information and communication technology) initiatives provided for gifted and talented students (Moltzen *et al.* 2001b). The government also established funding for research on existing provision for gifted and talented and provided local MoE contacts and an advisory committee, charged with plotting future directions in this area.

Does a learner–centred curriculum enable teachers to provide education for the gifted?

Despite the presence of a flexible, learner-centred national curriculum, according to Moltzen (2004) New Zealand's efforts towards its best and brightest have been beleaguered by two major constraints. The first of these is based on notions of egalitarianism and 'fair play', and the second is the lack of a national policy. The net result of this is that even with the flexibility available in the New Zealand school-based curriculum model, provision of education for the gifted has struggled. More broadly, perceptions of the egalitarian nature of New Zealand society meant that education for the gifted was not always seen positively (see e.g. Walters 1991; Moltzen 1996a, 1998). Indeed there were perceptions that among other things gifted children would make it on their own, and special programmes for the gifted are thereby undemocratic and unjust (Moltzen 1995). It is worthwhile noting here that some authors apparently felt that even in the regime of the old rather heavily prescribed school syllabi, there was enough flexibility to cater for special needs learners, including the gifted. Whether or not this could have happened is debatable, and Mitchell and Singh (1987: 319) note that in practice programmes are made for all exceptional special needs students '*except* the gifted and talented' [original emphasis].

Moltzen (2004) notes that changes in government attitude towards provision of the special needs for the gifted were dramatic and unexpected.

It is interesting to ponder on reasons for these changes. Looking at the historical situation of education in New Zealand generally, and education for the gifted, it seems that something of a critical mass was generated in which a series of interrelated events conspired to bring about change. As noted above, New Zealand somewhat prides itself on the egalitarian nature of its society. In truth New Zealand society in the 1980s in particular became much more diverse, in terms of wealth and ethnicity at least. The rich–poor gap was exacerbated dramatically during the free-market, far-right economic reforms of the 1980s and 1990s (Moltzen 1995). The development of a 'knowledge economy' and a shift away from vulnerable primary produce-based industries was seen as critical to New Zealand's future economic health. The importance of education in these areas heightened. A further feature of the times was fairly rapid immigration meaning New Zealand society became more socially diverse. All of these factors are clearly pressure points. But any changes in attitude towards education for the gifted would not have been possible unless the education system possessed the flexibility to cater for diversity in the classroom and for students with special education needs, including the gifted. Hence, the devolution and decentralisation and acceptance of learner-centred education also were important elements. Advocacy of the special needs of the gifted, then, perhaps, finally fell on fertile ground. Moltzen (2004) attributes the then minister of education with credit for the final steps taken to provide for the special needs of the gifted. This is likely true; someone had to make the decisions if education for the gifted was to move forward. But the time was ripe, and the educational infrastructure was there so that the decisions could be made.

Facilitating factors and barriers to provision of education for the gifted in New Zealand

Reid (2004) comments that New Zealand has a lamentable record in programme evaluation studies about educational provision for the gifted. He goes further to note that the few reported studies about education for the gifted are 'long on description, unsupported opinion, and unsubstantiated conclusions . . . [and] woefully short on quantitative and/or qualitative evidence of efficacy' (p. 426). Interestingly, an ERO report in the late 1990s claimed that 90% of some 336 schools investigated were 'providing suitably' for special needs students including the gifted (ERO 1998). Research by Riley *et al.* (2004), including a survey of all New Zealand schools, reported on a variety of aspects of education for the gifted:

- How common is policy or specific school-wide plans for provisions to meet the needs of gifted and talented learners in New Zealand schools?
- What types of methods are stated in school-wide policies or plans as being used to identify?

- What types of approaches are used in schools to provide for the needs of gifted and talented?
- Are there any patterns (i.e. differences between regions, between schools with high and low socio-economic profiles, for different ethnic groups) in provision of support for gifted and talented learners?

The survey comprised some 1,272 participants with a demographic mix reasonably reflective of New Zealand schools. The survey data were complemented by intensive case studies of ten schools and a comprehensive literature review. This survey represents a fairly comprehensive picture of education for the gifted in NZ schools as of 2004. The results from Riley *et al.* (2004) are summarised below, and complemented where data are available with reports of other case study research (Moltzen *et al.* 1992; Moltzen 2000a, b).

Provision of education for the gifted: overview

There is ostensibly growing awareness in schools of the need to provide for gifted students with a learner-centred education programme tailored to their needs. The defining characteristic of the gifted is that he or she is 'out of step with their peers' (Riley *et al.* 2004). Unlike overseas, in New Zealand multiple approaches to identification of giftedness and talent are reported by New Zealand schools (Moltzen *et al.* 2001a). In support of this proposition, Riley (2004) observes that for rural New Zealand some 67% report using two or more methods of identification. The three most common approaches are a combination of: standardised measures of aptitude, achievement and creativity; observations by teachers, parents, students and others; and, standardised evaluations of portfolios or performances (Frasier 1997). However, there is still heavy reliance upon teacher identification and standardised testing across all areas of ability. In particular, cultural, spiritual, and emotional giftedness are often overlooked. Additionally, many of the reported definitions, identification practices and provisions do not embody Māori perspectives and values. For example, research by Bevan-Brown (1996) suggests that the Māori see gifted as encompassing exceptionality in academic performance and general 'intelligence', but also the arts, sport, leadership and service to the Māori community as well as spiritual and emotional qualities and pride in Māori identity. Keen (2000, 2001) reports Māori and other Polynesian students being identified as gifted at about half the rate for New Zealand European and Asian students. The origins of this are unclear, but this disparity may be as a result of differing perceptions of gifted; i.e. based on definitions or mode of identification of gifted students.

There is a reported preference in New Zealand schools for implementing a combined approach of enrichment and acceleration, but the implementation of these is rather limited, with partiality to within-class provisions and withdrawal or pull-out programmes. Similarly, there is little reported use of individual educational planning (and related notions) in use in teaching of the gifted in New Zealand schools (Cathcart 1994).

There is awareness and recognition of the social and emotional needs of gifted and talented students; however, only isolated examples of provision specific to these are reported by New Zealand schools. Examples include creating physically pleasant learning environments suitable for gifted learners that are 'resource rich' (Clark 1997), and that encourage gifted learners to be 'natural' and take risks. This apparently can be achieved when such learners are able to build trust and develop self-confidence (George 1997). Additionally, some of the reported identification methods and provisions could have potential negative effects upon the social and emotional well-being of gifted and talented students. For example, feelings of isolation and segregation are reported (Riley *et al.* 2004).

Enabling factors in provision of education for the gifted in NZ schools

Riley *et al.* (2004) comments that there are strengths in both research and practice about provision of education for the gifted in New Zealand schools. However, any 'strength' identified is somewhat tempered by associated issues identified above. The strengths would appear to be a fairly strong awareness of the need to provide for the special needs of the gifted. This is not a trivial point, as noted above, New Zealand's notions of egalitarianism meant special needs education was provided to students deemed disadvantaged, especially Māori and those from lower socio-economic backgrounds. So this does represent a significant shift in attitude. This along with the flexibility (Riley *et al.* 2004) and learner-centred nature of the school-based curriculum development are enabling factors: schools do have the capacity to provide for the gifted special needs. As mentioned above schools do have considerable choice over content and delivery of curriculum – a key feature of the educational reforms (Milne 2004a, b). So, for example, a teacher can deliver biotechnology content in a fairly traditional teacher-centred manner or using challenging approaches such as using biotechnology to teach students about models and modelling in science (France 2001; see also Taylor *et al.* 2003 who talk about teaching astronomy using a model-based approach).

The multi-categorical interpretation of gifted (albeit tempered by reliance on standardised testing) is a strength: there is seemingly now at least some recognition of a liberal interpretation to the term 'gifted'. For example, a case study conducted by Riley *et al.* (2004) involved a whole school approach to identification and provision of education for the gifted. Identification while placing emphasis on academic ability also included evidence for creativity, aptitude for visual and performing arts, social skills and leadership. Gifted students, that is, those with such attributes, were still teacher identified but the push for gifted provision seemingly came from parents. In this case there was an element of serendipity with one teacher, the deputy principal, having recently completed a university course in education for the gifted and becoming the driving force behind the initiative. Provision consisted of a combination of electives, enrichment and extension programmes. A gifted child was traditionally seen as a 'clever' child; in other words the stereotypical prodigy – good at maths, or music, but mostly a child who excelled in school tests and examinations. It was hard to imagine schools bothering to cater for special needs of gifted students outside the traditional stereotype; so a more liberal interpretation of gifted is certainly enabling. Recognition of the need for professional development also is enabling. This is consistent with a clear perception that gifted students do have special needs, and that teachers need to understand how these needs might be best met. It seems unlikely that provision of guidelines such as the MoE (2002) document do more than highlight such issues, and perhaps raise awareness. Indeed the guidelines go on at some length about the need for professional development: which is mostly not accessible (see above).

Macleod (2004) notes that the flexibility of the new assessment regime (i.e. NCEA) also is an enabling factor in provision of education for the gifted in New Zealand. The fact that NCEA is an exit level qualification and criterion-based allows teachers to tailor programmes and assessment to suit student needs. Challenge for gifted students is provided at all levels of ability and in all subject areas the standards needed to obtain an 'excellence' in NCEA are very demanding, providing stimulating challenges for gifted students. For example, Hume (2003) notes that under NCEA assessment can take the form of a combination of formative and summative assessment regime, an unusual situation in a high stakes assessment regime, and probably only possible because of the flexibility of the curriculum (and NCEA). Clark (2001) explains how this can work using the example of classification of rock types, drawing on a constructivist-based vision of the teacher as a facilitator rather than transmitter of knowledge. Negotiated learning goals incorporating student self- and peer-assessment strategies (in this case on what basis rocks should be classified – size, colour, shape, etc.) resulted in highly contextualised success criteria which served to reinforce the students' understanding of the learning intentions by giving a clear indication of what successful learning looks like (in this case correct classification/identification of five 'mystery' rocks). In many ways this is an extraordinary situation. Here the students and teachers were able to negotiate on what basis the standards specified in curriculum documents would be satisfied.

This flexibility is also provided in the premier examination – the New Zealand Scholarship. Compared with previous versions, the new scholarship examination requires a broader and greater depth of understanding in response to open-ended questions in order to achieve, again, a more inclusive approach. Because scholarship is based on content within NCEA level 3 (i.e. the final and highest level of NCEA), potentially all students will have equal access and opportunities for scholarship. This is clearly more inclusive and consistent with multi-categorical notions of gifted. Hume's (2006) work illustrates how this can work with her research into an investigation of a specific NCEA achievement standard related to carrying out a practical investigation with direction. As noted above, the statements in achievement standards, which describe what students are able to know and do for credits, are written with comparatively non-specific performance criteria titled 'achievement', 'achievement with merit' and 'achievement with excellence'. Using the same content and the same tasks (e.g. Hume describes tasks such as 'Which Bunsen flame, blue or yellow, heats water the fastest?' and 'Rates of reaction between acids and metals') students have considerable freedom to design and conduct an 'authentic' scientific investigation (see Chapter 13 – cf. Gilbert and Newberry's comments in Chapter 2). For this achievement standard the students needed to conduct the investigation and produce a report which clearly specified the 'purpose', 'workable plan' and 'sources of error'. In this case the achievement and merit criteria are the same for a particular aspect such as planning, but a student might be typically expected to 'describe' at achievement level, 'explain' at merit level and 'apply' or 'evaluate' at excellence level. To achieve excellence, they would be expected to be able to identify relevant variables, suggest suitable ways to control variables, and distinguish between independent and dependent variables. In their planning they needed to appreciate the need for a suitable range of values for the independent variable, for repetitive measurements and for taking into consideration sources of error. They also needed to recall and apply basic and appropriate data gathering and processing skills, including observing, measuring time using a stopwatch, recording data in tables, averaging and graphing.

Inhibiting factors in provision of education for the gifted in NZ schools

There is a growing awareness of the need to provide gifted and talented students in New Zealand schools with an individualised and appropriate education, but this is impeded by a reported lack of professional development, access to resources and support, funding, time and cultural misunderstandings. Gifted and talented students from under-represented groups, especially Māori students and those of other ethnic minority groups, are not being readily identified in New Zealand schools, and culturally appropriate provisions are not being planned, implemented or evaluated. The reported involvement of parents, caregivers and extended family in the overall organisation, coordination, identification, and provisions for gifted and talented students in New Zealand schools is minimal. Schools in New Zealand are cognisant of the need for ongoing school-wide professional development for all teachers and consider the lack of these opportunities a barrier to identification and provisions. Resources, funding, time and access are reported as barriers to professional development. This is particularly relevant in the context of many school teachers perceiving a crowded curriculum (Riley 2004).

Conclusions and concluding remarks

The New Zealand 'experiment' with vast and rapid educational reforms has attracted worldwide interest. How successful these reforms have been in allowing for a genuine learner-centred learning environment, in this case for the gifted, is debatable. A description of how this experiment has progressed as presented in this chapter may nonetheless serve to aid others who consider provision for the gifted is inhibited by more regimented, prescriptive curricula regimes. Here I propose how teachers might build upon the New Zealand experience to provide for gifted learners:

- A multi-categorical view of gifted that takes into account social and cultural factors is essential.
- Science curricula require at least some flexibility in terms of content and pedagogy.
- Within-class and learning experiences outside the classroom provide social context for gifted students without isolation and feelings of being different. In science, activities such as science fairs and enquiry-based work allow catering for all abilities within the same educational environment.
- Adequate, ongoing professional development for teachers of the gifted is essential.
- A national-level requirement of provision for the gifted provides indications of government commitment to gifted education.
- In the absence of clear national commitment, school-wide commitment to provision for the gifted is required; lest any programmes are lost when teacher advocates of gifted students move on.

Interestingly, many of these issues are common in any educational context, be it learner-centred or otherwise. On the face of it a more flexible curriculum regime would appear to offer more capacity for provision for special needs; reality suggests that perceptions of a 'crowded curriculum' mean non-compulsory education provision is unlikely to be pursued in many schools. Analysis of the enabling and inhibiting factors suggests much could have been achieved in provision for the gifted under almost any regime: provided there were suitable incentives or teachers and schools dedicated to catering for gifted students.

Chapter 6

Developing the thinking of gifted students through science

Keith S. Taber and Vivien Corrie

As Chapter 5 made clear, an enabling curriculum still relies upon teachers having the understanding, skills and desire to challenge their most able learners. Whether in an open-ended 'learner-centred' curriculum context, or a tightly prescribed and monitored teaching context, meeting the needs of gifted learners depends upon effective planning. In this chapter, Vivien Corrie and I consider principles that should inform such planning.

This chapter considers how science education can contribute to the development of thinking skills, with particular attention to the needs of the highest achievers. We will consider what is meant by the term 'thinking skills' when used in educational contexts, and will briefly consider a number of commonly used models for planning teaching designed to develop student thinking.

Developing thinking as an imperative for the school curriculum

It is easy to think of curriculum in terms of timetabled subjects, so that the school curriculum consists of science alongside mathematics, history and so forth. The science curriculum may then be primarily conceptualised in terms of the science topics to be 'covered': energy, electrical circuits, acids, green plants etc. Although it is important for teachers to be able to think about their teaching in this way, it is also very important for all teachers to keep in mind the wider aims of education. The curriculum is, after all, intended to be a programme to achieve more general educational aims. Any rationale for the importance of science in the school curriculum based primarily upon the need for students to learn about oxidation or photosynthesis or gravitational fields is likely to look quite unconvincing to many educational stakeholders – to many taxpayers, to many parents, to many school children themselves.

The rationale for schooling, as a means to collectively educate young people, is based on an assumption that schools can effectively help develop the whole person – at least in those ways that society feels are important.

Although acquiring specific knowledge and understanding *is* important, the perceived importance of any specific knowledge for its own sake is likely to change over time. This has always been the case, but is even more pertinent at a time when scientific knowledge is accrued at a vast rate, and school children are used to readily accessing (if not always appreciating) information via the internet.

Since the nineteenth century, education has been expected to support the individual's intellectual, aesthetic, moral/ethical and physical development (Hirst and Peters 1970). Science can certainly contribute in all these areas (see Chapter 10). However, it is in terms of intellectual development that science is expected to play a major role. Science is well placed to do this, but – as Howard Gardner (1993) points out in the context of developing his notion of multiple intelligences – it is just one of a wide range of 'academic' school subjects that can all be seen to primarily develop this aspect of the person.

Although the principle of developing the whole person and related notions of the 'liberal studies' curriculum – 'concerned with the comprehensive development of the mind' (Hirst 1972: 408) – have a strong tradition in educational thinking, science education has passed through phases where this imperative has become obscured by other foci. School science is not a given delivered by fiat from on high, and nor is it simply 'science' taught in schools. Rather the school science curriculum is the outcome of political processes (Kind and Taber 2005) – political in the sense of being shaped by various interest groups who have the power to have influence in the matter (e.g. see Chapter 5). School science in the UK has passed through phases when enquiry was a key concern (e.g. at the time when Nuffield curriculum projects were having a strong influence), and in the 1980s when process skills were a prime concern – something reflected in the work of the government's Assessment of Performance Unit at that time (APU 1988a, b, 1989). Since the introduction of the National Curriculum (NC) in England, it is probably fair to say that the main focus of science teaching has switched back to teaching and learning of specific (and specified) science content. Although more recent changes are to be welcomed (QCA 2005), both scientific enquiry and the nature of science have been in practice downplayed since the introduction of the NC in view of the way most teachers interpreted the assessment arrangements and set their teaching priorities accordingly (Kind and Taber 2005; Taber 2006b). In the US in recent years, there has been a move towards the establishment of national standards for science education (NAS 1996), which have, bearing in mind the federal nature of the US, approached the status of a NC. However, in the US, enquiry seems to have a much higher profile, presumably due to the way the standards have been developed and presented.

Enquiry, when done well (see Chapter 13), is certainly an excellent context for developing thinking skills. Teaching science subject content can also be an excellent context for developing thinking skills *when* there is a focus on looking at how ideas relate to, and develop in response to, evidence. Teaching for rote learning of science facts and for reproducing set answers in science examinations is much less likely to provide a useful context. It was never the intention of government agencies or examination boards to allow school science teaching to evolve towards being concerned primarily with 'transmission' of knowledge and rote learning, but that seems to have been one unintended consequence of the NC. It is certainly the case that the UK government has recognised the need for emphasising the teaching of thinking skills through the curriculum (e.g. McGuinness 1999; DfES 2005).

Approaches to thinking skills

There are a number of ways of conceptualising student thinking that can be helpful in teaching. Here we briefly consider three perspectives that can usefully inform thinking. These include the developmental perspective, the curriculum demand perspective and the metacognitive perspective. These are not mutually exclusive perspectives, but rather focus on different aspects of thinking.

The developmental perspective

The developmental perspective considers that cognitive abilities increase with age. The growing brain is considered to have the potential to develop 'higher' cognitive abilities over time. The extent to which this maturation process is dependent upon external factors has long been a matter of debate. Jean Piaget researched and wrote about this topic for many years and became very influential in educational circles in many countries. His work explored what he considered a natural unfolding of cognitive abilities. The environment played an important role, but largely through the individual's deliberate actions, interacting with aspects of the environment. Piaget's contemporary, Lev Vygostsky, focused on the role of others, peers and more advanced thinkers, in providing interactions that could scaffold development, enabling learners to acquire and develop cognitive tools (see also Chapters 4 and 8). A main outcome of Piaget's work was a theory of the stages through which human thinking tended to develop (Piaget 1972). Early stages took place pre-school and during the primary ages, but a particular distinction of interest to science teachers was that between 'concrete' and 'formal' operational thinking (see Box 6.1). Much of the thinking that teachers might consider as 'scientific' is at a level of abstraction that requires formal operations in Piaget's scheme.

For example, conservation of mass, conservation of energy, electricity, particle theory and the carbon cycle are just a few of the ideas and topic areas that demand abstract thought and are taught at lower secondary level. Teachers use a variety of techniques to help make the unfamiliar (abstract) familiar through concrete examples, demonstrations and activities.

Box 6.1 Concrete and formal operations

Concrete operations – actions on what can be directly experienced	Formal operations – working with concepts that are abstractions/generalisations
Pouring this water into another beaker	Water as an example of substance, which is a fluid and so can be poured
Observing the motion of this ball	The ball as a moving object, and so having associated kinetic energy
This plant died when we did not water it	Water being essential for the life processes of plants
There is a full moon tonight	The phases of the moon as a periodic change in appearance due to the shifting relative positions of the observer, moon and sun

---

As one example, the type of understanding of electric circuits we might hope for in secondary school requires an appreciation not only of the concept of electrical current, but also potential difference ('voltage') and resistance. These ideas (especially voltage) are abstract and for most students a deep understanding is unrealistic. When lower secondary students are taught about circuits, the teacher needs to provide a range of models (see Chapter 7), analogies (see Chapter 2) and metaphors for students to think with as they explore the practical effects of making changes to circuits (Taber *et al.* 2006). In introducing the notion of electric current to a class, the students might act out a role play of how electrons move through a circuit and then use this 'concrete' experience to model the effects on brightness of bulbs in series and parallel circuits. We might expect the most able students to go on to critique the various models and so show an understanding of the more abstract ideas.

Another example would be introducing particle theory, which is known to be extremely challenging to most learners: so computer simulations may be used to demonstrate (for example) factors affecting the rates of reaction in a way that less able students can access and explain because the abstract is made visual. Gifted science learners may well demonstrate they are able to visualise and mentally simulate such processes and so predict outcomes (cf. Georgiou 2005) without needing to be shown the computer simulation.

Piaget's scheme assigned nominal ages for the main transitions between different stages of cognitive development, based on the typical results found in his and his collaborators' research. In Piaget's original thinking there was a strict hierarchy in the stages, so that every individual passes through the same stages in the same order, albeit the actual ages at which stages were attained would vary between learners.

Clearly from a Piagetian perspective, a learner who had advanced to higher stages of cognitive development than her classmates would be capable of more abstract thinking, and might well be seen as gifted in this sense. The sciences offer a great many highly abstract ideas that many students find difficult, but may well offer a level of intellectual challenge that the most able would find engaging (see Box 6.2 for just a few examples).

There are clearly *many* more potential examples: often the very topics that are considered 'too difficult' for most students, and may be squeezed out of courses, or oversimplified by using selective examples that can be rote learnt for examinations.

Piaget's original work has been the subject of a great deal of scrutiny and criticism. His stage theory considers the core of intelligence as some form of

---

Box 6.2: A few of the abstract ideas in school science

Particle theory – appreciating how the properties of macroscopic matter may be explained in terms of the nature and configuration of particles (for an example, see Episode 4 on p. 109).

Energy as an abstract accounting system.

Plant nutrition – the relationship between photosynthesis and respiration.

Chemical equations – deducing feasible chemical equations from common types of reaction and balancing equations.

Deriving units – such as showing that a Newton is a kilogramme metre per squared second, or that power has the same fundamental units whether (work done ÷ time taken) or (p.d. × current).

Calculating specific heat capacities, from experiments where the thermal capacity of the calorimeter has to be factored in.

Evolution – appreciating the main principles of natural selection.

Periodicity – how and why properties of the elements vary as they do.

Structure of DNA, and the implications for cell division.

Mapping proton number versus nucleon number for radioactive decay series.

central processing capacity that is accessed regardless of the context being 'thought about'. In its purest form this suggests that individuals should demonstrate the same level of thinking across the board – and should not be found to exhibit higher-level thinking in some contexts compared with others. However, in practice, this variation was apparent – learners seemed to be able to think more abstractly in some contexts than others. Piaget introduced the notion of 'décalage' (or lag, e.g. Sutherland 1992). The modified theory suggests that learners attain a level of cognitive ability, that they can *potentially* apply in all areas, but where in practice they need to be familiar enough with material to demonstrate their abilities. (By extension, opportunities for immersion in a field are needed to develop sufficient familiarity to develop an 'intuitive' understanding: cf. Chapter 2.) This is quite reasonable, that thinking at a high level requires both cognitive ability *and* conceptual understanding, but can also be seen as something of weakening of Piaget's original ideas. (It makes the theory 'less falsifiable' if any differences in an individual's measured cognitive level can potentially always be explained away.)

Piaget's ideas were the basis of a very influential study in science education, where Michael Shayer and Philip Adey (1981) argued that the demands of much of the secondary science curriculum were pitched at a level of cognitive development that surveys (measuring Piagetian levels) suggested many of the intended learners would not have attained.

Shayer and Adey later applied Piagetian ideas to develop materials for 'cognitive acceleration'. The CASE (Cognitive Acceleration through Science Education) project was designed for lower secondary students (e.g. 11–14-year-olds), and provides experiences intended to facilitate the progression to the more advanced 'formal operations' (Adey 1999).

Cognitive acceleration though science education

There is little doubt that science requires the types of formal operations Piaget believed were only reached during adolescence: abstraction, classification, generalisation, the ability to work with various symbol systems and formalisms, are a key part of science, and of secondary and college science lessons.

To the extent that some secondary students are not using formal operations, or not consistently using formal operations, they will clearly be at a disadvantage in science lessons. A programme that provides lower secondary level learners with experiences that scaffold the development of such thinking earlier than they might otherwise be attained would clearly be to the benefit of those students, and their teachers. CASE is such a programme, which aims to use the context of science-based activities to help students make advances in Piagetian levels. It is claimed (based on research carried out by the CASE team) that when CASE is adopted and executed correctly during the lower secondary years (11–14) it leads to better examination performance – not limited to science – at age 16 (Adey and Shayer 1994). The evidence for these gains has been convincing enough for many schools to adopt the programme – including the purchase of materials, buying the specific staff training and finding time on the timetable.

The CASE programme is based on 'five pillars', derived from well-supported principles, and would seem to offer a sound rationale regardless of how convinced one might be about the validity of Piagetian levels (see Table 6.1). However, it is accepted by the CASE team that the programme may not be useful for the entire cohort. Those students who are still some way from developing formal operations may never experience sufficient cognitive conflict to facilitate the changes in thinking required.

Of more significance for our present concerns: if – on a Piagetian model – gifted students are those who have attained formal operations early, then there is likely to be little in the programme for them. These students will progress through the activities quickly and effectively (already being able to operate effectively with ratio, proportions etc.), but without being challenged to change their thinking in any significant ways. Perhaps for the gifted learner, CASE could offer cognitive stagnation rather than cognitive acceleration.

Formal operations and beyond

This does not mean that the developmental perspective offers nothing for teachers of gifted students, but rather that the popular Piagetian stage theory

Table 6.1 The CASE process (after Adey 1999*)

CASE 'pillar' *	CASE rationale *	Comment
Concrete preparation	The terms of the problem need to be established	Familiarisation stage, the problem is set in a concrete context
Cognitive conflict	Thinking develops in response to cognitive challenge	There must be something that the learner is motivated to understand/explain
Metacognition	Reflection on the process of problem-solving is essential	The 'real' intended learning concerns the thinking skill, not solving the specific problem
Construction	Students must construct their own reasoning processes	For meaningful learning, the student must make their own sense of the problem context
Bridging	Reasoning patterns developed in the CASE context must be bridged to other contexts	The principle behind the problem (e.g. ratio) must be abstracted so that it can be generalised, and so be available as a resource for future thinking

may not be the most useful approach. A number of commentators have observed that formal operations are most useful in contexts where there are clear patterns to abstract; where rules and schemes can be unambiguously applied; where evidence converges to clear conclusions. In these situations tidy logical thought is appropriate and readily applied. School science is often presented through curriculum models that are oversimplifications, and through practical work engineered to offer clear conclusions (Kind and Taber 2005; Taber 2006b).

However, 'real life' is seldom like this. To the extent that school may make science appear this way to learners, school science provides a less-than-authentic image of the way evidence is often collected and interpreted in scientific research, or debated among scientists (see Gilbert and Newberry's characterisation of the nature of science in Chapter 2). In real research the evidence is often partial, imprecise, unclear and even contradictory. Scientists have to be able to make decisions in the light of such situations – perhaps using a more 'fuzzy' form of logic. Similarly, when we explore socio-cultural issues in the classroom (see Chapter 10), we need to help learners appreciate that even when inherent scientific values suggest our knowledge base is robust and reliable, we then have to reconsider the relevance and significance of scientific evidence in a wider context, using a distinct set of values external to science.

For this reason it has been suggested that there must be a 'fifth stage' of cognitive development beyond the four main Piagetian stages (Arlin 1975). So-called post-formal operations (Kramer 1983) concerns making rational and pragmatic decisions when simple logical thought does not allow any firm conclusions to be drawn.

One theory that may be useful here is that of Perry (Finster 1989; Moseley *et al.* 2004), who developed a model of stages of intellectual development more suitable for college level students. In (over-)simplified terms, Perry considered how learners progress from assuming there are absolute right and wrong answers, to accepting that we may not *yet* know the answers, to recognising that different opinions may be justifiable to eventually appreciating the nature of commitments as current positions. For teachers of gifted learners, cognitive acceleration may well imply helping students move *beyond* formal operational thinking. This requires setting tasks that are open-ended enough not to have clear 'right' answers (see Chapter 14).

An example of such an activity we have used with KS4 students involves using data from Antarctic ice cores to find out if there is a relationship between temperature variation and atmospheric carbon dioxide over 400,000 years. Students have to make a number of decisions about what data they will select which requires them thinking about the true meaning of 'reliability' (since the experiment cannot be replicated in the way that they have experienced in their own experimental work). They are required to plan ahead in terms of the data they will want to plot, making decisions about what data to 'collect'.

This piece of work provides students with a challenge because there is no 'perfect' way of sampling the results. They learn that scientists may need to compromise when collecting data and take a pragmatic approach when a vast quantity of potential data is available. Superficially, the data that students collect shows a relationship between the variables: however, it is not an absolute match when they start looking at it in more detail. This provides able students with a genuine challenge when writing their conclusion. This piece of assessed work is particularly interesting given the implications of their conclusion for government energy policies.

Indeed, 'STS' (Science-Technology-Society) or 'controversial' issues offer considerable scope for providing open-ended challenges. For example, in a debate on the use of 'GM' (genetically modified) material in food-stuffs students must attempt to weigh up the costs and benefits on both environmental and socio-economic issues, many of which are still unknown. Students are asked at the beginning of the lesson to place themselves on a continuum line between agreeing and disagreeing that there should be research into developing genetically modified food. After a lesson in which students explore the issues, they are asked to review their position on the continuum line. However, this task can be made more challenging when they are asked to take a position from within a role (such as a research scientist; a politician; an agriculture development agency for an African country) such that they have to make a judgement from a given perspective, considering the complexities of the issue.

There are suitable materials available to support teachers in setting up this type of STS debate. For example the SATIS (Science and Technology in Society) materials – which although pre-National Curriculum, still used in many schools – are being recommended for teaching about 'How science works' in the revised curriculum leading to school-leaving examinations in 2008 (QCA 2005: 20). In one activity, the Limestone Quarry Enquiry students role-play a public enquiry into the extension of a quarry in the Peak District. Placing the most able students in the role of 'Inspectors' gives them an opportunity to listen to the conflicting arguments and make a pragmatic decision as to whether to support the appeal or reject it. The ASE's (Association for Science Education, www.ase.org.uk) 'UpD8' ('update') materials offer mini-projects on contemporary issues. This type of activity can be made personally relevant. So students are asked to research and find evidence to address the question 'are mobile phones dangerous to human health?' (see also Chapter 9), and then they are asked to apply it to their own decision making – i.e. 'will I continue to use my mobile phone?'. The English NC changes implemented for 14 year olds from Autumn 2006 (QCA 2005) allow examination courses, such as Twenty-first Century Science', which offer many opportunities for engaging in activities that encourage such 'post formal thinking'.

Bloom's taxonomy – a tool for planning teaching

Bloom and colleagues produced taxonomies of educational objectives in the cognitive and affective domains. The former was adopted by many teachers and others working in education, and reference to Bloom's taxonomy usually signifies the taxonomy of educational objectives in the cognitive domain (Bloom 1964).

Bloom proposed six levels of demand associated with tasks that learners might be set, and a revised version has been developed (Anderson and Krathwohl 2001) distinguishing the nature of the knowledge being processed, and the type of thinking required. In the revised taxonomy, the main classes of the cognitive processes dimension are:

1   remember: recognising, recalling
2   understand: interpreting, exemplifying, classifying, summarising, inferring, comparing, explaining
3   apply: executing, implementing
4   analyse: differentiating, organising, attributing
5   evaluate: checking, critiquing
6   create: generating, planning, producing.

The knowledge dimension was divided into four main types of knowledge: factual, conceptual, procedural and metacognitive. The separation out of two distinct dimensions allows the taxonomy to be presented in the form of a table (with each cell representing a type of operation upon a type of knowledge) that may be used as a tool for planning teaching and assessment. If learning activities (or assessment items) are categorised in the table, it provides an immediate visual impression of the kinds of demands being made of learners.

A key to challenging learners is to ensure that learning activities include the higher levels of cognitive processing. For gifted learners in particular, it is important that the profile of activities is rich in analysing, evaluating and creating. An effective way of ensuring that the most able students are consistently challenged in their thinking, particularly when differentiating in a 'mixed ability' context, is to write lesson/topic objectives using the taxonomy, and ensuring there is a spread of objectives across different levels.

For example, when Y7 students (11- to 12-year-olds) study adaptation of animals and plants, students are asked to design a hypothetical animal or plant that would be adapted for a specific environment (such as deep in the ocean, where it is very cold and dark). This allows students to be creative while working with the key science ideas. In a Year 8 lesson (for 12- to 13-year-olds) when students are studying the changes in length of day during changing seasons, the most able students are given data from the southern hemisphere, but without telling them where it is from.

General points that can be applied within the science curriculum include always asking the most able to critique methods in practical work, and suggest modifications, and – wherever possible – asking them to produce their own models (see Chapter 7) and analogies (see Chapter 14) for concepts being studied.

Metacognition and independence in learning

One of the key changes in the revision of Bloom's original taxonomy is the inclusion in the knowledge dimension of consideration of metacognition: 'knowledge about cognition in general as well as awareness of and knowledge about one's own cognition' (Krathwohl 2002). Metacognitive knowledge is the knowledge an individual has about their own learning and thinking processes.

Traditionally school learning was planned and managed by teachers, with students expected to follow directions: being told what to study, when to study, how to study. However, such an approach had a number of obvious disadvantages. For one thing, when the locus of control over learning is retained by the teacher, the process breaks down as soon as the student needs to make decisions in the absence of the teacher. It has long been clear to teachers both that students needs study skills to (for example) revise effectively for examinations, and that part of the school teacher's role is to equip students to be effective learners once they leave school. In terms of the wider aims of education, which it was suggested above should provide the rationale for including material in the curriculum, it is clearly important that students are supported in developing into self-regulated learners.

Acquiring 'study skills' (Bulman 1985) is now a well-established feature of tutorial or personal development programmes in many schools. This may include knowledge about the best ways to schedule review sessions informed by memory studies. Often students are taught about such notions as learning styles. This may be limited to rather simplistic approaches such as designating students as 'visual', 'auditory' or 'kinaesthetic' learners based on commercially available questionnaires. Such 'VAK' schemes are poorly supported in terms of research evidence (Coffield et al. 2004) perhaps explaining why they are often inappropriately linked by proponents to Gardner's well-developed theory of multiple intelligence. However, even such a highly flawed approach focuses both teachers and students on (1) the importance of individual differences among learners and (2) the availability of different 'channels' for receiving teaching.

Again modelling may be a very important activity in this regard. The process of building physical models (e.g. with different coloured plastic modelling materials) not only allows students to demonstrate high levels of creativity, but also facilitates learning through visual and tactile/kinaesthetic modes. Such opportunities may be especially useful when students have limited language comprehension or level of literacy – but can also be valuable for gifted learners who suffer specific learning difficulties such as dyslexia (see Chapter 3). These learners may have particular difficulty producing written texts which can demonstrate their level of understanding. Sometimes offering such tasks as elective alternatives to written work for all students can also provide students with a choice of learning activity (see Chapter 12).

Another key concern is the 'myth of class teaching'. It is possible for a skilled tutor to closely monitor the thinking of an individual pupil and carefully make effective pedagogic decisions to steer learning. However, it is obvious to anyone familiar with the reality of class teaching that it is clearly unrealistic to expect a teacher to effectively monitor and manage the learning of perhaps thirty or more individual learners concurrently without help 'from the inside'. Classroom teaching is more effective when aims are shared with individual learners, and they take some role and responsibility in monitoring their own learning, and even making decisions.

This thinking is strongly represented in the assessment for learning movement (Harlen 2006). So, for example, students are given feedback on their work with the stress on what they have achieved and what they need to do to improve, rather than how well they have done in terms of some grade or score. With students who are already attaining high standards, it is important to acknowledge that, but still offer comments that encourage them to achieve more:

> Dan, your written work is of a very high standard, I would like you to share your ideas verbally in class. Articulating your ideas will help to develop your thinking.

> Peter, you showed me that you understood the ideas of conservation of mass fully by what you said in class, you now need to develop your written explanations so they give full answers to the question. You need to include more scientific terms.

In particular, the most able students can be set targets to challenge their thinking: 'Sarah, in the box below, I want you to think of a question about this topic for which nobody knows the answer.'

Having students involved in assessing their own work can help them appreciate both requirements and their own levels of attainment. For example, 11- to 14-year-old students may be asked to write a scientific explanation (some examples of the questions used are: what happens to the mass of iron when it rusts?; what happens to sugar when it dissolves?; how are identical twins formed?; what would happen if you dropped a feather and hammer at the same time on the moon?). The students are then given a contextualised mark scheme and asked to assign a level to *their own* piece of work, before then peer-assessing *another student's* work and suggesting one way in which the peer could achieve the next level. Students are given the opportunity to rewrite the explanation before handing it in for the teacher to assess.

In the context of the English NC, the prescribed NC 'levels' may be used as indicators of attainment and progression. The levels 'mountain' (Newberry *et al.* 2005 – see also Chapters 7 and 15) provides a guide for developing specific mark schemes that can be used in this way. For example in 'levelling', an explanation of the measured change of mass when iron rusts, the following criteria may be used to award levels:

- Level 3: the mass of the iron goes up.
- Level 4: the iron reacts with oxygen which makes the mass go up.
- Level 5: the iron reacts with oxygen to form iron oxide. Explain in terms of the *concept* of conservation of mass – particles having mass, oxygen being added.
- Level 6: use the word 'equation' to represent the reaction. Explain in terms the mass of reactants = the mass of products. Use the theory of conservation of mass in the explanation *or* use a model/analogy to explain the increase in mass.
- Level 7: use the chemical equation and chemical formula to explain the increase in mass quantitatively.

Such an approach can mean that the teacher spends more time explaining ideas to students and focusing minds on the nature of what is considered 'good' work, and less time in 'marking' piles of student work. The most able students soon learn to access the marking criteria and effectively apply criteria for evaluating (a high level cognitive skill) their own and other students' work.

It is also important to point out that student involvement in the monitoring and management of learning, and particularly in being empowered to make choices (see Chapter 12), can engage them in learning and improve their attitudes to classes (see Chapter 4). There is also a particular link here with those learners that we may consider gifted. The ultimate self-regulated learner is the autodidact: the self-taught learner (such as the Nobel laureate cited by Gilbert and Newberry in Chapter 2). Autodidacts are the small proportion of learners who seem able to master complex material without the formal structure provided by teachers and instruction. The self-taught, whether in mathematics, piano, or anything else, are generally considered to be of exceptional ability.

It is quite likely that many gifted students have highly developed meta-cognitive skills that enable them to plan, organise, monitor and evaluate their own learning to a higher level than most peers. To some extent teachers may be tempted to differentiate 'by support' by spending time with struggling students, and allowing the gifted to use their strengths to find their own way through work. This may *sometimes* be appropriate – as long as the gifted students are given work of a suitable level of demand.

However, we suggest here that just as more dependent students need to be supported to become independent learners, the gifted also need to be helped to develop their existing levels of metacognition. Gifted students should not only be set work that requires them to use higher level thinking skills, but also be given work that makes increasing demands of their abilities to regulate their own learning – such as concept mapping a topic (Taber 2002: 33–49).

This may mean, for example, that gifted learners are sometimes set work with a much more open brief, and having longer timescales than other students. Another potentially very powerful approach is through peer tutoring. Many teachers and student teachers come to the view that they only really came to understand key features of their subject, and especially aspects of the structure of disciplinary knowledge, once they were charged with teaching others (Taber 2001). From this perspective peer tutoring can be a valuable experience for gifted learners. This does not mean just using gifted learners who finish early to explain the work for slower peers, but building up their responsibilities for analysing and organising the material in order to teach it to their classmates.

Conclusions

This chapter has offered perspectives on thinking skills that teachers may find useful in planning science teaching for their most gifted students. To the extent that the gifted in secondary schools may often be those who attained formal operations early, and so indeed may be those most ready to meet the challenge of tasks requiring and facilitating 'post-formal' operations, it is important to plan work that helps develop their ability to deal with complex, ambiguous, poorly defined and nuanced situations.

A tool such as the taxonomy table, developed from Bloom's model of levels of cognitive demand, can help teachers check that they are including sufficient higher level thinking in lessons for all students, and can provide a tool to help differentiate for the most able who need a profile of work skewed towards evaluative and creative activities.

Finally, planning teaching to develop metacognition is important for all students, but is especially crucial for gifted learners who may already be highly self-regulated, and so have the potential to become effective autodidacts and so effective learners when they move on to less structured learning situations after school. It is the most independent learners who are likely to have the type of idiosyncratic intellectual life that may be both personally satisfying and potentially able to lead to original contributions to society. Science education has to contribute to the development of the whole person, to help all learners reach their potential. In the case of the intellectually gifted, science needs to stimulate new ways of thinking, and new levels of awareness and control over that thinking. This is a major challenge for the teacher, but we hope that the perspectives illustrated in this chapter will help inform effective planning and stimulating science teaching.

Chapter 7

Challenging able science learners through models and modelling

Andrew Grevatt, John K. Gilbert and Matthew Newberry

Chapter 6 discussed ways of planning for meeting the needs of the most able within the expectations of following a prescribed curriculum. One of the tools discussed, the 'levels mountain,' derives from the work of the Cams Hill Science Consortium – an action research group helping teachers develop challenging science teaching within the requirements and expectations of the English National Curriculum. In this chapter Andrew Grevatt, John Gilbert and Matthew Newberry discuss the work of the consortium, and how it is informed by scholarship in science education into the roles of models in science, in curriculum and in teaching.

Rendering the science curriculum more coherent

The four component 'areas of science studied' in the National Curriculum (NC) for England (DfEE 1999) for 5- to 14-year-olds – 'scientific enquiry' (Sc1), 'life processes and living things' (Sc2), 'materials and their properties' (Sc3), 'physical processes' (Sc4) – consist of a large number of facts, concepts, skills, and the relationships between them. It is therefore not surprising that students find 'science' difficult to learn (Osborne and Collins 2000). A close inspection of Sc2–4 showed that four 'key ideas' underlay the mandated content at Key Stage 3 (KS3, for 11- to 14 year-olds): 'the particulate nature of matter', 'forces', 'energy', 'cells' (Moore and Gilbert 1998). These four key ideas were adopted by the 'National Strategy for Science at KS3' and a fifth, 'interdependence', added (DfES 2002b). We are of the belief that 'interdependence' is not needed, the original four only being both necessary and sufficient for a full coverage of the curriculum. All the required facts, concepts, skills, in the three sections of the curriculum could be related to and explained with the use of one or more of these four key ideas. Furthermore, it was possible to identify the core features for each of those key ideas that was both 'good enough' for the purposes of the 11–14 curriculum and which would not be an impediment to more advanced study. Each set of core features constitutes a *model* of a key idea, where: 'A model in science is a representation of a phenomenon (an object, idea, system, event, or process) initially produced for a specific purpose' (Gilbert *et al.* 2000: 11). For any key idea, a model may have a range of ontological statuses. A *scientific* model is one currently   in use at the cutting edge of research in a given field of enquiry. For energy this is currently a quantum mechanical equation. A *historical* model is one that was accepted by a community of scientists at one time but which has now been superseded for research purposes. For energy, one such model is composed of Joule's mathematical equations based on the paddle-wheel experiment. A *curriculum* model is a simplified version of a scientific or historical model (usually the latter) that is included in the curriculum. For energy this could be either the 'transfer' or the 'transformation' model (Millar 2003) or a hybrid between them. These curriculum models are contenders for the right to represent energy in the science curriculum. A *teaching* model is an analogy that is created by the teacher (or students) in order to help in the understanding of a curriculum model. The 'chain of students with arms linked' is a teaching model for the 'transfer' curriculum model for energy.

The programme of study for KS3 for energy (DfEE 1999: 35–6) is:

> Energy resources and energy transfer. Pupils should be taught:
> - about the variety of energy resources, including oil, gas, coal, biomass, food, wind, waves and batteries, and the distinction between renewable and non-renewable resources
> - about the sun as the ultimate source of most of the Earth's energy resources and to relate this to how coal, oil and gas are formed
> - that electricity is generated by means of a variety of energy resources
> - conservation of energy
> - the distinction between temperature and heat, and that differences in temperature can lead to transfer of energy
> - ways in which energy can be usefully transferred and stored
> - how energy is transferred by the movement of particles in conduction, convection and evaporation, and that energy is transferred directly by radiation
> - that although energy is always conserved, it may be dissipated, reducing its availability as a resource.

From these curriculum models teachers devise their own teaching models in order to communicate the key aspects of the scientific phenomena using a format that children can both understand and then can apply themselves within their own explanations. To meet the requirements of the statements above teachers tend to use a variety of resources and approaches that make use of the transfer and transformation models of energy. From lesson observations and audits of departmental schemes of work most teachers that we have worked with tend to use bits of both models and often form a hybrid

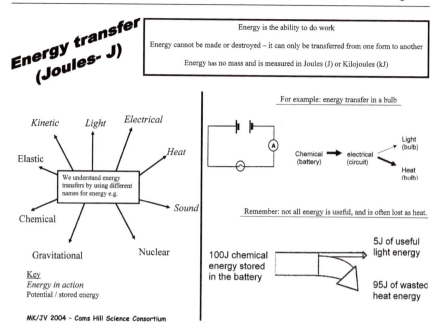

Figure 7.1 A curriculum model for energy (by Mel Kirk of Court Moor School)

model to explain energy. A curriculum model for energy (the 'good enough' model) developed by schools within the Cams Hill Science Consortium (CHSC) is given in Figure 7.1.

Finally, a *mental* model is an entirely private and personal cognitive representation. Getting a close relationship between a student's mental model of energy and the corresponding curriculum model is a central goal of school science teaching.

The challenge of models and modelling

The great attraction of an emphasis on models in science education is that, by each one acting as a representational focus for a large number of disparate facts, they can drastically reduce the 'cognitive load' (Johnstone and Al-Naeme 1991) of both teaching and learning the curriculum. Rather than deal with many separate, isolated, items of information, the teacher and learner who understand a model can readily forge mental links between it and those items and hence between them. In a sense, a model enables analogies to be drawn between separate items of information (Gentner 1983, 1988). Moreover, by being capable of representation in one or more *modes* (concrete, visual, verbal, symbolic, gestural), a model enables the learner to mentally visualise the entities and relationships of which it consists. This is of central importance for all learning, as visualisation is a major form of all thinking (see Chapter 2), especially so in science given the nature of the phenomena with which it deals (Gilbert, 2005a). So the acquisition of an understanding of a curriculum model (e.g. of 'energy') by students must be a major goal of science education.

Case studies of action research conducted by teachers within the CHSC have shown that focusing upon the interdependence [sic] of the four different models in explaining an everyday abstract phenomenon can provide a very effective method of providing challenging learning opportunities for able science students. It has been argued in Chapter 2 that students should not be identified as 'gifted and talented', rather they should be given a learning environment which provides them with opportunities to demonstrate this themselves. Teachers engaging with models and modelling has proved to be a successful way of doing this.

Acquiring a good understanding of a curriculum model involves a student in forming, through the mechanism of visualisation, a mental model that is demonstrably very close to the original, i.e. closely matching vital elements of that model. This process of formation is that of *modelling*, i.e. it involves *creating* a mental model (Justi and Gilbert 2002) and not just memorising the curriculum model, even though that is what superficially appears to happen. Modelling involves bringing together the mental consequences of experience and expressing these, internally and perhaps externally, in language. The acquisition of these experiences, their interrogation and the output in the form of expression, can take place at a wide variety of natural paces for different individuals. However, this pace can be increased by the teacher adopting a pedagogy in which he/she repeatedly demonstrates the process of modelling in action. The assimilation of this approach by students will lead to them being able to 'metacognitively model' the process of modelling itself. Those students who are most readily able to do so may properly be referred to as 'gifted and able in science' (see Chapter 2).

Levelness and the most able in science.

In the NC in Science for England at Key Stage 3 (11–14 years), learning is assessed in terms of the attainment of seven *levels of understanding* thought desirable. It has been found possible to represent the development of the notion of 'model' in terms of these sequential levels (Newberry *et al.* 2005; see Figure 7.2).

This representation was developed after a pooling of classroom experience by the teachers in the CHSC, and by lesson observation and analysis conducted by the science inspectors and advisors working across schools within the Hampshire Local Education Authority. It is a qualitative repre-

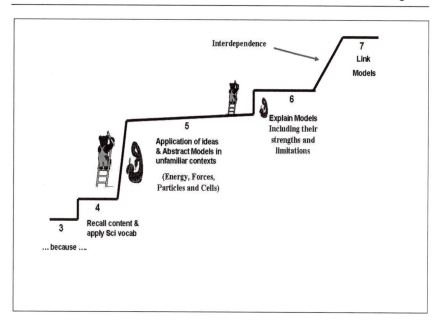

Figure 7.2 National curriculum in science for England: The 'levels of attainment' in terms of the notion of 'model'

sentation showing relationships and trends only: the vertical axis gives the successive 'levels' and the horizontal axis the successive phases over time in the development of the notion of 'model'. The unevenness of the steps in the vertical axis is an indication of the relative intellectual demand made by the successive levels. The variation in the slopes of the horizontal elements is an indicator of the different times over which the next level develops and the length of time in one level an indicator of the range of experience needed before the next level is attained. A student who shows attainment at:

- Level 3 is able to describe immediate experiences in everyday terms.
- Level 4 is able to recall those experiences and to use appropriate scientific vocabulary in the process.
- Level 5 is able to use the 'good enough' models of 'energy', 'forces', 'particles', 'cells' to describe the content of the curriculum.
- Level 6 is able to discuss each of these four models and to evaluate their strengths and weaknesses as the basis for providing explanations of phenomena.
- Level 7 is able to explain complex phenomena by using several or all of these models.

In terms of attainment of the notion of 'model', Level 5 is the major step, with Levels 6 and 7 building on that foundation. Formation of explanations of phenomena at Level 7 requires students to have an understanding of the interdependence of different models and to apply different models within an explanation. An example is that of forming their own detailed understanding and explanation of photosynthesis through the application of the energy transfer model, the particle theory model and an understanding of specialised cellular structure. Pupils in KS3 who are gifted and talented can demonstrate that they are able to combine and apply more than one model within their explanations

An example of how this works is given in Table 7.1, where the development of the model 'energy' is used to progressively explain the evolving use of 'particles' in respect of electrical phenomena.

What are the implications of a 'model-based curriculum' for the education of the gifted and talented in science? This approach readily facilitates the introduction of *extension* work (Freeman 1999) i.e. having students studying the content of the current curriculum at a greater depth than usual. In the case of 'models' it would mean at KS3 (lower secondary) developing student understanding beyond the expected Level 5 or 6 to Level 7.

Table 7.1 Explaining how a torch works (from Grevatt 2005)

To get Level	You should have . . .
3	Drawn a simple circuit diagram of the torch.
	Shown where the electricity comes from.
	Stated simply how the torch works.
4	Drawn a circuit diagram using standard circuit symbols.
	Stated the job of the cells, wires, bulb and switch.
	Identified which materials in the torch are conductors and insulators.
5	Drawn a circuit diagram using standard circuit symbols.
	Described the job of the cells, wires, bulb and switch.
	Described materials in the torch as conductors and insulators.
6	Drawn a circuit diagram using standard circuit symbols.
	Explained the job of the cells, wires, bulb and switch.
	Drawn a model of electricity to explain how the circuit works, using the terms current and voltage correctly.
	Explained why the parts of your model are like the real circuit components.
	Described limitations of the model circuit compared with the actual circuit.
7	Drawn a circuit diagram using standard circuit symbols.
	Drawn a model of electricity to explain how the circuit works, using the terms current and voltage correctly.
	Explained why the parts of your model are like the real circuit components.
	Explained limitations of the model circuit compared with the actual circuit.
	Used a model of electricity to describe the energy transfers in a circuit.

Energy: a case study of models and the gifted and talented in science

A student who is gifted and talented in science will most likely (but not exclusively) have attained Level 5 in terms of the notion of model by the final year of primary school, and will be able to communicate at Level 6 in Year 7. The toughest test of this attainment would be in respect of the key idea of 'energy' for this is both an abstraction and is based on a word that has many everyday uses (Millar 2003). The topic of 'energy' is also of great importance in the toolkit of the aspirant scientist because it is taught explicitly in 16% and is required implicitly in 70% of the topics in the widely used teaching package 'Key Stage 3 Sample Scheme' (QCA 2003). So the capability to communicate at Level 6 in respect of 'energy' in Year 7 is a realised expectation of any student who is 'gifted and able' in science.

In order to see whether this is so, two case studies (one of a male, one of a female) were conducted with students who had been identified as 'gifted and talented' in terms of their scores in a cognitive attainment test and the KS2 SATs in science, English and mathematics (i.e. national tests taken by all students in the final year of primary education, aged 10–11). These case studies were embedded in work with a 'top set' Year 7 class in a rural comprehensive school. The students completed an open answer questionnaire consisting of three questions (What is energy? How is energy involved with the human body? How is energy involved with electric current?) on three occasions over the school year. These were:

- before any teaching of 'energy' had taken place (Probe 1);
- after a 'hybrid' model of energy had been taught. (Probe 2);
- after both the 'transfer' and 'transformation' models has been taught (Probe 3).

A question about the operation of a CD player was also asked, between Probe 2 and Probe 3.

The hybrid model was taught because this was the accepted model within the science department at Uckfield Community Technology College as it was with most science teachers at this time. During this year (2004–5), the 'KS3 National Strategy for Science' advised that all students should be taught the transfer model instead of the transformation model or hybrid model (KS3NS 2003b). The teacher (AG) was concerned that using use one teaching model in preference to another conflicted with principles of good science teaching i.e. that it must mirror good science by testing out the value of different models. The reason AG chose to challenge gifted and talented students with the two energy models was to see if students had a preference for which curriculum model to use, or whether they preferred a hybrid model.

The teaching of this hybrid took the form of three lessons. As a starter activity, in the introductory lesson, the teacher (AG) developed his own hybrid teaching model. This model aimed to encourage pupils to adopt the language and conventions of the energy transfer and transformation models and become aware that energy is often perceived in different ways by different observers/by taking different measurements. To explain the 'my mum' teaching model, AG wrote 'Why is energy like my mum?' as a title and a stick person 'mum' was drawn in the middle of the whiteboard. Arrows were drawn from this to words to help students evolve a 'mind map' of terms that can be used to describe AG's mum: mum, wife, daughter, nurse (her occupation), sister, friend, etc. It was explained that these are all different roles/forms that 'my mum' takes, but she remains the same person. Then 'ENERGY' was written in the centre of the other half of the board. Students are asked to suggest forms or types of energy (nine were identified). Students often volunteered energy resources throughout this phase, which were listed separately and used to challenge any misconceptions in naming forms of energy and energy resources. Once the forms of energy were listed, the teacher explained that, like 'my mum', energy is the same 'thing', but can be seen doing a variety of different things. The students were then asked to explain this in pairs using their own words to allow discussion and development of ideas. The energy 'like my mum' model used 'forms of energy' but these were transferred from one form to another.

Energy rules

Students were then introduced to a model of energy in the form of a list of rules. Students read through these rules, wrote them into their books, and produced a poster for display in the classroom for easy reference. It was explained that these simple rules can be applied to energy whenever they mention it in any topic. Simple energy transfers were introduced at this point, and students learned to use an arrow to show the direction of energy transfer.

Energy chain cards

A series of colourful clip art cards were presented to students to be cut out and laminated. Students were introduced to the cards by showing energy transfer from an apple to a human, then from some meat to a human. This idea could then be developed to show how energy is transferred from the sun to get generated electricity via a number of resources. Students worked in groups to make energy chains for a variety of energy resources. The materials that formed the basis of this teaching are given in Figure 7.3.

At the end of this teaching, the students were asked to draw an energy diagram, to explain that diagram in words and to evaluate the 'good' and 'bad' points of both the 'transfer' and 'transformation' models.

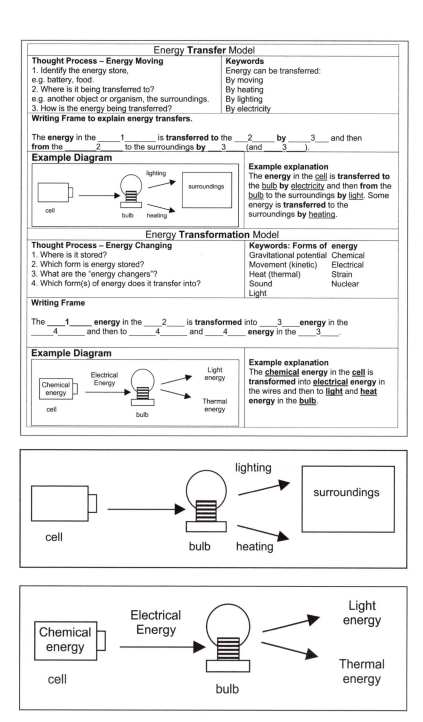

Energy **Transfer** Model

Thought Process – Energy Moving	Keywords
1. Identify the energy store, e.g. battery, food.	Energy can be transferred: By moving
2. Where is it being transferred to?	By heating
e.g. another object or organism, the surroundings.	By lighting
3. How is the energy being transferred?	By electricity

Writing Frame to explain energy transfers.

The **energy** in the ____1____ is **transferred to** the ___2___ **by** ___3___ and then **from** the ___2___ to the surroundings **by** ___3___ (and ___3___).

Example Diagram

	Example explanation
(diagram: cell → bulb → surroundings, with lighting and heating)	The **energy** in the <u>cell</u> is **transferred to** the <u>bulb</u> **by** <u>electricity</u> and then **from the** <u>bulb</u> to the surroundings **by** <u>light</u>. Some energy is **transferred** to the surroundings **by** <u>heating</u>.

Energy **Transformation** Model

Thought Process – Energy Changing	Keywords: Forms of energy	
1. Where is it stored?	Gravitational potential	Chemical
2. Which form is energy stored?	Movement (kinetic)	Electrical
3. What are the "energy changers"?	Heat (thermal)	Strain
4. Which form(s) of energy does it transfer into?	Sound	Nuclear
	Light	

Writing Frame

The ____1____ **energy** in the ____2____ is **transformed** into ____3____ **energy** in the ____4____ and then to ____4____ and ____4___ **energy** in the ____3____.

Example Diagram

	Example explanation
(diagram: Chemical energy cell → Electrical Energy → bulb → Light energy, Thermal energy)	The <u>**chemical**</u> **energy** in the <u>**cell**</u> is **transformed** into <u>**electrical**</u> **energy** in the wires and then to <u>**light**</u> and <u>**heat**</u> **energy** in the <u>**bulb**</u>.

Figure 7.3 The 'transfer' and 'transformation' models of 'energy' (KS3NS, 2003B)

Case studies: Luke and Jemma

In these case studies AG intended to find answers to two questions:

- Does explicit teaching of the energy transfer models enhance the teaching and learning of more able pupils?
- Does the use of the energy transfer models help reveal any other characteristics of able and talented students?

Two such students – Luke and Jemma – were selected to be case studies (see Table 7.2).

Luke: prior data

Age	Sex	Verbal CAT	Quantitative CAT	Non-verbal CAT	Average CAT score	KS2 Science Level
12	male	131	127	119	126	5a

Luke stands out from his peers as being self-motivated, having a strong desire to 'do well', and is very interested in science both inside and outside school. He grasps new concepts very quickly and asks questions about their applications after initial instruction, whereas most students require time to assimilate and accommodate these concepts. Luke is recognised as being gifted by most of his subject teachers, not only those of science. Using numerical indicators, in comparison to the year group, Luke is identified as gifted and talented because his average CAT score was in the top 5% of the year group and his non-verbal CAT score was also in the top 5% of the year group. Within his science class, Luke had the highest CAT scores.

Jemma: prior data

Age	Sex	Verbal CAT	Quantitative CAT	Non-verbal CAT	Average CAT score	KS2 Science Level
12	female	95	125	126	115	5a

Jemma is also self-motivated, has a strong desire to do well and has interest in science both inside and outside school. She also grasps new concepts with relative ease, though does require some time for consolidation before she is able to apply what she has learnt. She does not have as much confidence about her own knowledge and understanding as Luke does. Jemma was identified as gifted and talented because, compared with the year group, she was in the top 10% for her non-verbal CAT and average CAT scores. She was one of two girls who had the highest CAT scores in this particular class.

Luke: explanation of the operation of a CD player

Luke (see Figure 7.4) has taken the model he was given, but has broken it down further into its mechanistic parts and then applied the model to each of these components of energy transfer. There are inaccuracies in his explanation and diagram, for example, he suggests that a lens 'turns the light into electrical impulses'.

When asked which model he preferred, he stated the transfer model because it 'shows where the energy is transferred and where it goes.' He does not like the transformation model so much because it, 'doesn't tell you where the energy is'. He concludes that 'both diagrams are basically the same'.

Jemma: explanation of the operation of a CD player

Jemma (see Figure 7.5) has used the energy transfer model in her diagram and in her explanation, using a diagram following the format that she was given as an example. However in the diagram, she chose to use the words as types of energy (transformation model) rather than the 'by heating' suggested in the model. Jemma has done what was expected, but has not used the model in its entirety. This led us to ask whether this is a deliberate choice or because she did not understand the task completely. When asked which model was best to use, Jemma stated that she preferred the transformation model because

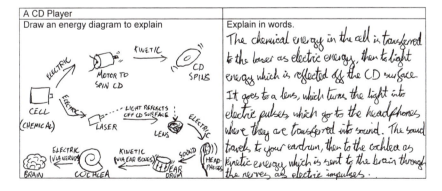

Figure 7.4 Luke's diagram and explanation for the CD player

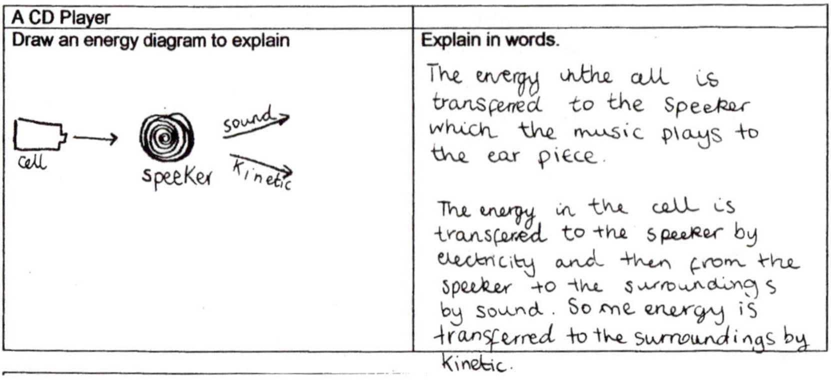

A CD Player	
Draw an energy diagram to explain	Explain in words.
cell → speaker sound → kinetic →	The energy in the all is transfered to the speaker which the music plays to the ear piece. The energy in the cell is transfered to the speaker by electricity and then from the speaker to the surroundings by sound. Some energy is transferred to the surroundings by kinetic.

Figure 7.5 Jemma's diagram and explanation for the CD player

'it is explaining the chemical energy' and 'it is more scientific'. She identified this as a weakness in the 'transfer' model, '[The transfer model] doesn't tell you what the chemical energy is flowing through.'

What does this data show about the transfer and transformation models?

The pupils did not use the different models separately and tended to use a hybrid in their explanations of the CD player. Neither pupil was able to describe any significant differences between the two models. Both pupils liked being able to 'name' forms of energy, as this appeared to make explanations easier. They were able to move between both models depending on which suited their needs at the time. AG felt that the hybrid model had given them flexibility to use each teaching model to help with their explanations for new situations. In both cases, their explanations were not wrong, though highlighted some misconceptions. There is no real scientific reason to teach one model in preference to the other since these models are teaching models. The students here have taken their first steps at evaluating and comparing alternative explanations, a valuable scientific skill in itself.

Does the explicit teaching of energy transfer models enhance the teaching and learning of more able pupils?

The QCA (QCA 2006) has produced a list of the characteristics of the gifted student of science. Those identified in this study are italicised below.

The task, at first glance, seems very closed and specific. It requires pupils to apply the model to a new situation. Jemma was able to apply the model to the new situation with relative ease. This indicates that she *was able to think*

Table 7.2 Luke and Jemma: outcomes of probes 1–3

Question	Pupil	Probe 1	Probe 2	Probe 3
1 What is energy?	Luke	A force that causes things to happen. Without energy, nothing would move or do anything.	Energy is a force that makes things happen, nothing could work without it.	Blank
	Jemma	Energy is something that can help things move and work e.g. cars, the human body, turbines, boilers, pylons.	Energy is something that gives other objects power to make electricity.	Makes things happen.
2 How is energy involved with the human body?	Luke	There is electricity in the body, that is sent as pulses to muscles etc. to tell them what to do (through moves). Food is also turned into energy, that the body uses to function.	Chemical energy is consumed in food. The energy is used to power the body, so the energy is turned into kinetic.	Energy, in the form of electricity, is sent round the body as messages in your nerves.
	Jemma	Working (energy) keeps the blood flowing round our bodies.	Energy helps us move and think.	Energy in food is transferred to our body to move.
3 How is energy involved with electricity?	Luke	Electricity is a form of energy.	Electricity is a form of energy. It can be made in a power station by different forms of energy, and can be used to make heat and light energy, along with others.	Electricity is a form of energy.
	Jemma	Energy will power electricity that humans need.	Energy in the boiler makes steam that makes the turbine move then goes into the generator that then goes to electric wires to our home, energy in the boiler started the chain.	Blank

abstractly and apply these ideas to new situations. Luke took the idea and *applied it in more depth to the new situation.* This suggests that he could have been dissatisfied with what he saw as a 'basic idea' and took it much further in his model. This shows that the apparently closed task allowed pupils to express their ideas with freedom, making the task more open ended.

Both students were able to *engage with this task*, were keen to put forward their opinions about each of the models. This supports the QCA criteria that gifted and talented (G&T) pupils *'enjoy talking to the teacher about new information or ideas'.* They were both able to use the abstract models to explain their ideas and observations. Luke took this further by applying ideas from other areas of science by including the biological ideas of hearing.

There is clear evidence of *logical thinking* and both provide plausible explanations for the phenomena of energy transfers. Luke shows particular *imagination* and although not all of his explanation is scientifically correct, he is able to use knowledge, understanding and imagination to give an explanation using abstract ideas.

In both cases, the students were able to give *coherent arguments* for their preferred model and question the models that they were presented with. This is another characteristic highlighted by the QCA.

It appears that the explicit teaching of both models for 'energy' is beneficial to more able pupils. This approach provides a range of learning opportunities including applying abstract ideas, evaluating models and concepts, and using imagination to explain phenomena in new situations. This provides challenge and motivation to what can be seen as a difficult and dry concept to teach. It also opens the opportunity for students to discuss evidence and question scientific models, getting them involved in the scientific process.

Does the use of the energy transfer models help reveal any other characteristics of able and talented students?

The characteristics listed by the QCA are not intended to be all-inclusive. These case studies suggest that a characteristic not listed by the QCA is the ability of gifted and talented students to deal with uncertainty (cf. 'post-formal thinking', see Chapter 6). Providing more able pupils with the opportunity to compare, discuss and evaluate models allows them to engage with the scientific processes. This is a key to developing scientists of the future.

Discussion

Both these students found the hybrid model useful as a bridge towards an understanding of the 'transfer' and 'transformation' models and hence to an attainment of Level 6 in respect of the notion of 'model'. Luke was the more secure in this respect, for he had a firm command of the 'transformation' model prior to the lesson. He retained a preference for this model until near the end of the lesson sequence, by which time an understanding of the 'transfer' model had been attained. He declared a preference for the 'transfer' model after having tackled the 'CD explanation' problem. He could be said to have reached Level 6 in respect of 'model', and, by virtue of having used it to explain 'electricity', of being well on the way to Level 7 generally. Jemma, under the stimulus of the 'CD explanation' problem, was able to use both models, but seemed to prefer using only one of them i.e. 'transformation'. She may be thought to have been on the verge of, rather than firmly within, Level 6 for 'model'.

By adopting a pedagogy which supported the development of the capacity to 'metacognitively model' the process of modelling the notion of energy, and by planning in detail for its implementation, AG was able to support the progression of these students to Level 6, thus enabling them to be recognised as 'gifted and able in science'. This pedagogy would have to be adopted consistently if future progression was to be made by these students.

The next step for the teacher, AG, was to challenge the students to compare each other's models. They would be encouraged to identify which aspects of their models related to the transfer model or the transformation model and discuss why they had used these ideas to explain the CD player. Other 'energy' situations could then be introduced, where the students applied their energy model, refined it against each of the teaching models and, in so doing, would be able to discuss the limitations of each model, accessing Level 7 (see Figure 7.2). Using this approach allows for the assessment of the students' current attainment and informs planning for future lessons. Opportunities for these students to consolidate Level 6 concepts through their models and access Level 7 could be planned using the pedagogy discussed above.

Both the case-study students were able to understand the basic Level 5 electricity concepts with ease: how to construct and draw a circuit diagram for series and parallel circuits, explain the functions of the components and simply describe how a battery powered device works. The CD task challenged these students to question their ideas about electricity by explicitly linking the concept of electricity with the Big Idea of Energy. This pedagogy challenged their ideas and allowed AG to develop both their understanding of concepts such as current and voltage as well as scientific processes in using models to explain abstract concepts and be critical of these models. These features of this approach are valuable when teaching and looking for suitable approaches to extend gifted and talented learners within the context of the classroom.

Chapter 8

Challenging gifted learners through classroom dialogue

Phil Scott

The previous chapters stressed the importance of planning science lessons so that learners, and especially the most able learners, are challenged in their thinking. A key feature of lessons, including science lessons, is talk. Language is the major tool of teachers, albeit a tool we are sometimes too reluctant to hand over to our learners. In this chapter Phil Scott draws upon research exploring classroom talk in science to suggest how more careful planning of the 'rhythm' of types of classroom talk may help stretch learners' thinking.

Talk and meaningful learning

In a Science PGCE (Post-Graduate Certificate in Education) class, some teacher trainees were reflecting on their own learning experiences at university. One of them commented that very often they took notes in lectures but 'hardly understood a word of it!', and this was met with nods of agreement from the others. Another student described how, as examinations loomed, she and her two friends formed a group to 'talk through' their lecture notes. This proved to be a common approach, with students 'talking their way' to an understanding of demanding scientific ideas. Indeed, one student described how he would take a walk *alone* and talk aloud the science ideas to himself. As he said, 'If I can't explain something to myself or to others then I don't really understand it'.

Such reflections point to the intimate connection between language and learning and to the fundamental importance of talk in coming to an understanding of ideas. Given this connection between language and learning, it is somewhat paradoxical that in science lessons in schools (and even more so in universities!) it is often the teacher (the expert) who does all of the talking while the students (the novices) say little.

The central theme of this chapter is to consider how gifted learners might become engaged in more *meaningful* learning through extending the kinds of talk carried out in science classrooms. Meaningful learning is taken as involving making connections between ways of thinking (Ausubel 2000). Such connections might be between the everyday views which students bring to science lessons and the scientific views which are taught. They might be between the taught scientific view and other scientific concepts which are already known by the students. This process of seeing similarities and differences between ways of thinking is key to developing a meaningful understanding of new knowledge and it is precisely this outcome which we should aspire to for gifted students.

Language, learning and Vygotsky

Over the last twenty years or so, Vygotsky's sociocultural perspective on learning and development has become increasingly popular as a framework for researching the link between language and learning. Central to Vygotsky's approach is the idea that learning involves a passage from social contexts to individual understanding. Thus according to Vygotsky's 'General Genetic Law of Cultural Development', higher psychological structures (such as scientific conceptual knowledge) appear: 'first between people as an inter-psychological (social) category and then inside the child as an intra-psychological (personal) category' (Vygotsky 1978: 128). What does this mean? Quite simply that we first meet new ideas in social situations where those ideas are rehearsed between people, drawing on a range of modes of communication, such as talk, gesture, writing, visual images and action. Vygotsky refers to these interactions as taking place on the *social plane*, which may be constituted by a teacher working with a class of students in school, or involve a parent explaining something to a child. As ideas are rehearsed during the social event, each participant is able to reflect on and make individual sense of what is being communicated. In other words, we don't all end up with precisely the same understanding. Furthermore, the words, gestures and images used in the social exchanges provide the tools needed for individual thinking. Thus, there is a transition from *social* to *personal* planes, whereby the social tools for communication become internalised and provide the means for individual thinking. This intimate relationship between talking and thinking becomes very apparent when we start 'talking to ourselves' or 'thinking aloud' about difficult or stressful problems (as did the 'walking and talking' PGCE student referred to earlier). It is no coincidence that Vygotsky's most influential book is entitled *Thought and Language* (Vygotsky 1962). According to this socio-cultural perspective, if we want to promote meaningful learning of scientific knowledge by gifted learners, then the starting point involves engaging them in the kinds of talk where ideas are explored and connections made between those ideas (see also Chapter 2).

A framework for analysing classroom talk

Although science lessons appear in lots of different shapes and sizes a common feature of all of them is that teacher and students (to various extents) engage in talking. As might be expected this talk takes different forms and in this section a framework (Mortimer and Scott 2003) for identifying different kinds of classroom talk is presented. This framework is based on two dimensions: interactive/non-interactive and authoritative/dialogic.

Interactive/non-interactive

According to this first dimension, *interactive* teaching involves the verbal participation of both teacher and pupils, while *non-interactive* teaching excludes the participation of the pupils, as the teacher adopts some form of lecturing style. An interesting and frequently overlooked feature of interactive talk is that, although it may involve lots of question and answer turn-taking, it is often played out in such a way that the teacher takes no account of the pupils' points of view. This brings us to the second dimension.

Dialogic and authoritative

What do we mean by 'taking account of pupils' points of view'? The idea here is that the teacher asks pupils for their points of view and explicitly takes account of them by, for example: asking for further details ('Oh, that's interesting, what do you mean by . . . '); or writing it down for further consideration ('Let's just put that down on the board, so that we don't forget it . . . '); or asking other pupils whether they agree with it or not ('Do you go along with what Anita has just said . . .?'). In a nutshell, the teacher makes room in the classroom talk for a whole range of ideas. This kind of classroom talk, where the teacher takes account of pupils' points of view, is referred to as being *dialogic* in nature (Mortimer and Scott 2003). Generally, in dialogic talk there is an attempt to acknowledge the views of others, and through dialogic approaches the teacher attends to the pupils' points of view as well as to the school science view.

Of course, classroom talk is not always dialogic in character, there are many occasions when the teacher is not interested in exploring pupils' ideas and taking account of them in developing the lesson. Here the teacher is likely to focus on the science point of view and if ideas or questions, which do not contribute to the development of the school science story, are raised by pupils they are likely to be reshaped or ignored by the teacher. This kind of talk is taken as being *authoritative* in nature. We therefore have a second dimension which can be used in thinking about teacher talk in science lessons: this is the authoritative-dialogic dimension.

The communicative approach

The two dimensions identified above can be combined to generate four ways in which the teacher might communicate with pupils in the classroom (Table 8.1). Thus any episode of classroom talk can be identified as being either *interactive* or *non-interactive* on the one hand, and *dialogic* or *authoritative* on the other, generating four classes of *communicative approach* (Mortimer and Scott 2003):

Table 8.1 Four classes of communicative approach

	Interactive	Non-interactive
Authoritative	Interactive/Authoritative	Non-interactive/Authoritative
Dialogic	Interactive/Dialogic	Non-interactive/Dialogic

With an *interactive/authoritative* communicative approach, the teacher is likely to focus on the school science view and lead the pupils through a question and answer routine with the aim of establishing and consolidating that point of view. The *non-interactive/authoritative* approach involves some kind of presentation by the teacher. An *interactive/dialogic* approach sees teacher and pupils talking about a range of points of view. Finally there is the *non-interactive/dialogic* approach which at first glance may appear self-contradictory. How is it possible to communicate in a way which is both non-interactive and dialogic? The idea here is that the teacher might be reviewing different points of view in a non-interactive way: 'Now, John said X, but Anita had a rather different idea when she argued for Y'.

Talk in science classrooms

How might the different communicative approaches outlined above appear in science lessons? Let's look at examples of interactive/authoritative and interactive/dialogic communicative approaches in action.

Interactive/authoritative communicative approach

The following episode is taken from a Year 8 science class in a comprehensive school in a large city in the North of England:

> Episode 1: From the sun
> 1. Teacher: Where does the coal get its energy from?
> 2. Student 1: Trees.
> 3. Teacher: Sorry?
> 4. Student 1: Trees.

5. Teacher: Trees. Dead plants, yes. Do you remember doing this at primary school? Trees and dead plants. Now the difficult part . . . where do these trees and dead plants get their energy from in the first place?
6. Student 2: Ground.
7. Teacher: The ground. How did the ground give it energy?
8. Student 2: Put things in it.
9. Student 3: Grow.
10. Teacher: Right they grew. What do you need to make something grow? What one thing that we've . . .
11. Student 4: Water!
12. Teacher: Water? Where did all that energy come from?
13. Student 5: Sky.
14. Teacher: What?
15. Student 5: Sun.
16. Teacher: The sun! So if we say . . . if we trace back the electricity from here. Electrical energy. Going back to the power stations. That came from the coal. That coal gets chemical energy from plants that have all died and so on. The plants originally got their energy from the sun.

You will probably recognise this kind of question and answer routine, where the teacher is searching for the idea that the sun is the ultimate source of the coal's energy. One pupil suggests that the energy comes from 'trees' and the teacher accepts this response, asking where the 'trees and dead plants' get their energy from. Another student responds with 'Ground' and the teacher poses a further question, 'How did the ground give it energy?' The notion that plants get their energy from the ground is a common alternative conception, but the teacher does not pause to explore this pupil idea. Rather he continues with his questioning, eliciting the responses, 'grow', 'water' and 'sky' before finally getting to the target answer, 'sun'. Throughout this interaction, the pupils' contributions are limited to single words, while the teacher acknowledges these contributions, 'Water?', but takes no further account of them. In this way, the teacher adopts an *interactive/authoritative* communicative approach. The talk is interactive in the sense of there being lots of questions and answers and it is authoritative as the teacher focuses on just one acceptable answer.

Interactive/authoritative talk is the most common form of communicative approach in science classrooms, not only in the UK, but around the world (see, for example, Wells 1999; Alexander 2001). Some observers reckon that it accounts for as much as 90% of the talk in science classrooms. In other words the teacher spends most of the time in asking streams of questions whilst the pupils respond with short, often single word answers, as they are required almost to 'guess what the teacher is thinking'.

This form of classroom talk is identifiable in a second way. Look back at the transcript. The teacher starts by asking a *question*: 'Where does the coal get its energy from?' The pupil *responds*, 'Trees'. The teacher then makes an *evaluation*: 'Yes', before moving on to ask another *question*: 'where do these trees and dead plants get their energy from in the first place?' A pupil *responds* with 'Ground' and the teacher *evaluates*, 'The ground' and moves on to ask the next question, 'How did the ground give it energy?'

In this way a clear *pattern of discourse* emerges where:

Teacher asks a question:	INITIATION	[I]
Pupil responds:	RESPONSE	[R]
Teacher evaluates:	EVALUATION	[E]

This 3-step, triadic pattern, I-R-E, is the ubiquitous 'dance-step' (1–2–3, 1–2–3, 1–2–3. . .) of science lessons (Edwards *et al.* 1987). Once you become aware of it you can't fail to notice how common it is.

Interactive/dialogic communicative approach

The following episode took place during the *first* lesson of a teaching sequence on heat and temperature, with pupils aged 14–15 years. An initial activity involved students immersing one hand in cold water and the other in warm water before plunging them both into a tank of water at room temperature. During this activity the teacher noticed that students were talking about what was happening in various different ways. In the subsequent whole-class plenary the teacher encourages the students to explain, in their own terms, what happened in the activity:

Episode 2: Hot and cold
1. Teacher: So, how do you explain it? What happens when we feel hot and cold?
2. Student 2: Maybe the temperature of the water passes to your hand when you put it in the water.
3. Teacher: What passes to your hand?
4. Student 2: The temperature.
5. Teacher: The temperature? Do you agree with that?
6. Student 3: There was a heat change.
7. Teacher: Heat change. What's that? Can you explain please?

Here, Student 2 (turn 2) uses the idea of *temperature* in a way which is closer to the school science concept of *heat*. Student 3, on the other hand, refers to a 'heat change'. The discussion continues (some turns later) with different students making contributions:

29. Student 1: I think there is a heat change because our body is always around the same constant temperature.

30. Teacher: Hmm . . .
31. Student 1: So, if you put your hand in a bowl of warm water your temperature remains more or less the same, it doesn't change. There is a change of heat. Heat relates to what you feel, so there is a heat change and not a change of temperature.
32. Student 4: That's it. And heat can be cold or hot. It can be a cold or hot heat.
33. Teacher: Do you agree with that? Movement of cold heat and hot heat?
34. Student ?: No.
35. Student ?: Temperature is only a measure.
36. Teacher: But she is saying that. Please [Student 4], explain again, because when you were saying hot and cold heat I saw someone looking surprised.
37. Student 4: I think that heat, when we talk about heat it does not mean just a hot heat, it can be cold, cold heat. For instance, in cold water we have cold heat and we felt it cold.

Throughout this episode (which continued for a further 10 minutes), the teacher adopts a neutral stance in not offering evaluative comments as she explores the pupils' views of heat and temperature prior to any teaching on this topic. She prompts the students to present their ideas and asks for elaboration and justification of points of view. She also helps the students to recognise the existence of different possible interpretations of the phenomenon. For example, in turn 36 the teacher gives special attention to Student 4's explanation, which is based on the existence of two kinds of heat. Although Student 4's explanation is not fully explored at this point in the sequence, the teacher returns to it later. In this way the teacher develops an interactive/dialogic communicative approach and the 'two kinds of heat' idea is foregrounded as a theme to be revisited.

The distinctive *pattern of discourse* in this case involves chains of interaction rather than the I-R-E pattern of the authoritative talk. Thus the teacher starts by asking a question, 'What happens when we feel hot and cold?', and Student 2 responds, 'Maybe the temperature of the water passes to your hand. . .'. The teacher makes a *prompt* in asking for clarification, 'What passes to your hand?' The student responds and the teacher makes a further *prompt*, seeking others' views, 'The temperature? Do you agree with that?' In this way we see a pattern emerging in the discourse:

Teacher asks a question:	INITIATION	[I]
Pupil responds:	RESPONSE	[R]
Teacher prompts:	PROMPT	[P]
Pupil responds:	RESPONSE	[R]
Teacher prompts:	PROMPT	[P]

A chain of interaction, I-R-P-R-P-R-P-, is set up as the teacher encourages responses from different pupils. The key feature of the interactive/dialogic approach is that the teacher makes room for and explores pupils' ideas.

Communicative approaches and teaching purposes

There are striking differences between these two episodes. In the first episode the students' contributions are limited to single words whilst in the second the students make much more extended and complete utterances. In comparing the episodes it is tempting to suggest that the interactive/dialogic communicative approach of the second is 'better' than the more limited (in terms of student contributions) interactive/authoritative approach of the first. Is non-interactive teaching bad, simply because it's the teacher who is doing all of the talking? The short answer is that it depends on what the teacher is trying to do. It depends on the *teaching purpose*.

Experience indicates that expert teachers demonstrate a *rhythm* to their teaching, whereby: now they open up matters for discussion (interactive/dialogic); now they work on the science point of view (interactive/authoritative); now they present the science view (non-interactive/authoritative) and link it to the pupils' thinking (non-interactive/dialogic). There is no special order for these approaches but there is a strong sense of rhythm as ideas are opened up for discussion and then closed down. The challenge for the science teacher is to make appropriate use of the full repertoire of communicative approaches as they play out the *tension* between promoting authoritative and dialogic interactions (Scott *et al.* 2006).

Gifted pupils in action: Jamie and the plunger

Let's now draw on some of these ideas in considering a short episode which involves a science teacher talking with an individual student, Jamie. The episode occurred in a Year 8 lesson at the start of work on 'air pressure'. The class is working on a circus of activities and the teacher asks Jamie, in an interactive/dialogic approach, why the plunger of a *sealed* air syringe springs back to its original position after being pulled outwards.

Episode 3: Thinner air
1. Jamie: Well, it was like, er . . . you're making the space bigger and it's only got a small amount of air [inside the syringe]. So it's trying to get more air in and it can't cos that's [the plunger] there. So instead of bringing more air from there, it's bringing that [the plunger] in.
2. Teacher: Mmm . . . you know when you say, 'it, pulls in the plunger' . . . what is it that is doing the pulling?
3. Jamie: I don't know . . . [5 seconds]

4. Teacher: Cos normally if something's doing the pulling . . .
5. Jamie: Mmm . . . [7 seconds]
6. Teacher: A bit of a problem, eh?
7. Jamie: Yeah. Is it the small amount of air [inside the syringe] that's pulling and trying to get a bigger amount of air? . . .
8. Teacher: The only bit that I don't understand is what . . . how air can do any pulling . . .

Jamie starts by suggesting that the air inside the syringe brings the plunger in and the teacher *prompts* him (turn 2) to elaborate on what he means by 'it'. There are two lengthy pauses as Jamie reflects on the problem and the teacher draws attention to the central problem of 'how air can do any pulling' (turns 6, 8). Jamie now sets off in a different direction:

9. Jamie: You know when there's air in . . .
10. Teacher: Mmm. . .
11. Jamie: and you know when . . . you pull it out?
12. Teacher: Yeah
13. Jamie: What's in there then? [inside the syringe]

Further discussion led to agreement that there is 'thinner air' inside the syringe when the plunger is pulled back:

14. Teacher: So the air is thinner and fills the whole of that space.
15. Jamie: like if you're higher up.
16. Teacher: Yes, exactly like that. There's a bit of a problem here, isn't there? How thinner air can do any pulling at all?

Jamie introduces the idea that the air inside the syringe is thinner, 'like if you're higher up' at the top of a mountain. The teacher returns to the question of how the 'thinner air' inside the syringe 'can do any pulling at all?'

17. Jamie: was it that . . . the thinner air [inside the syringe] just trying to make itself thicker air because it's thicker air all around it, so . . . it was trying to adapt . . .
18. Teacher: Mmm . . .
19. Jamie: to the normal air . . . around here? So it's like if you fill that with air here and you kept it so as no air could get in or out and you pulled it and took it high up . . .
20. Teacher: Yeah . . .
21. Jamie: it doesn't go back in. It doesn't come back because the air's the same.
22. Teacher: Yes.
23. Jamie: Right I understand.

Jamie now develops an elegant 'thought experiment' which involves the plunger of the syringe being drawn back down 'here' (at sea level) and then taken 'high up' (to the top of a mountain), where the plunger is released. On release the plunger 'doesn't go back in . . . because the air's the same'. In this way Jamie makes the step from an everyday, common-sense view of the phenomenon (based on the air inside the syringe pulling) to the scientific point of view (involving differences between the air inside and outside the syringe).

Challenging gifted learners: 'working the gap'

Episodes of this quality are unusual in science classrooms, so how was the teacher able to set up and sustain the interaction?

First, the teacher *recognised* that Jamie's initial explanation was based solely on the action of the air from inside the syringe. He then *challenged* this view with the key question: 'how air can do any pulling', leaving plenty of *time* for Jamie to think it through. When Jamie asked what happens to the air inside the syringe, the teacher was happy to use Jamie's suggestion that the air is 'thinner' rather than insisting on the correct scientific concept (density) – which might have created a distraction. Throughout the interaction the teacher *sustained* this interactive/dialogic exploration of ideas with a series of prompts (turns 10, 12, 18, 20, 22). The teacher in the 'hot and cold' episode took a similar approach as she allowed space for students to talk through their points of view and drew attention to the key issue of 'hot and cold heat'.

The success of both of these interventions depended not only on the teacher's knowledge of the science but also on their ability to recognise the student's starting points *and* to pose key questions in challenging the students' thinking. In each episode the teacher demonstrated their considerable expertise as they worked the *gap* between everyday and scientific views.

Gifted pupils talking in groups

If we take seriously Vygotsky's perspective on language and learning then there is a clear priority not only for promoting dialogue between teacher and students but also for setting up situations where students talk science to each other. The following episode occurred in a Year 9 class on the particulate theory of matter (an especially abstract concept: see Chapters 6 and 7). A group of students is considering the question of how the bonding between atoms returns as a gas is cooled to form a liquid and then a solid.

    Episode 4: Bonding
    1. Paul: I mean we're more or less clear how things go from solids to liquids to gases, but not from gases to liquids to solids.
    2. Jane: The point is, in the gas the bonding has totally gone.

3. Paul: So, how does it happen that bonding comes back?
4. Jane: I suppose it works vice versa, when it's heated it destroys the bonding, when it's cold . . . you know . . . it remakes it.
5. Clare: But how does it remake it? What does it remake it with though?
6. Alan: When they're hot they [atoms] vibrate more, so that the bond isn't as strong.
7. Paul: Yeah, I know, but they vibrate more and break the bonding and then they finally get to a gas and that's as far as they go . . . but how does it get the bonding back? Ah! . . . when it starts to cool down, they don't vibrate as much.
8. Jane: Ah yeah! When they cool down the bonding will be increased so they won't be able to move around as much. That fits in doesn't it?
9. Paul: Yeah . . . but the point is, how do we get the bonding back?
10. Alan: Slow down the vibrating . . .
11. Paul: Slow down the vibrations.
12. Alan: I suppose it's ever-present there, but . . . yeah! It hasn't got a chance to like grip, grip them, you know and keep them together. Well, where it slows down, you know, it might get to grips with . . .

Once again we have a situation where students are engaged in talking science, this time moving impressively towards an understanding of how bonding reappears as a gas is cooled. The teacher is not directly involved in the dialogue but has framed the task in such a way that the students can have a productive discussion. This framing involves specifying clear purposes, fixing time limits and ensuring that the students have a range of appropriate ideas to draw upon (it's no use asking students to discuss matters of which they have no knowledge). In addition, the students must have some sense of what is involved in developing a dialogue in the context of science, and here the idea of 'modelling talk' is crucial. Put simply, if students participate exclusively in authoritative talk in science lessons then the chances of establishing rich, thoughtful dialogues in small-group settings must be low. The students in the 'bonding' discussion had lots of experience of talking science with their teacher in class (following an interactive/dialogic approach), and it shows in the high quality of their group discussion.

The impact of engaging gifted students in science dialogues does not end with the students being better able to progress towards meaningful learning through talking. Following Vygotskian theory, it is clear that if students engage in dialogic talk then they will become more skilled in *thinking* in a dialogic way, considering different points of view and making connections. From a Vygotskian perspective the link between the quality of talking and the quality of thinking and learning is inescapable: if we want gifted students to improve in their ability to think through problems, then we need to start by putting them in situations where they are encouraged to talk through problems.

Final thoughts

In this chapter a case has been made for the fundamental importance of talk in supporting the meaningful learning of gifted students. A recurring feature of the examples of dialogue presented here is the sheer high quality of the students' contributions. Through such examples we are reminded of the difference between what children are capable of achieving in classroom settings and the more modest outcomes which routinely follow from so many science lessons. These student performances were prompted, not through invoking some form of relevance (to sport or music or whatever) but by posing key questions which engaged with the students' thinking about natural phenomena, thereby invoking a form of 'intellectual relevance'.

Whilst acknowledging the high quality of the students' contributions, it is important to recognise the deep and insightful teaching expertise which made those contributions possible. This teaching expertise involves in large part breaking free from the authoritative grip of triadic (I-R-E) patterns of discourse and moving towards chains of dialogic interaction (I-R-P-R-P-R ...). Equally important is the need to get students talking science for themselves, exploring, and thinking through, ideas in a dialogic way.

Of course such shifts in practice are not trivial, requiring the confidence, skill and knowledge to 'work in the gap' between everyday and scientific views. These shifts in practice may well be challenging but are also likely to be immensely rewarding and liberating for both the teacher and their gifted students.

Chapter 9

Asking questions in classroom science

Mike Watts and Helena Pedrosa de Jesus

As Phil Scott pointed out in Chapter 8, teacher questions are a major feature of the tactics of teaching. In typical classrooms, most of the questions are asked by those who know the answers, rather than those who are seeking to learn. Yet, in science itself, asking questions is a vital activity. In this chapter, Mike Watts and Helena Pedrosa de Jesus explore how learners can be encouraged to ask the questions, something that can not only link learning to students' interests, but also develop metacognition and engage higher level thinking.

Introduction

In this chapter we argue for the importance of encouraging students to ask questions in science, as a way of challenging their thinking. We make a series of early points and then go some way towards exploring how these might be worked out in practice.

Our first point: schools are places of conformity. This is not necessarily always a cause for anxiety – schools are organisations and, like most organisations, require a degree of conformity in order to function properly. That said, too much conformity can quell even the most robust of *creative* spirits and mute the most incisive of *critical* questioners. Since our interest lies in developing both these qualities, with a distinct emphasis on the latter, we are keen to provide 'zones of low-conformity' in schools, zones within the normal running of schools and classrooms where young people can give expression to their intelligent, critical, challenging and creative questions.

Second, teachers require uniformity. Again, this is not always a negative critique. Classrooms work effectively where there are both implicit and explicit agreements and understandings between teacher and taught that enable progress to be made. In our view, a good classroom is where learners and teacher are complicit in the 'orchestration' of teaching and learning (Watts 2004a; Pedrosa de Jesus *et al.* 2005). From this perspective, good teaching implies orchestrating activities in order to maximise engagement with learning of the greatest number of students at any one time and place. However, in too many instances, teachers act and combine to repress creativity (Rutland 2005). And, when they do, they thwart original and therefore unexpected questions that they feel may be disruptive of routine, class control, orderliness, organisation, curriculum orthodoxy and so on. There is no doubt that learners' questions can be disruptive – even if they are not intended as such (Watts *et al.* 1997a). In some of our work teachers have described how an unexpected question has been disabling – not of the general smooth working of the lesson – but of their own smooth thought processes and understanding of science (Watts *et al.* 1997b). Better, on occasions, to resist such incursions into one's personal (and often private) conceptual systems and to ignore/sidestep/deflect the question!

Third, teachers are an important connection between intelligent questions and intelligent answers. They provide an important role in promoting 'creative questioning', providing a positive role model that reinforces critical questioning in learners. They can protect learners from conforming pressures and establish a learning environment that permits alternative solutions; tolerates and supports constructive error; and encourages effective surprise. Most important, they do not isolate non-conformity where it happens. Where the UK's government exhorts teachers to employ 'interactive teaching methods to promote questioning, reflection and observation, critical thinking, evaluation of pupils' own and others' work, discussion and dialogue' (TTA 2002: 58), we would exhort teachers to use 'interactive teaching methods to promote *and foster creative* questioning, reflective *questioning* and observation, critical *questioning* . . .' (emphasis added). Not an impossible task, as we hope to illustrate.

What kinds of questions are there?

There are a limitless number of possible questions to ask. The importance we attach to the asking of questions lies in the ways in which the composition and delivery of questions affects thinking and understanding, on the enhancement of learning that takes place in and around a question. Quite clearly, people can be differentially curious, differentially willing to ask questions: the 'epistemic hunger' (Dennett 1991) of some learners being more readily satisfied than that of others (Watts and Taber 1996). Some students ask questions easily, others less so. Some do so on the smallest contact between problem and explanation, others require more information before they can first form a question. Whatever the case, a question signals puzzlement, curiosity, perplexity, doubt, challenge, wonder, incongruity – and more. All of these states of thinking are worthwhile and a necessary prelude to the construction and development of meaning. In some cases, asking even poorly formed and tentative questions can indicate an active, interrogative attitude that not only looks for appropriate information and opinion, hunts for conceptualisation and meaning in the subject matter, but also seeks some determination of the worth of what is read or heard.

Our work has given rise to five main kinds of learner questions (Pedrosa de Jesus *et al.* 2004), as in Table 9.1. It might appear from our five types of question that some are better than others – that the types imply levels of questioning and that there is a necessary hierarchy involved in our taxonomy of questioning. This is a popular approach but not one that we adopt directly. To begin with, there are no *bad* questions, we see *any* question to be a good question! Each of our types of question begins from a basis in meaning-making, of attempting to construct frameworks of understanding.

Acquisition questions are those that seek to clarify information and detail, attempt to differentiate between fact and speculation, tackle issues of specificity, and ask for exemplification and/or definition. These questions are an attempt to decide which information is pertinent, check what basis it has for inclusion within a particular setting, and/or to determine the place and worth of particular data or evidence.

Specialisation and Integrative questions, on the other hand, seem to signal some restructuring or reorganisation of learners' understanding. They seem to be intended to get further 'inside' the ideas, be hypothetic-deductive, seek extensions to what is known, cross knowledge domains. These questions explore argumentative steps, identify omissions, examine structures in thinking, and challenge accepted reasoning. In our experience, Acquisition questions greatly outnumber Specialisation questions by a ratio of some 10:1 (Pedrosa de Jesus *et al.* 2004). We see this to be because learners need to clear a platform of understanding before they can begin to explore and to speculate.

There is no doubt that it is easier (and probably more necessary) to ask Acquisition questions at the outset of a topic of work – but this process tends to set the scene for the asking of more detailed Specialisation and Integrative questions. If there is to be a hierarchy, then this should lead from straight-forward questions towards increasingly complex questions, leading to more involved 'quality' learning. Here we turn to John Biggs' work in which he describes 'quality learning' as:

> the development of students' intellectual and imaginative powers; their understanding and judgement; their problem-solving skills; their ability to communicate; their ability to see relationships within what they have learned and to perceive their field of study in a broader perspective, to stimulate an *enquiring*, analytical and creative approach; encouraging independent judgement and critical self-awareness [emphasis added].
>
> Biggs 1988: 174

It seems to us that this is where good questioning should lead. So, while there is no sharp hierarchy involved, we do see some sense of progression taking place whereby learners need to secure a basis for understanding before

Table 9.1 A typology of questions

Acquisition questions	These are those questions that deal with relatively straightforward ideas, objects, processes, or concepts which do not require evaluation, judgement, or the drawing of conclusions. When asking questions of this kind, learners are attempting to clear up matters of fact, clarify ideas, confirm explanations or pin down some issues. These are 'stick-to-the-facts' questions, testing for information and reassurance.
Specialisation questions	These tend to go beyond an initial search for information; the learner establishes relations and tries to understand and interpret the meaning of related issues. These kinds of questions move beyond a specific or detailed level of understanding in order to generalise or relate these specifics into meaningful patterns. The learner has reached a 'base camp' in his or her understandings, and then uses the security of this to launch a few 'sorties' into the neighbouring terrain.
Integrative questions	The characteristics of this kind of question are the reorganisation of concepts into novel patterns and the hypothesis of new or different applications of principles. Integration questions are attempts to reconcile different understandings, resolve conflicts, test circumstances, force issues, track in and around complex ideas and their consequences. Such questions may have some direct relevance to the classroom topic being taught, though questions may be triggered by tangential issues or are stimulated by something from outside the class entirely.
Organisational questions	These can be thought of as the questions that marshal, and lead to, procedural knowledge, the *'Knowing how to . . .?* rather than the *'Knowing what . . .?* of learning. Questions like these (Holcomb 1996) guide learners in the preparation, focus, diagnosis, development, implementation and evaluation of their work. Specific questions (Pearson 1999: 28) can be used to guide these processes so that, for example in the 'focus' stage, the question might be: *Where do we want to go?* While implementing, monitoring and evaluating on the other hand, the questions might be: *How will we know we have got there?* (McGill and Brockbank 2004: 62).
Reflective questions	A reflective question is where a clear amount of 'internal contemplation' has taken place. That is, where a question has been consciously shaped by being mindful of the process of questioning, the audience and the social/academic context. A reflective question shows some understanding of the ways in which thinking can work, how questions can work, and can be designed through organising the nature and form of the question. It usually expresses feelings, beliefs, values about some issue of personal importance and is revealing of self-esteem, the self esteem of others, and shows empathy with other people in the vicinity.

they feel confident and willing to pursue more involved, analytical and speculative questions. In our view, it is important to appreciate that students frequently need to ask Acquisition-type questions before they can ask more complex questions. According to Biggs, once more, 'the quantitative stages of learning occur first, then learning changes qualitatively' (Biggs 1999).

What is critical questioning?

> The purpose of critical thinking is to achieve understanding, evaluate viewpoints, and solve problems. Since all three areas involve the asking of questions, we can say that critical thinking is the questioning or enquiry we engage in when we seek to understand, evaluate, or resolve
>
> Maiorana 1992: 5

Maiorana's position here seems fine by us. We see the process of question-generation and, in particular, the design and use of good, incisive, probing questions, as exercises in critical thinking and in the development of critical thinking skills. That is, critical thinking implies a clear propensity to ask questions and that 'critical thinking is the art of asking questions' (Hobson 2002). In this vein we enjoy questions like: 'Could you give me an example of . . .?', 'Is your basic point . . . or . . .?', and questions that probe assumptions: 'Is this the same issue as . . . ?'; 'You seem to be assuming . . . How would you justify taking this for granted?'; 'Is this always the case?'; 'To answer this question, what questions would we have to answer first?' (Paul 1993).

Moreover, in school science, we want youngsters to ask questions, not least since 'questioning lies at the heart of scientific enquiry and meaningful learning' (Chin *et al.* 2002: 521). We want critical questions, surely, such as: 'How could we go about finding out whether this is true?'; 'Is there reason to doubt that evidence?'; 'What effect would that have?'; 'If this and this are the case, then what else must also be true?'

We have argued elsewhere (Mallick and Watts in preparation) that critical questioning also entails being political (in the very general sense) in that teachers and learners must be aware of their own value commitments, the commitments of others and the values promoted by the work they are doing in class. Science itself – and certainly the technological development of science – is very 'value-laden', so embroiling the critical questioner in such questions as: 'How would other groups or types of people respond to these ideas/ issues?'; 'Why?'; 'What would influence them?'; 'How would people who disagree with this viewpoint argue their case?'

Critical questioning, then, involves constructing difficult questions, opening up issues, raising problems, hunting for clues, chasing faint trails, querying uniformity, questioning orthodoxy, challenging authority. Critical questioners should constantly ask of themselves (Paul and Elder 2006):

- Which questions should I ask?
- Should I question the answers to the questions that I ask?
- Should I question the question?
- Are some questions better to ask than others?
- How do I recognise a useful as opposed to an unhelpful question?
- If thinking is something I do inside my head, and I ask all these questions, do I have to come up with the answers?

What are the problems in learners' questioning?

We have just suggested that learners in the throes of a science lesson *should* ask the teacher such questions as 'Is your basic point . . . or . . .?' and 'You seem to be assuming . . . How would you justify taking this for granted?'. The mere asking of such questions would, in many classroom contexts, appear overtly challenging, if not downright rude and disrespectful. Much rests in the tone, of course, and tone is just one dimension of classroom context. In many instances these types of questions seem to be more the responsibility of the teacher than the student. And therein lie some of the problems of trying to promote learners' critical and creative questioning.

First, we are interested in developing learners who have the capacity to learn at pace and with a level of complexity, to increase the depth of their understanding and the interest they hold. In our view, these are learners who have:

- a natural curiosity about the world and the way things work;
- an enjoyment of hypothesising;
- an increasing ability to express scientific knowledge and understanding logically and coherently;
- a useful and appropriate scientific vocabulary;
- an ability to transfer knowledge and understanding from one situation to another;
- an ability to spot and describe the patterns in results;
- innovation in the kinds of questions they ask.

Clearly, these characteristics mirror those often used to define gifted learners (i.e. as presented in Chapters 1, 2 and 3). Higher order thinking (see Chapter 6) occurs when a person takes new information, and information stored in memory, and rearranges and extends this information to achieve the purpose or find possible answers in perplexing situations. However, it is 'well documented that student questions in the classroom are very infrequent and unsophisticated' (Graesser and Person 1994: 105). In fact, studies at different educational levels and contexts generally indicate that learners do have questions but *avoid* asking them (Susskind 1969; Pedrosa de Jesus 1991; Dillon 1998). There are many reasons for young people not asking questions

– the classroom environment itself can discourage question asking. It seems that many young people do not want to call attention to themselves, and asking questions in class can generate feelings of exposure and vulnerability (Watts *et al.* 1997; Pedrosa de Jesus *et al.* 2004). Putting a hand up in the middle of a class session brings a multitude of eyes to bear on the question-asker, and that level of scrutiny may often be avoided. One study of learners' questions found that questions were 240 times as frequent in small-group tutoring settings as in classroom settings (Graesser and Person 1994).

The very task of asking a question may not be easy for some learners (Costa *et al.* 2000). There are a range of processes that take place as a question is formulated, sometimes referred to as 'anomaly detection', 'question articulation' and 'social editing' (Graesser *et al.* 1992). The puzzlement that comes with detecting an anomaly, an error or false premise in something does not come equally to all. For example, if a learner skim reads a text, or pays only partial attention to a video programme, he or she may well miss some important clues that there are key issues abroad here. Articulating a question can pose problems, too. Some people can ask long and detailed questions seemingly at 'the drop of a hat', while others need to write their question and then reformulate it several times to make it clear and unambiguous. Most important, '*social* editing' implies that the question may or may not actually be asked, depending on the social circumstances. Class members who lack confidence may prefer to write and post their questions, ask their friend, catch the teacher at the end of the lesson – all rather than pose the question out loud in the class.

More worrying, in our view, is the suggestion that few questions are asked because, as we noted earlier, teachers often dislike and inhibit question-asking (Marchbad-Ad and Sokolove 2000). Perhaps not unnaturally, teachers themselves feel vulnerable when there are a large number of questions, or a small number of difficult questions, coming from the audience – it is often much easier to teach, to lecture, to transmit, without the distraction, disruption and delay of having to deal with a plethora of questions. In these circumstances, many young people are more likely to ask questions to other students than to their teacher (Dillon 1988). Our final point here is that learners' questioning is also influenced by instructional models and lesson structures (Pizzini and Shepardson 1991). A large class format is much more daunting than small-group work; a raked lecture theatre more inhibiting than a comfortable tutorial room; an OHP or PowerPoint™ lecture more restrictive than a participative role-play session. That is, a climate of enquiry is encouraged by the social structure of the classroom, the young people's roles as participants, and the controlling function of the teacher's own questions (Watts 2004b). Questions are asked when individuals are confronted with obstacles to goals, anomalous events, contradictions, discrepancies, salient contrasts, obvious gaps in knowledge, 'expectation violations', and decisions that require discrimination among equally attractive alternatives. So, questions are less likely when issues are presented as unproblematic, cut-and-dried and uncontentious. The reverse is true where students are challenged in their thinking, values and beliefs.

What is a climate of enquiry?

A climate of enquiry is one of the 'zones of low-conformity' we mentioned at the start. The direction we take in this chapter places the burden for classroom questioning on the learner, but facilitated by the teacher. We see such a climate, such a zone, in the building of a co-operative enterprise from the start, one that strives for a long-term, self-directed view of learning (see 'Metacognition and independence in learning', Chapter 6) . The more the classroom context enables the process of enquiry the better, so that no one has to feel particularly vulnerable about not knowing – neither the teacher nor the learner. Sessions are constructed around clear and genuine student and teacher questions, questions that open up the classroom to critical enquiry. This calls for good organisation, thoughtful planning, well phrased questions from everyone, a sequencing of questions distributed around the class, acknowledgment of pauses and 'think time', and considered responses. Learners are encouraged to interact with each other, with the teacher, with texts, resources, the internet, in a relaxed atmosphere. In turn, the teacher's intervention in the classroom is to orient and encourage learners to ask questions, recognise difficulties that might arise and find then adequate and efficient strategies to meet these.

If, at first blush, this seems enormously idealistic, we can only point to our examples below by way of illustration. Before we reach these cases studies, we need to set the stage a little.

Our own work has shown that teachers can encourage student questions by systematically making room for questions within the usual class agenda, welcoming and inviting questions, and waiting patiently for them. Where a class is about to spend several days or weeks studying a particular topic or concept, there comes the opportunity to begin by listing what the class members think are the questions that could be asked within and about the topic (Pedrosa de Jesus *et al.* 2004). On occasions we have asked the class to categorise the questions recorded, asking them how they might group the questions (Watts and Alsop 1997). These categories have then provided the basis for organising and structuring work for the next few days or weeks. This also allows questions to be raised that 'fill in gaps' between categories, to evaluate the priorities of questions and to extend the questions being asked. Some questions have been relatively easy to answer, some more difficult; for some the resources will be available, others will require considerable searching; some will ask for contextual information (Specialisation questions) and others will require evaluative and critical thinking.

In the course of other sessions we devised a Question Box for the collection of written questions (Pedrosa de Jesus *et al.* 2004). These boxes were placed in each classroom and laboratory, and sometimes in the corridors outside. They are acrylic containers, very much like ballot boxes, with an outer compartment where a notepad is available for students' questions posted at any point in the session or during the day. The Question Boxes were emptied at the end of each day and collected together for responses to be made on a weekly basis. As part of this same study, one of our number devised an intranet system across the department and available to students off-site. This software system was accessible through the use of an appropriate password, operating within the science building and other parts of the site. It also enabled those who had internet facilities outside to work at home and access the system. Throughout our work the email system prompted a large number of questions, largely because this gave time and privacy in which to formulate and ask questions.

Others have suggested that teachers can improve classroom learning by helping students to learn good questioning skills (Gall 1970; Kloss 1988; Graesser and Person 1994). There are an enormous number of instructional packages aimed at teaching learners to ask questions, and in teaching critical thinking skills. The examples we present below are not of this type; we rely here on strong classroom management, good orchestration of learning, on consistent modeling and encouragement by teachers, so that learners increasingly take responsibility for asking these questions of themselves and their peers.

Case 1: Scientist in the hot seat

We have been labouring the point that learners' questions are important because they encourage and facilitate creative thinking and curiosity. They are important, too, because they provide markers of the progress each learner is making within science – they give insight into thinking. For us, curiosity and creativity are related to levels of interest; a willingness to be excited by events; a tendency to want to know more and to positively seek imaginative possibilities and hypothetical outcomes or relations in events. It is likely that young people vary greatly in their natural tendency to be curious or creative, depending on how these things might be encouraged and measured. The suggestion here is that science lessons might teach, or at the least encourage and develop, this natural tendency to be curious and creative.

Curiosity, from a common-sense point of view, is shown by pupils wanting to know more, pupils being willing to enter into an issue within a lesson, pupils spontaneously questioning the ideas being developed, pupils just demonstrably being interested and excited, being intrigued by the events and wanting to know more. In our view this entails learners being in a conducive social context, in which demonstrable creative and curious activities will be rewarded, without fear of failure. Our example describes a 'zone of low conformity' and concerns the use of a virtual learning environment (VLE) that encompassed, for this exercise, five centres:

- three geographically dispersed secondary schools, in Hampshire, Liverpool and London;
- the Natural History Museum, London, the location of the 'hot-seat' scientist;
- Roehampton University, the hosts of the VLE called 'Think.com'. We also engaged the services of an eminent and prestigious science educator from Reading University.

The scientist, Dr Matt Genge, is a noted expert at the Museum on comets and asteroids, and agreed to be in the 'hot-seat' whereby a class of thirty children in each of the three schools could direct questions at him for a period of one hour. Each class of thirty 12 year olds worked through a series of connected terminals so that their questions appeared not just on their own screens in their own school, but also on those at the other centres: the schools, Matt's computer at the Museum and ours at the University. In this way, everyone could see which questions had been posted and see Matt's answers as he worked down through the questions (See Box 9.1).

Some 100 young people can ask an enormous number of questions in one hour, firing off both the scientist's answers and the other questions arriving from youngsters in the other schools – many more than a solitary scientist can answer. While considerable duplication in the early stages allowed Matt to respond only to the 'most frequently asked' questions, this quickly gave way to increasingly more targeted and sophisticated questions as the youngsters digested his responses as they appeared on the screen. Moreover, while we had proposed that the class in each school should collaborate to share their

---

Box 9.1 Examples of 12-year-olds' questions about comets and asteroids

What is a comet? What is an asteroid? Which is the nearest asteroid? What is it made of? Could humans land on it? Would an asteroid ever hit the Earth? What would happen? Are asteroids made of useful minerals? Could they be mined for human use? Could life exist on an asteroid at present? Where did asteroids come from? How easy are they to detect?

questions, such collaboration only came into its own midway through the session, as the youngsters grew in confidence with the process and began to pool their questions – often prompted by questions and answers to questions from the other schools.

The questions flew unrestricted and unguarded. Whereas the teachers and lecturers involved may have felt an early need to set the ball rolling, and then monitor and 'care-take' the question-asking, this was largely unwarranted. The youngsters experienced frustration because the competition to get their question asked (before it was asked by some else) was fierce, and because the system slowed as the volume of questions increased rapidly – not least because the hot-seat scientist was a lone respondent. As the hour progressed it became increasingly difficult to ask new and original questions, pushing the youngsters to pool their thinking, challenge their understandings, increase the sophistication of their enquiries and elevate the tone of the session. In the language we used earlier, the questioners moved through a plethora of Acquisition questions, became increasingly more Specialised in the technical details of comets, and then began to increase in range and implication as they became Integrative of a wide variety of associated issues. The session finished with several questions to Matt personally – 'What made you become a scientist?'; 'Why did you decide to specialise in comets?'; 'Why do you work at a museum?'

The overall consensus of these children and teachers undertaking this project was that it was very valuable, enjoyable and well worth the time and effort invested in it. The questions generated were highly facilitative of the active learning of science.

Case 2: Communicare nelle scienza

This European project connected schools from Torino, Italy; Poitier, France; and London in the teaching of science and languages. It was aimed at 15- and 16-year-olds in each country, linking schools though a project website and email correspondence. Teachers in the schools were drawn from science departments, modern languages and, not unusually, ICT (information and communication technology) specialists, pooling resources to develop their common interests. The website was in the three languages but navigation around the system was simple and straightforward. The overall structure was that the teaching teams generated and developed materials around three chosen themes: the increasing use of electric cars, the development of satellite technology and the health risks attached to using mobile phones. Paired schools in different countries began their interactions around one of these themes and used the teachers' resources as the basis for constructing their own materials and presenting each other with questions and challenges.

The teachers' questions appeared in the form:

Activity
Imagine you have a brother who is 12 years old, and a sister who is 8 years old. Both want to have mobile phones. Your task is to advise them about the safety of using phones. So:

1   Would you advise them to have mobile phones at these ages? Why would you give this advice? Should the older brother have a phone but not the sister? Why?

2   What advice should they be given about the length of time each day that they might use a phone? How would you justify the advice you give them? What length of time per week, per month or per year? Why?

3   Some mobile phones are advertised as having low specific energy absorption rates (SAR). Do you think this would make a difference to your advice? Would you allow the two young people to have phones if they were fitted with a 'hands-free' kit?

The challenge for the youngsters was to collaborate within and between their schools to research the issues and respond in their own ways. Their responses were then posted onto a 'showcase' page of the website for the other project participants to explore and use. In the initial stages, they found the tasks easier when framed within the usual format for language lessons and asked their questions of each other as a series of 'mini-quizzes', crossword puzzles and other language games. In our terms, these were largely Acquisition questions, with some Specialisation questions interspersed. As their inter-actions increased, so levels of debate increased. This activity was posed by the teachers of a school in London:

What is the link between using mobile phones and the smoking of cigarettes? According to two researchers in the UK there is a strong link, but it is a 'reverse link'. As the use of mobile phones has increased, so the habit of smoking among 15 year olds has fallen. For example, between 1996 and 1999, the prevalence of smoking fell from 30% to 23%. During this same period the use of mobile phones has increased dramatically.

So, what could be the link? 'We hypothesise that the fall in youth smoking and the rise in ownership of mobile phones among adolescents are related' say the authors of the report. There are several reasons for this. First, there are financial reasons – the researchers suggest that both activities are expensive and teenagers cannot afford to do both – so one must go. Most young people prefer the advantages of technology and so choose to have a mobile phone. A mobile phone is attractive because it gives a sense of individuality and sociability, it allows young people to be independent and to also bond with their friends. What do you think?

Similarly, the youngsters' increasing familiarity with the process meant that they, too, raised the levels of the questions they posed to each other:

'Mobile phones on public transport systems such as trains and buses, and in public areas such as theatres and cinemas are an infringement to people's rights. They are annoying and irritating.' What do you think? Do you agree with our statement? Do you have a personal opinion on whether mobile phones should be banned from public places because they intrude on other people's personal space? Write your views to us from UK and France to see if you agree with us, telling us of a situation that you were in where a mobile 'phone was a nuisance.

While these activities tended to begin within the structures of standard lessons, whether within science, language or ICT lessons, their continuation depended upon those motivated youngsters who quickly took responsibility and management of the activities and used before, during and after school time to engage with the projects. In our view, designing enquiry-based-learning with and for these learners has developed their problem-solving skills, logical reasoning and reflective thinking, let alone their ability to engage in science in – sometimes – two other languages. Also, it has involved working as a member of a team, questioning, being challenged, being critical, creative and shaping skills for continued intellectual development.

Case 3: The thermochemistry of fitness

Our third case takes us out into a university foundation chemistry course in Portugal for students who would then continue into other more specialised degree programmes (Pedrosa de Jesus *et al.* 2005). The teaching staff had been working hard to encourage a climate of enquiry and, among the range of activities available to the students, had included the opportunity to engage in a small research project. These 'mini-projects' existed in parallel with the students' more routine studies and, while participation was voluntary, it did enable students to enhance their grades by a small margin, where they felt this additional work might benefit their overall assessment. In the event, some fifty students formed a total of thirteen groups of three, four or five students each. The groups met in and around their normal timetable over a period of some six weeks. The 'grande finale' to this work comprised an oral 'poster presentation' by each group in turn to the teachers and other students, followed by questions from the audience. The work was undertaken with gusto and enjoyment, moving though several phases as the students accumulated ideas and then designed poster presentations.

As we observed one particular group in action, it became clear to us that their questions performed several important functions in the structure of their work in, for example, organising ideas, delimiting the scale of the theme,

> **Box 9.2 Organisational questions and points to investigate**
>
> Why does the percentage of corporeal fat vary differently during the course of a day?
>
> Aerobic and anaerobic exercises
>
> Human calorimeter/Calorimeter (maqueta)
>
> Supplements
>
> Bio impedance
>
> New food pyramid
>
> Measure percentage of fat of colleagues
>
> Does a person who takes exercise expend more energy when asleep?

identifying and discussing the many strands and sources of information available to them, and in their reflections on the whole theme (see Box 9.2).

These Organisational questions became useful tools in the self-management and organisation of the group's work. The group created a character they called 'Lara'. Using Lara they were able to ask sometimes naive questions which they then used to organise both the remainder of the work and their reflections as the group. One of the questions asked by Lara was: 'Am I fatter than my friends?' and this was used as a way of introducing a range of answers in the poster format. In addition, their question structure led to experiments using a rudimentary lab calorimeter and measuring the relative amount of fat in a small sample of students.

For us, these Organisational questions (see Box 9.3) prompted a greater convergence and a more systematic approach to the mini-project. Shaping their work in this way allowed the trio to stage their activities and provide sufficient structure to accommodate shifting participation and roles between them.

The group presented a poster introducing the character 'Lara' and showing her reflecting on the problems of perceiving herself as fat and asking questions such as: 'Why don't these trousers fit me! Am I *that* fat?' These give way to more deliberated questions such as: 'How can I know just how fat I am?' Questions such as these were used throughout the presentation as a means of introducing each element of their research, connecting sub-themes and serving as 'organising' subtitles:

- How can I know my own level of fitness?
- What is impedance? And 'How can I determine the percentage of fat in a body from its impedance?'

Box 9.3 Refined organisational questions

What is Lara's fitness?

Which is the most precise method to evaluate fitness?

Am I fatter than my friends?

How I can be fit?

How many joules do I expend with exercise?

Where does the energy that I use come from? (food is fuel, food calorimeter)

What food I should eat?

What kind of routine do I need to have for having a healthy life?

How to determine the energy of the food? (calorimeter in practice, study impedance better?)

- How many calories are in a piece of cake?
- How many calories are expended in different physical activities?
- How can I calculate this?
- Does the human body obey the first law of thermodynamics?

The class reacted extremely well to the presentations and a swell of questions and debate arose at the end of the presentation. The overall consensus of those students that undertook the mini-projects was that these were valuable, enjoyable and well worth the time and effort invested in them, and that the questions generated in-group and by audience responses to the presentation were highly formative of thinking and learning.

In this sense, these Organisational and Reflective questions have been useful incentives to promote the active learning of chemistry. Designing enquiry-based-learning with and for university students has developed their problem-solving skills, logical reasoning and reflective thinking. Also, it has involved working as a member of a team, questioning, being creative and shaping the skills for continued intellectual development. Again, the links to commonly cited characteristics of gifted learners are clear.

Where to go from here?

There are always worries in using examples and it is often tricky to generalise from brief case studies such as these. What works as a developmental project may not work in the routines of a school day, what works in one phase of education may be inappropriate in another, what works in one school may be a disaster elsewhere. What examples do, though, is bring to life some of the issues at hand. In our case these concern the creation of 'zones of low conformity', organised periods of schooling when the implicit and explicit rules change to allow learners to be critical and challenging through questioning – time out from the usual orthodoxies of schooling. There are no guarantees of answers, nor is the teacher bound to respond to questions any more than other members of the group. The teacher's role becomes that of helping find routes to explanations and solutions rather than necessarily having those to hand. Moreover, many questions are allowed simply to 'hang in the air'. Subsequent sessions can be geared around the most pertinent or persistent of questions; assignments, tasks, projects, homework, can all be shaped by the chase for answers, and the raising of the next questions.

In each case we have also shown how building on other people's ideas can be encouraged, and how it is possible to 'ramp up' the quality of learners' questions. While patience is sometimes needed with a welter of Acquisition-type questions, the goal is a large number of ideas and questions. In some sessions, as we have indicated above, the objective of the session may simply be geared to 'clearing the ground' and using such Acquisition questions as the preparatory work for future sessions. In many instances, teachers have found that such questions are similar, which can indicate general problems with a particular topic and can be dealt with along the way, or at the start of a subsequent session, as a 'frequently asked question' (FAQ). Then moves can be made to shape questions towards greater specialisation, integration and reflection. Organisational questions can be encouraged, along with more unusual, creative, critical and challenging questions.

We believe that 'critique' and 'challenge' lie in the eye of the beholder, and what might seem like the asking of a proper but challenging question may feel threatening and disturbing to the person questioned at the other end. There is a spectrum that leads from questioning to confrontation. Our examples have attempted to show interactions of a much gentler tone leading to questions from all quarters that are challenging but not threatening. The intention is that contributions are accepted without judgement. Nothing could be more inhibiting of question-asking than when initial questions are met with impatience, exasperation or irritation, let alone dismissiveness or 'put-down humour'. In others, questions can be written and responded to as the sessions progress.

But, without doubt, we want also to give reign to the difficult questioner, to those 'off-the-wall' questions, the profound, cheeky, technical, bare-faced, testy, uncomfortable, rhetorical, political questions – perhaps those likely to originate from gifted learners. Critical questioning has variously been described as 'questioning authority', as 'engaging in critical enquiry', 'reflective questioning', 'identifying critical questions' and 'critical-thinking-as-asking'. One list of thirty-five dimensions of critical thought includes 'questioning deeply: raising and pursuing root or significant questions' and 'clarifying and questioning beliefs, theories, or perspectives' as important ingredients (Paul 1993). These seem like suitable goals to us.

Chapter 10

Teaching controversial socio-scientific issues to gifted and talented students

Ralph Levinson

A curriculum for the most able learners in science (if not all learners) needs to move away from a focus on learning a lot of things about many topics, to learning to think, and argue, with science in contexts that are relevant to young people. The move to incorporate more discussion of contemporary and controversial issues in science may engage many students currently having limited interest in science. When done well, as Ralph Levinson's chapter makes clear, it can also offer sophisticated treatments of complex issues. Classroom activities based on socio-scientific issues offer considerable opportunities for differentiation by task; by support; and by outcome; and provide an ideal context for challenging the most gifted learners.

Introduction

White Couple Have Black IVF Twins

MMR – The facts, claims, realities and the unanswered questions

Scientists Find How to Stop Ageing

These are headlines dated 30 April 2004, 24 February 2004, and 8 July 2002 from *The Independent*, *The Sun* and the *Daily Express*. I will leave you to work out which newspaper and dates correspond with each headline (the answers are at end of the chapter). Controversial socio-scientific issues are now commonly front page news and an inescapable part of contemporary life.

This article will discuss ways in which controversial socio-scientific issues can be fruitfully taught to all students, particularly drawing on abilities associated with giftedness. In so doing it will:

* describe a teaching model for addressing controversial socio-scientific issues;
* exemplify how such issues can be taught in the classroom;
* identify learning opportunities and possibilities for all students to demonstrate exceptional levels of achievement.

Contemporary socio-scientific issues such as the environmental effects of transgenic plants, xenotransplantation and global warming engage many secondary school students (Osborne and Collins 2000; Murray and Reiss 2005). Although the science is often complex and uncertain, the issues are topical with social, ethical, economic and political elements. While studying contemporary socio-scientific issues might inspire students to find out more, science teachers are understandably wary of addressing such issues precisely because of their difficult and tentative nature. In dealing with the social and ethical impacts, many science teachers feel they are leaving their comfort zone (Levinson and Turner 2001). It is enough of a challenge teaching atoms, forces and photosynthesis, let alone complex science on which experts disagree. Teachers ought to be cautious and so aware of the constraints and what might be reasonably achieved. Where a manageable approach is taken towards teaching these issues it can have the effect of enhancing the interest of all students in science; reinforcing investigatory skills; making young people aware of the key elements of a controversy; and developing an understanding of how different disciplines can illuminate ideas. Specifically, learning about controversial socio-scientific issues helps students understand the tentative nature of science (see Chapter 2) and allows gifted students to engage in some depth with complexity.

What is a controversial issue?

I will start by trying to make sense of what exactly a controversial issue is. A useful reference point is the description from the Citizenship Advisory Group. According to this definition a controversial issue is one: 'about which there is no one fixed or universally held point of view. Such issues are those which commonly divide society and for which significant groups offer conflicting explanations and solutions' (Crick 1998). There are plenty of examples that can be used to illustrate this with the news at the time this chapter is being written: Should the British government pull its troops out of Iraq? Should parents be able to choose the sex of their baby? And, should triple injections for MMR be obligatory? According to the Crick depiction all these are controversial because people hold differing views on what should be done and they are or have been prevalent in the media and therefore in the public domain. This description of controversial issues tells us how we can recognise a controversy through the behaviour of individuals or groups of people. Under the umbrella of this definition would come disagreements and conflicting explanations about which is the best soccer team in Europe, who should be thrown out of the Big Brother house and why the UK does so badly at the Eurovision song contest. While these are all issues which may well be worthy of discussion in the classroom, there are no criteria which can help us decide which issues have a significant educational value. If we do address contemporary controversial *socio-scientific issues*, what is it that can be learned which has some enduring value? After all, controversies come and go and there seems to be no conceptual thread which links them.

Having identified some problems with a *social* description of controversy, is there an *epistemological* justification which gives some insight into the intrinsic nature of controversies? What is it of value to know and understand about controversial issues? A matter is controversial 'if contrary views can be held on it without these views being contrary to reason' (Dearden 1981). This takes the characterisation of controversy forward because it is now based on reason bringing with it tests of truth, such as the validity of generalisations and predictions in science and the logical steps which support a moral judgement. But a problem still remains: people hold opposing views based on rational thinking, so why support one viewpoint over another? There are world views, beliefs and values informed by experience which help in swaying the decisions we make. Thinking rationally is a necessary but not a sufficient step in characterising controversial issues.

On the basis of rationality we can make certain kinds of decisions. A car manufacturer might decide that a higher than average level of risk has to be factored in to the design of a new model of a car otherwise the costs of manufacture become unacceptable and the company will lose out to competitors with resultant loss of jobs and profits. The problem is that there is a 1 in 50,000 chance that the flaw will result in a fatal accident. On a cost–benefit basis this can be construed as a rational decision.

But many people would argue, rightly, that a cost–benefit basis is only one element of decision making; reason must go hand in hand with reasonable behaviour. As well as people having views which are rational, these views would also have to be *reasonable*. They would have to meet the basic ethical requirement that it is insupportable having the view that it is all right to do to others that which we could not accept being done to ourselves. Rather than attempting to define a controversial issue, McLaughlin has suggested categorising the kinds of *disagreements* that occur in a liberal democratic society based upon reasonable behaviour. These categories move from levels of broad consensus about what it is the disagreement is about, to fundamental differences of worldviews (McLaughlin 2003). I have simplified McLaughlin's categories into those where:

1   people might settle a disagreement based on forthcoming evidence;
2   people agree broadly about a matter but disagree about priorities;
3   people's judgements about an issue are influenced by their llife experiences;
4   people have very different philosophies and worldviews.

The case study on the facing page illustrates these categories.

Case study – embryo selection

When young children are suffering from a genetic condition such as thalassaemia, they have a chance of cure through a transfusion of healthy and genetically compatible cells from a 'saviour' sibling. A 'saviour' sibling is genetically selected as an embryo. Embryos produced through IVF (*in vitro fertilisation*) are tested to check that they are free from the genetic condition of the child and that their cells are compatible. Embryos that meet these conditions are then implanted into the mother-to-be, and if the implantation and resulting pregnancy are successful, cells are extracted from the umbilical cord of the 'saviour' sibling at birth, harvested and transfused into the older child. The genetic testing of IVF embryos is called pre-implantation genetic diagnosis (PGD).

Thalassaemia major is a single gene disorder which results in insufficient production of haemoglobin to enable the red blood cells to carry oxygen to the body's tissues. Patients are normally given regular blood transfusions (usually every three weeks or so) to make up for their own lack of red blood cells. A side effect of this treatment is that excessive iron levels build up which the body cannot deal with and, as adults, sufferers need to take medicines to regulate the iron levels. People who suffer from thalassaemia major usually have an average life span of 40 to 50 years but there is every chance this will increase. The condition can be cured by a bone marrow transplant but the donor must have an exact tissue match otherwise the donated blood cells will be rejected. Finding a matching donor is a very difficult task.

Zain Hashmi is a little boy who suffers from thalassaemia major. His mother opted to undergo PGD to conceive an embryo which would both be free of the condition and would provide cells which were an identical match for Zain. At the donor baby's birth, cells would be harvested from the umbilical cord which would be transfused into Zain. The Human Fertilisation and Embryology Authority (HFEA) granted permission to a clinic to use PGD to help Zain. After a number of cycles of treatment an embryo which was free of thalassaemia, and a perfect tissue match for Zain, was implanted into his mother's womb. But there was a miscarriage a few months later. The Hashmis are determined to continue the treatment until a baby is born to term who is a perfect match for Zain.

The Hashmis have been criticised by the society representing thalassaemics, for undergoing PGD (UKTS 2003). Thalassaemics, it is argued, live contented and fulfilling lives and, as treatment improves, so will the quality of life and average life span. In highlighting the Hashmi case the media have tended to over-egg the unpleasantness of thalassaemia major, alarming those who have the condition and ignoring the many positive and life-affirming attributes of those who suffer from thalassaemia. To use PGD to cure Zain, the UKTS argues, is to stigmatise thalassaemics, to suggest that the life of a thalassaemia sufferer is not worth living and to possibly divert attention from the need to ameliorate the condition. This argument has resonances with those from disability groups who maintain that the elimination of a genetic condition carries with it the implication that their lives are less than satisfactory and that, had the technology been available earlier, they would not have been born.

In 2001 Comment on Reproductive Ethics, CORE, brought a high court case arguing that the HFEA had gone beyond its remit in licensing a clinic to select an embryo for the correct tissue match. While PGD can be legally used in the UK to screen prenatally for genetic disorders, this did not allow licences to be granted for tissue typing. The problem for the Hashmis is that they needed both. Although CORE won its case, it was overturned by an appeal court.

This is clearly a complex issue. In organising any discussion about this issue we could break it down into different categories discussed in the previous section.

Evidence

Where could evidence be used in settling a disagreement in this case?

Suppose that people agree that PGD is a good technique to relieve the suffering of children with thalassaemia but there is as yet insufficient evidence to indicate how successful this treatment is. The question which students might consider is 'what constitutes success' (see Box 10.1).

The teacher needs to emphasise that what is being considered is *evidence*, whether in support of or against the effectiveness of 'saviour siblings' in curing genetic conditions. Students might find data which supports the effectiveness of PGD while others could find data which rebuts the data or provisos which might indicate limitations on the effectiveness of the treatment. Useful resources would be the internet with accounts of other treatments, condensed reports from journals such as the *British Medical Journal* and newspaper

---

Box 10.1 Evidence-gathering questions about the case study

If it is a complete cure, how much time should elapse before we can be confident it is successful? How much is known about other cases of 'saviour siblings' and the progress of the genetic condition? If it is a gradual improvement in quality of life, how would we measure this lifestyle? Which stages in the cycle of treatment – fertilisation, implantation, transfusion – could be difficult and then put progress at risk? What are the medical risks and how might they be quantified? What interpretations could be put on the data gathered so far?

reports. It is unlikely that students will be able to collect sufficient evidence to demonstrate the case one way or the other but that is not the point. What is crucial is that students know that:

- the decision they are trying to make is based on evidence;
- the evidence has to be interpreted;
- the question they are trying to answer is not whether PGD should be used but whether it works;
- by asking the right kinds of questions they will know where to gain access to data and evidence; and
- the evidence is likely to be complex and uncertain (and that is usually the case with contentious issues).

Difference of priorities

At present there is no definite evidence to suggest that PGD is unequivocally successful in saving the lives of sick children. It will be some time before that can be decided, not only in terms of the physical benefits for the sick child but also whether there are psychological effects on the 'saviour sibling'. Even at this stage, however, given the potential of PGD, it could be asked whether it should be available to everyone on the National Health Service (NHS). In the last few years, people have paid for PGD outside the UK where they have a preference for a male or female. Now PGD is effectively available it will be those with money who will be able to use it either for purposes of sex selection, or possibly for other physical attributes and for saviour siblings. If this is the case then it comes to be a resource available for those who can afford it leading to social differentiation – wealthier people will be able to use the treatment to cure genetic conditions or sex-select their children whereas others will not.

Making PGD available on the NHS, say for those who have children with potentially fatal genetic conditions, will have ramifications for NHS expenditure. Resources might have to be shifted from other areas, for example, geriatric care, nursery provision for sick children or hospitals acquiring high technology equipment. In other words it will become a matter of priorities – given limited resources, however large or small, what should we give priority to? Whatever decision will be taken there will be potential consequences (what would happen to those services which lost resource investment as a consequence? who would be affected? who would gain? who would lose?), issues of social justice (should we strive to ensure equality of provision or that the most deserving get what is needed?), rights (do people have a right to certain kinds of treatment, however expensive?) and cost–benefit analyses (how do we assess benefits against costs?).

These are primarily *ethical* issues. Again there is no simple answer but the purpose is for students to give due consideration to particular questions. Since there are so many aspects to consider the teacher should help students focus on one particular question. There are a number of values that need to be thought through in such a situation:

- Is the action or decision being taken beneficent. For example, will the potential good being done to the thalassaemic child and his parents, outweigh the possible psychological harm to the saviour sibling and other affected parties?
- Are individuals' rights being respected? Do the rights of the person receiving treatment (and his family) impinge on the rights of others? What are the responsibilities that go along with these rights?
- Is everyone being treated fairly?

Students should appreciate that:

- There are no simple answers to these questions; it is often a matter of balancing out many different demands.
- Priorities might change over time.

Differing life experiences shaping judgement

The way we feel, act and believe about something often has a lot to do with our life experiences: events and circumstances that have had a crucial effect on the way we think and feel. Parents will want to do anything to ease and save the life of their child and many will think that PGD and the production of a saviour sibling are justified in helping this to come about. But there are disabled groups who feel that the emphasis on cure and eliminating the disability, rather than amelioration of the condition, threatens the status of disabled people. It can detract from the need to support disabilities if the emphasis is on eliminating it at birth. While no one would begrudge the Hashmis in their very distressing quest, there is certainly a need to examine the implications of such treatments for all disabled people.

To understand this difficulty, students need to be able to understand the broader effect of this technology on the rights of disabled people as well as being able to empathise with people in the plight of the Hashmis. Some students will have relatives with disabling genetic conditions and will want to discuss treatment and how they feel about it with their peers. Others might be a little more reticent, so this needs handling sensitively. Teachers will need to find out first whether students are happy to talk about their experiences and to ensure there is a respectful and attentive atmosphere in the classroom. There will also be a literature on disabled rights in which students could be encouraged to read critically, whilst correctly summarising the views of the writer.

This is a good opportunity for role play or dramatic enactment. A group could develop a story of a child receiving cells from a saviour sibling: possibly told from the experience of the child being treated, and from the viewpoint of the saviour sibling many years later. Afterwards a class audience could question the actors on their points of view. A film dealing with this topic has been made by Y-touring (see www.ytouring.org.uk).

The idea is to make sense of a life experience using narrative and imagination. Individuals or the group as a whole might not be able to come to any decision but the point is to gain an insight from people with different interests as to how they would view the situation.

Different worldviews

In terms of embryo selection these arguments almost always revolve around abortion. One perspective is that an embryo is a living thing, and it is not right to create and take one life in order to help another: the best of ends, namely to cure a sick child, does not justify the means. On the other hand, those who take a utilitarian point of view often base their argument on maximising happiness: saving or improving the quality of life outweighs the harm in destroying a non-sentient embryo. The embryo is not perceived as a person or of equal status to a living child. Being able to dispassionately explore issues through the lenses of world views we do not share might be considered to require well-developed intellectual skills (see Chapter 6).

If people have thought about these things at all they are unlikely to change their minds overnight. The danger with such positioning in the school classroom is that students may just repeat the same positions without moving on. A way forward is to take the Platonic approach by trying to ensure one has understood the opposing point of view. A way to do this is to ask, for example, someone who thinks that the embryo is a person and that destruction of an embryo is murder to articulate their argument. Ask the opposing part, e.g. utilitarians, to repeat the argument back with the condition that not only should they repeat the argument accurately but try their best to improve it. Then the utilitarians advance their argument and their interlocuters have to repeat it accurately with improvements. Students with opposing viewpoints can then think of critical questions they would like to ask each other. The purpose of this approach is to illuminate – to ensure that whatever point of view is expressed, that it is critical, rigourous and informed.

How categories can be represented in other issues

The case presented above shows how the four categories can be explored in one context. There are many other socio-scientific issues that can provide contexts for exploring controversial issues within these four categories (see Boxes 10.2–5).

Box 10.2 Issues suitable for exploring at the level of evidence

Siting of nuclear power stations – What is the link to leukaemia? How do we distinguish between correlations and causations? What is meant by risk and perceived risk? What kind of evidence would we be looking for to point towards cause and effect?

Electric cars – Do electric cars consume fuel? If the pollution from electric cars is simply displaced can they be said to be 'cleaner' than cars with petrol engines?

Animal experimentation – How can we assess pain and suffering in animals? What is the evidence that experiments on animals lead to useful and valuable knowledge?

Recycling – What processes are involved in recycling aluminium cans? If we look at the life-cycle of any product what is the evidence that recycling the product will be less damaging environmentally than making it anew?

Distribution of fuel resources – How do different countries compare in their use of fossil fuels? Which type of data should be used – gross national consumption or per capita? How could we compare consumption fairly given different climates, industrial productivity and living standards?

Fluoridation of water supplies – How could evidence be collected to demonstrate that fluoridation of the water supplies is (1) improving dental health, and (2) not harmful?

Implications for gifted and talented

Reflecting on the categories we have identified two points stand out:

1   There are few demands on content-specific scientific knowledge such as would be found on the national curriculum, although there are concepts such as risk, and scientific procedures, associated with the issues.
2   There are skills associated with giftedness in exploring controversial issues.

Relatively little knowledge of science content is needed to start grappling with many socio-scientific issues. In the case of PGD discussed earlier, students will need to know the basics of IVF, why a tissue match is important and that there is a technology to identify single gene conditions in embryo cells. But in

---

**Box 10.3 Issues suitable for exploring at the
level of priorities**

Energy resources – Given the problems associated with global warming
should the UK rethink the development of nuclear energy? Should there
be increased investment in renewable resources? Should we prioritise
investment in energy conservation?

Electric cars – Should the government subsidise the use of electric cars
in large cities to reduce smog and local pollution?

Xenotransplantation – With the possibility of using pigs' hearts to
replace malfunctioning human hearts should the emphasis be on
prevention of heart disease and improved quality of life rather than
xenotransplantation and the possible risks of infection?

Genetic screening – Should all women be screened for breast cancer or
only those most at risk? Why aren't all women screened for breast
cancer?

Animal welfare – How can the humane treatment of livestock be
balanced against the increased demand for meat?

**Box 10.4 Issues suitable for exploring at the
level of different life experience**

Genetic modification of foods – Why do some farmers in third world
countries resist the introduction of GM crops even though such a change
is likely to improve their output?

Nuclear power stations – How can you weigh employment at nuclear
power stations with the risk of increased incidences of childhood
leukaemia in the local area?

---

considering evidence, they will need skills in interpreting data, for example
from a variety of graphs; in examining priorities they will be addressing ethical
issues; and in looking at life experiences and diverse world views they will be
drawing on social and ethical questions, but also using techniques such as
drama and role play to imagine the points of views of others. These are not
strategies frequently used in science lessons, but they are likely to be used in
RE, English and drama. There may then be a case for planning such lessons

---

Box 10.5 Issues suitable for exploring at the level of diverse world views

Animal experimentation – Should there be a complete ban on the use of animals in medical experiments even where this might save human lives and where treatment of the animals is fully regulated?

Xenotransplantation – If xenotransplantation can save the life of a loved one should it be allowed if the transplantation of a pig's heart into a human violates religious principles?

---

across the curriculum. Time, expertise and cross-curricular planning are crucial in supporting this process (Ratcliffe et al. 2004).

The second point is that there is a great deal of scope for deploying sophisticated skills such as interpreting complex data, critically dealing with ethical judgements and developing narratives from a wide variety of perspectives. In many of these issues students will come to understand that there are rarely simple answers to questions, and thereby come to understand the complex nature of such issues. Appreciating complexity is a sophisticated aim but it is not beyond the capacity of most students, and enhances understanding of the multifaceted nature of controversial socio-scientific issues. Given the complexity and breadth of these issues, students will be supported if they focus on one particular aspect in one of the categories identified in the previous section. So far, I have explored the ways in which socio-scientific issues can be broken down and the nature of the arguments made explicit, with suggestions as to how these can be approached in the classroom. All of these issues involve some kind of discussion and I now wish to turn to this.

Running discussions on socio–scientific issues

Studying the nature of these disagreements and possibly arriving at some decision about them can only be achieved through people talking to each other. In any exchange of views involving reasonable people in democratic debate there are some important principles which need to be adhered to:

- Students must be attentive and listen to each other.
- No one should be debarred from contributing to the discussion and we should put forward our views truthfully.
- All contributions must be respected, that is they should be listened to thoughtfully and critically.

While this seems to be straightforward, such dispositions are not always evident in the classroom and need to be encouraged. One way is to have clear procedures in class and group discussions – turn-taking for talking needs to be recognised, speakers should not be interrupted until they have finished nor should they take up an unreasonable amount of time in saying what they think. Listeners should be able to formulate contributions to clarify what a speaker has said or to point out an inconsistency in their argument. These procedures can be adhered to by the whole class if they are made explicit and if the students themselves help formulate the procedures.

A common way of organising talk is through small group discussion. How to take turns in speaking, listen to another point of view, ask clarifying questions and work co-operatively are all skills that can be learned and practised. The teacher can set up group tasks that make these procedures explicit. For example, asking one member of the group to read a short passage while others in the group prepare questions from the passage for discussion could enhance listening. Small tasks can be set at first where students work in pairs or threes and have to take on certain roles, e.g. presenting, feedback, taking notes.

When you set up a group discussion task it needs to be clear and tightly focused. It could be in the form of a dilemma (see Box 10.6).

Along with a specific task the teacher has to make it clear to the group what a desirable outcome would look like, e.g. a dramatic episode which includes two reasons why Ailsa feels she should risk having children if they are both CF carriers, two reasons why she should not.

Each student should be assigned a role, e.g. in larger groups, someone who will chair the discussion and ensure everyone in the group has an opportunity to speak, someone who will present conclusions at the end, someone who will research and access resources for factually correct information (often the most complex role and one that deploys skills of a high order), someone to take notes and bullet point what the group wants to say. It is vital that these roles are changed for the next group discussion so that students can experience different ways of working within a group.

Where students do need to access information the necessary resources should be readily available and at the right level, e.g. a useful website,

---

Box 10.6 A dilemma for discussion

'Should Ailsa have children with her partner if they are both carriers of genes for cystic fibrosis (CF)? What are the reasons for? What are the reasons against? What would you do in her situation?'

newspaper cutting, books, periodicals. You should ensure that the information is localised and that students can access it without much trouble and interpret it, otherwise a lot of time will be spent looking for information and if it is not found quickly, students will move off-task. A range of resources can be made available, to provide for different literacy levels, and to include more demanding sources to challenge the most able (see Chapter 11). Use a framework to structure reasoning and decision making, as below (Wellington and Osborne 2001):

Some people think . . . is a good idea because . . .

Others think it is a good idea because . . .

Further arguments that are in favour are . . .

But some people think that it is not a good idea because . . .

Others say . . .

Further arguments against are . . .

Having looked at the arguments for and against I think . . .

Recounting a point of view

The third part of the framework after categorisation and discussion is to elaborate possible ways students can validate their points of view. Bruner elaborates on two modes of convincing others of one's perspective. He calls them modes of thought (Bruner 1996). These are the narrative mode in which we draw on a series of events to contextualise our point of view, to make it more real. It is a way of telling a story to make a particular point. Only when we have heard somebody's story do we realise the problems they have overcome and, even if we do not agree with them, at least there is chance that we can understand them better and talk to them on a different level.

The second mode of thought is logico-scientific. It is the ways in which we draw inferences from evidence, make predictions based on patterns of data, generalise, hypothesise; in other words how we might draw scientific conclusions. Logico-scientific thought is indispensable in socio-scientific decision making but it can be fruitfully complemented by the narrative mode. What I am pointing out here is that opportunities should be made both for students to tell their stories where relevant in a sensitive and attentive environment, and that scientific modes of thought need to be encouraged and deployed where relevant.

Summary

In this chapter I have attempted to show how controversial issues can be broken down and focused into manageable chunks. There are opportunities to deploy skills and knowledge associated with giftedness: investigations using scientific procedures, interpreting complex and uncertain data, imagining the experiences of others, narrating experience in a vivid and convincing way, thinking scientifically. All of the examples allow all students to engage with the issues; some might explore the issues in greater depth – although not necessarily those who are generally recognised as gifted. Making connections across different subject areas might stimulate the interest of those who are not necessarily high attainers in science.

Newspaper headlines

White couple have black IVF twins: *The Sun*, 8 July 2002.
MMR: *The Independent*, 24 February 2004.
Ageing: *Daily Express*, 30 April 2004.

Chapter 11

Context-based science: a 'gift horse' for the talented?

Vanessa Kind

Chapter 10 suggested that the discussion of socio-scientific issues can provide useful contexts for challenging gifted learners. In this chapter, Vanessa Kind considers the move towards complete science courses where the science is fully contextualised within such issues. Whereas traditional courses tend to introduce concepts first, and then discuss how and where the concepts are applied to demonstrate relevance, context-based courses start with a context of obvious relevance, and then introduce the science concepts through their relevance to the context. Science courses based upon topics about food, transport, clothing, medicines, etc. may give the impression of being less rigourous than traditional courses exploring organ systems, acids, electromagnetism, the rock cycle, etc. The chapter offers an account of the rationale and nature of context-based science, and what the experience of existing courses suggests in terms of meeting the needs of the most able students.

The task of this chapter is to assess whether gifted and talented students may benefit from use of a context-based approach to teaching and learning science. In approaching an answer, we will look at the effectiveness of the current curriculum, explore a curriculum model designed for gifted and talented students and look at what we mean by 'context-based' science together with examples prior to drawing conclusions.

To start, let us frame what we mean by 'context-based' courses. These:

- adopt what may be termed 'everyday' or 'real-life' applications for teaching science;
- offer an active, 'student-centred' approach to teaching and learning (cf. Coll, Chapter 5); and
- use a 'spiral' curriculum, introducing scientific concepts by revisiting them in varied settings (after Bennett and Holman 2002).

In contrast, 'traditional' or conventional-style curricula offer applications as 'bolt-on' additions, leading teaching and learning with abstract factual or theoretical data. Material relating to one topic is taught in a continuous series of lessons, with no opportunity to revisit later.

By way of introduction, it is worth noting that the question of 'what and how to teach' gifted and talented students in science is open, in that collectively researchers and curriculum developers agree that there is no set formula that has been 'proven' as specifically effective in ensuring gifted and talented students' achievements match their abilities (Tomlinson 2005). Hence, there is a case to answer as to whether the specific context-based courses available in the UK serve gifted and talented students' needs 'better' than the mainstream 'traditional' approach in use in the majority of schools.

To begin our discussion, we will look at the current situation, assessing points of dissatisfaction and using this to formulate aspects of science provision that may contribute favourably to raising students' achievements.

The current position: what students and teachers think about school science

The science National Curriculum adopted in the UK over the last fifteen or so years takes a content-led approach, supported by an assessment system widely regarded as domineering, overly summative and burdensome. Together, the curriculum content and its assessment have encouraged use of a didactic style of teaching, leaving 'little time' (to paraphrase many teacher colleagues) for activities such as genuine open-ended investigations, project work, experiments and experiences that may lead to extra-curricular or 'irrelevant' material being covered. Montgomery (2000) condemns this system, taking the view that the UK curriculum has led to:

> a cadre of teachers who are educationally illiterate and pupils who are becoming repositories of fact but who lack the ability to put their knowledge to any useful real-world purpose . . . . the highly able and the more creative are rejecting such 'schooling' and are switching off.
>
> Montgomery 2000: 130–1

This critical, strident statement merits further examination. Two major projects, Osborne and Collins (2000) and Jenkins and Nelson (2005), provide substantiating evidence. While not specifically focused on gifted and talented students, these studies offer a rich student and teacher 'voice' lending broad support to Montgomery's claim.

Osborne and Collins used focus groups to gather the views of 15- to 16-year-old students, teachers and parents about the science curriculum. The researchers' evidence indicated that science was described by all parties as an important, prestigious subject that contributes to students' self-esteem, in part by providing insights into how the world works (pp. 5–6). Students expressed a general lack of intrinsic interest in science, valuing it mainly as an aid to achieving career aspirations. Chemistry in particular was singled out for criticism as being 'abstruse and irrelevant to contemporary needs' (p. 5), although physics was also poorly regarded, especially by girls. Students also cited factors such as lack of practical work, a general lack of relevance, repetitive content, a heavy rote learning requirement and an over-reliance on copying activities as influencing their opinions (pp. 5–6). However, students found science interesting when they did practical work, were offered challenge and stimulation (but not to the point of finding work too difficult and hence frustrating), and when they sensed awe and wonder (p. 6).

Teachers acknowledged the legitimacy of students' views, but considered themselves as working within the constraints of a content-dominated and overloaded curriculum. The ruthless pursuit of monitoring pupil performance was seen as a contributing factor to removal of the 'fun' element. Teachers thought that students overstated the case for too much copying, and considered repetition was needed to consolidate understanding (p. 6).

All participant groups in Osborne and Collins's study believed that change was needed. Their collective 'wish-list' included more choice post-14; a less repetitive curriculum and much closer links between science in school and in the media; and more practical work, including extended investigations and opportunities for discussion (p. 6). The report's authors concluded, in a tone nearly as damning as that of Montgomery, that the result of the content-dominated science curriculum was that:

> science teachers rush their pupils across the scientific landscape and offer an unvarying experience from the latter stages of primary school to the final days of secondary school, often repeating material and eliminating time consuming activities such as practical work or the discussion of contemporary science.
>
> Osborne and Collins 2000: 6

Jenkins and Nelson (2005) in their report on the large-scale survey Relevance of Science Education (ROSE) project (Schreiner and Sjøberg 2004) provide supporting quantitative data drawn from 14- to 16-year-olds. This survey was established to enable informed discussion about possible improvements to school science curricula and was undertaken internationally. The data gathered from UK students confirm that a majority found the subject interesting (61%), relevant (around 65%) and important (around 58%). Students were evenly divided on the issue of whether science is 'difficult', although more girls than boys thought so. The survey also identified other points relevant to this discussion. Only around 39% of students, despite the aims of the National Curriculum, found the science they were taught in school encouraged them to be 'more critical and sceptical' (DfEE 1999: 15), stimulated them to consider a scientific career (21%) or increased their appreciation of nature (42%). About 34% were at all attracted to the notion of having 'as much science in school as possible'.

These two major studies lead us to certain conclusions about qualities that might constitute an appropriate experience of school science. First, students don't seem to mind science being difficult per se, although they do not like it to be too hard. Some Collins and Osborne respondents (2000: 19) saw possession of a GCSE (the school leaving qualification taken at age 16) in science as a 'status symbol', indicating significant achievement. Second, students expect teachers to provide a variety of learning experiences, including practical work to help maintain high interest and stimulation. Their perception is that science involves extensive copying and note-taking activities to help them learn 'facts' when they would prefer to discuss ideas and be able to express opinions (cf. Chapter 10). Third, the evidence points to the notion that relevance is important. Students of all types in both studies valued the opportunity to work on science topics that related clearly to their everyday lives, inspired a sense of awe or touched on 'the unknown'. Osborne and Collins (2000: 44–5) found that students wished to know more about natural environmental disasters including hurricanes and volcanic eruptions, climate change, genetic engineering, cloning and other medical advances. Jenkins and Nelson (2005: 49) list topics of interest to boys and girls separately: boys would like to know more about topics such as explosive chemicals; how it feels to be weightless in space; black holes, supernovae and other spectacular objects in space; how computers work; and brutal, dangerous animals. The girls' preferred topics have a more human flavour, including: why we dream when sleeping and what dreams may mean; how to exercise and keep fit; how to perform first aid; and what we know about cancer.

Thus far, we can see that UK teenagers are dissatisfied with many aspects of school science, even though they believe the subject is important, confers esteem and is needed for various careers. We can, then, suggest three criteria that students might regard as important qualities of a science course:

- Teaching methods must be varied.
- Topics must include a balance between contemporary and abstract issues.
- Difficulty is acceptable, provided it is related to something worth learning.

We will return to these when we consider context-related courses and materials in more detail. Next, let us look at possible provision for gifted and talented students and see how a context-based approach might fit into whole school strategies.

Providing whole school experiences for gifted and talented students

Provision for gifted and talented students tends to operate in one of two stances, as shown in Table 11.1 (see Montgomery 2000: 135). Schools may adopt a 'structural' approach, in which children are subjected to one or more strategies for accelerating their progress by carrying out work designed for older students. At the simplest level, this involves giving 'extra work' taken from schemes for older students to gifted and talented children as 'extension' material. At the next level, schools use test results from primary (5- to 11-year-olds) school and 'CAT (cognitive abilities test) scoring' to create 'streams' or 'sets' of children of different abilities, one of which (often referred to by teachers as 'the top set') includes gifted and talented children. This group will have greater expectations placed on them in terms of accepting faster lesson pace and quicker accommodation to complex language structures, including technical terminology and higher levels of academic achievement.

Significantly, the expectation is often that 'top set' children are more capable of rapid note-taking, fact learning and accurate recall than their peers, so teachers do not necessarily perceive a need to change established didactic practices in favour of a wide variety of alternative teaching strategies – rather, the concern is to ensure these children achieve the high grades expected using traditional procedures.

At a more complex level in terms of in-school organisation, a structural strategy means setting up one or more groups of high ability students to take their GCSEs in a different pattern from their peers. Typically, this means taking one or more GCSEs, often mathematics, 'early', that is, one or even more years ahead of their cohorts at the usual age of 16, or, in science, taking 'Triple Award' GCSE. This means instead of taking a qualification equivalent to two GCSEs, the standard 'Double Award', such students take three separate science examinations in chemistry, biology and physics. At an extreme level that is rarely seen in the UK state (government-funded) sector, a structural strategy would mean placing a gifted and talented child in a year group older than his/her chronological age.

Table 11.1 Approaches to provision for gifted and talented children (Adapted from Montgomery 2000: 135)

Structural	Integral
Acceleration	Differentiation
Streaming	Enrichment
Setting	Mentoring
Grade skipping	Layering (Inputs)
Enrichment	Assessment (Outputs)
Segregation	
Product-based	Process-based

The stance named 'integral' includes strategies that affect events more generally at a classroom operations level. It is here we see the impact of curriculum choice more forcefully. Integrated strategies provide an insight into the way many schools approach formulation of their gifted and talented 'policy', as these require no structural alterations and retain an impression of what might be termed 'fairness' to all children. Common integral strategies include provision of systematic extension or enrichment material and differentiation by task, similar to the lowest level of the structural stance. Activities from a different (but intended for the same age group) 'off-the-shelf' package are selected for provision of higher level or more open-ended tasks.

Sensitive handling is required to avoid resentment among non-gifted and talented students due to not being given the more challenging and perhaps more appealing tasks, while the gifted and talented children may also resent being singled out as 'special'. A more common, but often less satisfactory, strategy is differentiation by outcome. This approach allows all children to perform on the same task at the level that best suits them. This may result in underachievement, particularly by gifted and talented students, if tasks are too simple or the class atmosphere is for some reason oriented 'against' high achievement. A fourth but probably less common strategy may be to assess the work of gifted and talented children by tougher criteria, making clear that different, higher academic or cognitive expectations are required, thus distinguishing this group from their peers.

Context-based material is implemented mainly within the integral strategy in one of two ways. For example, schools may use context-based self-standing units (for example, College of William and Mary 1997) or activities (such as Kind 2004) to provide extra work for gifted and talented students to help extend their achievement beyond the average attainment expected for the cohort. Second, a context-based course (such as those described later) may be selected for an entire cohort, providing activities undertaken by everyone and completed according to students' varying abilities.

Next, we examine a curriculum model in depth that adopts the integral stance, linking to teaching units specifically for gifted and talented students to be implemented as extension material.

The integrated curriculum model (ICM)

The ICM was proposed and developed by VanTassel-Baska (1986, 2003) in response to typical characteristics of gifted and talented children, namely their precocity, intensity and complexity. The model has three dimensions: *advanced content*; *higher level processes and product development*; and *interdisciplinary concepts, issues and themes*, all of which are intended to be applied generally to all curriculum subjects. The model provides a useful structure against which context-based courses may be judged as appropriate for gifted and talented students.

By *advanced content* the model means that a suitable curriculum should: present interesting and challenging ideas; indicate more than one source for information; show the notion that knowledge is open-ended and to some extent tentative; provide advanced readings and include abstract concepts.

The requirement here is to provide material that stimulates children's imagination, creativity and cognitive skills. Material that is 'open' rather than 'closed' in the sense of issues, topics for discussion or problems to solve are more challenging than factual 'list'-type areas of knowledge. The idea that knowledge is being created and is incomplete or fixed is important. The provision of reading material at a higher level than that of the class average is needed to support gifted and talented children's learning.

In practice, a science curriculum would need to provide ideas that are relevant to students, but not immediately obvious in terms of how these may be resolved or understood. For any topic, the model requires a range of documents or sources to be made available with a higher reading age (VanTassel-Baska suggests two years higher) than that of the whole class. The open-ended view of knowledge fits well with changes to the English Science National Curriculum (QCA 2005), as the 'How Science Works' section is designed to include the notion that scientific knowledge is not 'just' a body of facts to be learned, but that there are 'fuzzy' boundaries. School science already includes a requirement to learn abstract concepts – the mole, particle model of matter, the periodic table, laws of motion and inheritance patterns are simply a few that come immediately to mind.

By *higher level processes and product development* the model means that a suitable curriculum should: permit independent research; stimulate metacognition and articulation of thinking; include opportunities for concept mapping; include problem based learning.

This dimension focuses specifically on children's cognitive skills. Independent research sits alongside the open-ended qualities of knowledge presented in the first dimension, providing a means by which a student could take his/her understanding further, perhaps by extended reading or experimental work. Metacognition (see Chapter 6) and articulation of thinking ensure that children are given the chance to appreciate the processes by which knowledge is acquired, perhaps by reflecting on several competing theories about the same topic, or by assessing a range of data that may point to several different explanations. They should be given the opportunity to discuss their views with others, perhaps in an open forum or by circulating discussion papers for comment. Concept mapping is a recognised tool that can assist with development of mental schemata for interrelated ideas. A map in itself can be the result of significant cognitive effort, as well as being a flexible 'aide memoire' that can be adapted as more knowledge is acquired. Problem-based learning involves wrestling with a variety of different types of data and other materials presented in such a way that there is an issue, question or point to resolve.

In science, the independent research aspect of this dimension could mean including opportunities for students to undertake a practical research project, attempting to answer a genuinely open-ended question. The study would take place over an extended period, rather than being the subject just of one lesson's worth of work (cf. Chapter 13), and build on an area of particular interest to a student. To assist with metacognition and articulation of thinking, students may learn how scientists have used research evidence to develop new theories and ideas, as well as current thinking about these theories. A good example for post-16 might be the demise of classical physics based on analysis and persistent research about sub-atomic particles and the consequent development of quantum theory.

Concept mapping may be used at all levels. Used most effectively, this technique could help students develop their thinking as maps may be changed as a unit of work progresses and more concepts are added. The requirement to include problem-based learning implies a range of possible strategies: analysis of empirical data arising from practical work; decision making procedures about how to solve an environmental or industrial issue; resolution of a molecular structure given a complex set of data; and conversion of tabular data to graphical formats with associated questions.

By *interdisciplinary concepts, issues and themes*, the model means that a suitable curriculum should show how ideas and concepts relate to other subject areas.

This dimension draws on links between subject areas, indicating that subject boundaries rather than appearing fixed and immoveable are in fact diffuse. This permits gifted and talented students to stretch their thinking beyond the traditional, rather false curricular frameworks assembled for timetabling and teachers' conveniences.

Thus, applied to science, this means exploring social, economic and political issues and consequences associated with scientific ideas. Typical examples may include the debate surrounding the MMR vaccine; the impact of climate change and energy supply on social behaviour and household costs (e.g. see Chapter 10); and perhaps issues surrounding the competing expense versus value to society of particle physics and space exploration. More prosaically, students may be given opportunities for cross-curricular work, looking at links between science and history, geography, English and art.

VanTassel-Baska and her team have developed curriculum units based on the model in a range of different subjects, including science. We will look at the science units next.

'Extension' materials based on the integrated curriculum model

The curriculum units (for example, College of William and Mary 1997) are specifically designed to provide support for teachers working with gifted and

Table 11.2 Science curriculum units based on VanTassel-Baska's integrated curriculum model (source: http:// cfge.wm.edu/curriculum-kendallhunt.php, accessed 6 March 2006)

Title	Age group	Content summary
Dust bowl	6–8	Students act as 'apprentice scientists' building a model ecosystem and analysing the factors that can influence their system. Opportunities to solve problems and recommend solutions based on 'scientific process' are included.
What a find	8–10	Students act as trainee archaeologists in a research museum. They discover that historic artefacts have been discovered at a school during a rebuilding programme. Students learn to excavate and conduct the dig, discovering the pre-placed artefacts.
Acid, acid, everywhere	8–12	Students solve a problem involving interdisciplinary systems centred around an acid spill on a road. Knowledge and understanding about habitats, chemicals and transport systems are required.
Electricity city	10–12	Students have the role of planning the electricity needs of a major urban recreation complex. This requires analysis, research, practical work and evaluation.
Hot rods	12–14	The impact of nuclear waste is explored in this unit through the eyes of a mayor of a town where a nuclear power plant is located. The biological implications of radiation and the potential benefits of nuclear power generation must be weighed in order to decide on recommendations for the use of the power plant.

talented children in primary and lower secondary school (approximately ages 6–14). Brief descriptions of the contents of the science units are given in Table 11.2. A scan of the outlines reveals common aspects – a context-based setting; a range of activities, use of a 'child as scientist' model, assumption of major decision making role; and connections to wider aspects surrounding the science. The implications are that students will be required to communicate their findings to others and demonstrate an ability to reference a wide range of materials in solving the 'real-world' problem posed.

The publisher's briefing about one of the units, 'Acid, acid everywhere' (Box 11.1), gives a more detailed indication as to its content. The description shows that an acid spill is being used as the context within which to explore scientific concepts in several different areas, together with the interactions these have with the wider implications of a major accident.

The authors claim (VanTassel-Baska, personal communication) that the blueprint adopted in the development of these materials has included:

- ensuring a standardised format for representing parts of the curriculum;
- clarity about the areas the units cover;

Box 11.1 Context for a unit on acids

'There's an emergency! A tanker truck marked 'corrosive' is overturned on a local bridge, and liquid is spewing from it into the stream below. An ominous steam now rises slowly from the once-clear water source. This introduction sets the tone for Acid, Acid Everywhere, which is a simulated, interdisciplinary problem-solving unit introducing fourth-through sixth-grade students to chemistry, biology, ecology, and transportation systems. These systems are overlapped not only to graphically illustrate the interactions between them, but also to give students an opportunity to learn all of the real-world problems associated with a serious acid or oil spill.

College of William and Mary 1997

- clear information about the developmental levels, differentiation features and other special features that the units provide.

The materials have been thoroughly trialled, with key follow-up in terms of professional development to teachers implementing them, thus providing good levels of support. Thus, teachers have been aided in transferring the units and the skills needed to teach them into their repertoires. This, VanTassel-Baska asserts, is essential to ensure successful implementation.

Next, we will attempt to apply the ICM to 'whole course' context-based materials that were developed in the UK to improve the quality of science teaching and learning, rather than specifically for gifted and talented students. We need first to know a little more about these materials.

An introduction to 'whole course' context–based materials

The 1980s saw the development of the first context-based science courses in the UK through Salters Chemistry, a course for 14- to 16-year-olds. Sponsored by the Salters Institute, curriculum developers wrote a series of units each taking an everyday setting as a theme for teaching chemistry. An introduction to the unit 'Transporting Chemicals' (Box 11.2) illustrates the approach.

Already we can see similarities with the College of William and Mary units – the contextual setting is clear, and the use of 'case studies' implies an active approach likely to result in some sort of product. There is clearly an issue being addressed here, through which the chemistry necessary to understand the contextual setting is taught. Other units include titles such as *Food for Thought, Mining and Minerals, Burning and Bonding* and *Making Use of Oil.*

Box 11.2 A Salters Chemistry unit

A survey of road tanker lorries shows that codes are used to convey information about chemical and any associated hazards. Experiments illustrate the meaning of hazard warning signs, and students see how chemical formulas and equations can be used as international codes to convey information about chemicals and reactions. Case studies of chemical manufacture reveal the scale and importance of the chemical industry. Students take part in a role play exercise to consider the factors which influence how chemicals are transported. Finally the Periodic Table is introduced as a way of collating information about different elements.

UYSEG 2001

Following the original Salters Chemistry course, a full suite of courses comprising Salters Double Award GCSE and single subject GCSEs in Chemistry, Physics and Biology (see for example UYSEG 2001) was developed. The range of provision was extended to include post-16 in the early 1990s, initially with Salters Advanced Chemistry, SAC (Burton *et al.* 1994, 2000), Salters Horners Advanced Physics, SHAP (UYSEG 2000) and culminating with Salters Nuffield Advanced Biology, SNAB (UYSEG 2005). The Institute of Physics devised its own context-based post-16 provision, Advancing Physics (for example, Ogborn and Whitehouse 2000) launched in 2000. A 14–16 course, 21st Century Science (see for example, Burden *et al.* 2006a), was developed and piloted in the UK, and became available nationally from September 2006.

Salters Advanced Chemistry illustrates the post-16 approach. The course features units based on 'Storylines' with titles such as *The Atmosphere*, *The Polymer Revolution* and *What's in a Medicine?* In terms of teaching and learning, only the necessary concepts and ideas relevant to these contexts are taught in each unit, fragmenting the curriculum material into small parts. The full 'core' chemical knowledge is covered by revisiting concepts and ideas in various units throughout the course, so students' experiences of one particular topic build up over long periods of time. Hence, the curriculum 'spirals' the development of students' knowledge and understanding. A traditional teaching sequence would give a topic such as 'chemical bonding' full treatment for an extended period of, say, three to five weeks, covering this to the level of detail required by the end of course assessment. Revisiting the topic in this case is mainly for final revision purposes only and applications are supplementary rather than fundamental.

Advancing Physics also adopts a unit-based structure. In this case, each unit takes an aspect of physics, but with a modern slant. Four topics, *Communication, Designer Materials, Waves and Quantum Behaviour* and *Space and Time* feature in the Advanced Subsidiary (AS) course taken by 16- to 17-year-olds. Each unit focuses on physics in use in contextual settings. For example, in the *Communication* unit students learn about the background to the development of a variety of sensors. The physics involved in the development and use of the sensors is discussed, gradually building students' knowledge and understanding of key physics ideas and principles.

For 14- to 16-year-olds, 21st Century Science, developed by the Nuffield Curriculum Centre and the University of York Science Education Group, offers a new context-based approach at this level. The topics include *You and Your Genes, Air Quality, Material Choices* and *Radiation and Life* (e.g. see Burden *et al.* 2006a). The unit themes are designed to be of particular interest to young people, with much content being written in answer to typical questions they ask. In *You and Your Genes*, for example, questions such as 'What are chromosomes made of?', 'How do you inherit your genes?' and 'Why don't brothers and sisters look the same?' are answered. Contextual settings are used to approach more complex issues: in this unit, a 'Dear Doctor' section focuses on cystic fibrosis, using an imaginary letter from a parent whose child has been diagnosed with the disease. Issues such as the ethics of pregnancy termination and genetic screening are discussed, as well as up-to-date topics such as gene therapy and cloning (cf. Chapter 10). Besides teaching science in a context-related way, the course aims to enhance students' understandings of the nature of science and scientific literacy.

Do 'whole course' context–based materials match the integrated curriculum model?

To answer this question we will revisit the three dimensions described on pp. 147–9 and demonstrate the extent to which these materials may meet the ICM's requirements.

The advanced content dimension

All the courses offer interesting and challenging ideas, although the level can vary between topics. The post-16 courses, for example, offer the most complex and more difficult topics in the second year, that is, for 17- to 18-year-olds. 21st Century Science uses the 'Higher' level text (see Burden *et al.* 2006b) to offer more challenge to higher ability students, although not specifically those identified as gifted and talented. The notion of openness in ideas is also seen – the opportunity to discuss ethical issues, for example, offers a range of answers, none of which can be seen to be 'right', forcing children to accept alternative ideas and see their own thoughts against those of their peers (see 'Formal operations and beyond', in Chapter 6). The 'fuzziness' of knowledge comes through in the post-16 work, particularly in physics and biology, where the edges of scientific research are touched on in topics such as 'Grey matter' (SNAB) and 'Reach for the stars' (SHAP). Reading materials are consistent for all students with no special provision for high ability students. The reading level of the post-16 course texts appears to be relatively high, while that of 21st Century Science seems to aim for the 'middle ability range' child.

The process/product dimension

The Salters post-16 courses all include an individual investigation (e.g. see Box 11.3). The inclusion of this project requirement fits well with the ICM, in that students are expected to work over an extended period on a topic of personal interest, with a view to using research evidence and a range of strategies including practical work to achieve viable results.

The issues/themes dimension

Here, whole course context-based materials are in some respects less successful in matching the ICM than in the other dimensions. The UK curriculum has been highly specific in terms of the expected content to be examined, and parity between conventional and context-based courses is essential. There is therefore less flexibility to undertake extensive cross-

---

Box 11.3 Individual investigation in a SHAP unit

Planning and carrying out [of] an individual two-week investigation and the writing [of] a report on their work. It is assessed on the basis of the criteria mentioned below:

A Research and rationale
B Planning
C Implementing
D Observing and recording
E Interpreting and evaluating
F Communication

(http://www.york.ac.uk/org/seg/salters/physics/
assessment/coursework_assessment.html,
accessed March 2006)

curricular work in the sense intended by the ICM. However, the Storylines (SAC, SNAB and SHAP) and unit contents (Advancing Physics) adopted by the post-16 courses and the unit contents of 21st Century Science adopt a stance firmly rooted in socio-scientific and socio-economic issues, so boundaries are more greatly reduced between science and other areas than is normally seen in a 'traditional' type course.

Additionally, a characteristic of context-based courses is the wide variety of teaching and learning experiences offered through the prescribed activities. Salters Advanced Chemistry, for example, includes model building, role play, practical investigation and problem-solving as well as laboratory experiments as strategies to teach key ideas. Other sources of information such as newspaper articles, scientific papers and different types of data are also used to support students' learning. These can provide alternative ways of introducing links with other subjects.

So, do context–based courses constitute a 'gift horse' for the talented?

Finally, we can return to the question that forms the title of this chapter. Do we have sufficient evidence to indicate that adoption of context-based courses can provide a suitable science curriculum for gifted and talented students?

The evidence presented by Osborne and Collins (2000) and Jenkins and Nelson (2005) clearly suggests that the present situation is not entirely satisfactory. What we are doing at the moment for gifted and talented students is probably turning them towards humanities subjects, where opportunities for discussion, respect for different opinions and relevance to everyday life may seem more immediately apparent than in the abstract world of a physics laboratory. This is confirmed by the decline in recruitment to particularly physics post-16, a trend that, in 1997, served as the initial prompt to the Institute of Physics to develop Advancing Physics. More positively, the research studies indicated ways in which science curricula might change, and highlighted desirable qualities for new science courses that fit well with the general approach taken by context-based courses. In general, context-based courses are on the 'right track', providing challenge, relevance and variety.

However, we are in this text particularly concerned with gifted and talented students' needs, so we must go further. What is it that might mean these courses are suitable for this specific group of students?

The ICM indicates that context-based courses can be seen to make strong claims at matching two of the three dimensions, with the third lagging slightly behind due to UK National Curriculum constraints. Closer inspection of course materials is required to ensure the level of 'match', a task that keen readers concerned with the potential adoption of one of or more of these courses may wish to undertake for themselves. Clearly, the evidence presented here is convincing, in that context-based courses would provide suitable teaching and learning material for gifted and talented students. Bennett *et al.* (2005) offer supporting evidence from an entirely different perspective. Their study of over two hundred chemistry teachers revealed that SAC is perceived as more 'student-centred' (p. 1,534); that the individual investigation is 'very challenging' (p. 1,536); and that the course offers a 'greater variety of teaching methods . . . encouraging self-study' (p. 1,536). These factors, recognised by chemistry teachers, all match the earlier evidence suggested by the ICM.

However, before we all consider the issue 'solved', warning notes need to be sounded. VanTassel-Baska (1998) nominates three elements she regards as central to a successful science curriculum for gifted and talented students. The careful selection of materials is important, but insufficient. There also needs to be support for teacher development, and careful monitoring of any innovatory curriculum.

Bennett *et al.*'s (2005) study revealed concerns among teachers about the pedagogical content knowledge required to teach SAC. Comments such as 'some staff found it difficult to rethink their teaching' and 'it takes a while to get used to a spiral curriculum' (p. 1,533) were given by some teachers. In my own experience of SAC, teachers varied considerably in the degree to which they could genuinely adapt to the spiral curriculum and the range of activities they were expected to use, having first taught traditional post-16 courses.

VanTassel-Baska's third element is backed up by evidence showing that the implementation of context-based courses has been found to be most successful where it is well-supported by low-priced, readily available teacher and technician workshops. Bennett *et al.* report, regarding SAC: 'Many teachers mention the support and training workshops as important reasons for implementing the context-based course, and cite this as one of the main reasons why they would recommend the course to new teachers' (Bennett *et al.* 2005: 1,543).

The opportunity to reflect with others in similar situations and to learn and practice new skills is a vital factor that has contributed to the success of these context-based courses in the schools that have chosen to implement them.

The concern implicit in the above is that choosing a context-based course may offer benefits for gifted and talented students, but that these will be severely tempered unless a suitable teacher support network is in place and utilised. There is a danger that choosing a context-based course may simply generate another opportunity for 'differentiation by outcome' that does not fully realise its potential to meet the needs of the full ability range. Indeed, anecdotal evidence from teachers in pilot schools adopting 21st Century Science comment that the course has proved very beneficial for middle ability children, but has failed to stimulate higher ability children, who have, they felt, needed more intense content. The same teachers also report that 21st Century Science has not aided post-16 recruitment to science courses, as students have not been clear about, for example, the nature of 'chemistry' as a unique subject. These apparent disadvantages are being addressed in the schools concerned.

To summarise, we can see from the above that context-based courses offer the potential to satisfy the crying need for relevance, stimulation and variety demonstrated by two major research studies. Not only this, but there is evidence to indicate that the qualities of context-based courses match an established curriculum model designed for gifted and talented students. There is a suggestion, though, that use of modular context-based material specifically designed for gifted and talented students may bring greater intellectual benefits and thus be more satisfactory than a 'whole course' approach, in order to ensure these students are fully stretched. Successful use of any context-based science material depends heavily on the willingness of teachers to adopt practices that they may find challenging, difficult and profoundly different from what they are used to. Without this, the positive benefits that potentially could accrue for gifted and talented students will be lost.

On a final note, it needs to be said that context-based courses do, on the whole, offer intellectual challenge and rigour, particularly at post-16. No evidence to date has been found to suggest that these are any less 'difficult' than a conventional approach. The variety of teaching strategies and activities available makes them very attractive options that are likely to benefit the full ability range.

> If we design curriculum for our best learners and use it to stimulate a broader group of learners, then we will have succeeded admirably in our efforts to raise the ceiling for the gifted but [also] to provide a new set of standards for others to aim for.
>
> VanTassel-Baska, personal communication

Our horse, then, suitably handicapped, is mounted and ready to run.

Chapter 12

Choice for the gifted: Lessons from teaching about scientific explanations

Keith S. Taber

Chapter 12 brings together themes that are found in a number of contributions in the book. The chapter reports on student responses to activities designed around one specific aspect of the nature of science - explanations. It is argued that this is an example of a theme where students can be given activities with sufficiently open-ended demand to provide a potential challenge for even the most gifted. However, the chapter is also focused on an aspect of provision that can provide gifted (and other) learners opportunities both to follow interests, and to practise metacognitive skills: choice.

This chapter explores the potential value of 'choice' as a feature of science teaching planned for the most able in science classes. Student choice is one feature of learner-centred approaches to teaching (see Chapter 5). The context of the chapter is a sequence of activities focused on the notion of 'scientific explanation'. The approach taken is considered to offer a number of features that link to the needs of the most able science learners. In particular, there were a number of ways that the lesson activities offered 'choice', and positive student responses to the sessions seemed linked to this notion. It is suggested here that choice, as a principle to inform lesson planning, relates to a number of the issues that are considered important in teaching the gifted:

- creativity: by providing open-ended activities (Stepanek 1999);
- differentiation: by allowing students to respond at different levels (NDE 1997);
- engagement: by offering opportunities to link to personal interests (Renzulli 2004);
- metacognition: by requiring pupils to make judgements e.g. about which examples to tackle, and when to move on to another example (Shore and Dover 2004);
- task demand: by offering opportunities for higher level cognition (VanTassel–Baska 1998).

The activities discussed here were developed for use as curriculum enrichment for 13- to 14-year-olds, so the particular teaching sequence did not have to fit within a fixed scheme of work. Nonetheless, the general principle exemplified here can certainly be a consideration in planning more regular teaching.

The science context: the nature of scientific explanations

As discussed elsewhere in this book (in particular, see Chapters 2 and 14), the nature of science is considered to be: (1) a key focus for a science education that prepares young people for adult life in technologically advanced democracies; (2) an area where student understanding has often been found to be very limited; and (3) a potentially fruitful source of ideas and activities to engage and challenge the most able students.

Explanation would seem to be central to the essence of science. A naive view might claim that science *discovers* knowledge about the world, although it might be more accurate to suggest that science *creates* knowledge through the development of theories. The theories are used in turn to understand, predict and sometimes control the world, and in these activities, scientific explanations play the key role. We might consider theories and models to be the resources of science, but explanations to be the active processes through which theory is applied to contexts of interest (Gilbert *et al.* 2001). In science itself, as in an individual's science learning, the conceptual and the cognitive are complementary and interlinked.

An explanation is an answer to a 'why' question: but that in itself makes for neither a good explanation, nor for a scientific one. There is no simple answer to what does count as a good explanation, in science or elsewhere. Explanations have audiences, and to some extent, a good explanation is one that satisfies its audience – in other words it meets the explainee's purpose in seeking an explanation. Additionally, it has been known since at least Aristotle's time that we can talk of different kinds of causes, which suggests that many 'why questions' might have different *types* of acceptable responses, depending on the type of cause being sought.

For the purposes of the teaching episode considered here, pupils were told that scientific explanations needed to take into account *logic* and *theory*, i.e. that *the explanation needs to be rational, and the explanation needs to draw upon accepted scientific ideas.* As the notion of 'theory' is itself known to be difficult for students, they were also told that *scientific theories are ideas about the world which are well supported by evidence; are internally consistent; and which usually fit with other accepted theories.*

The teaching context: working with a top set with a wide ability range

The work discussed here was undertaken with a Year 9 (i.e. 13- to 14-year-olds) top science set in a maintained (state funded) 11–16 comprehensive school in the city of Cambridge, England. The school has a very cosmopolitan intake, and tends to have higher than average numbers of students who are considered to be able, as well as high numbers of those needing various kinds of learning support. Due to timetable organisation, the year group was split into two parallel half-years, and so the ability range within the top set was quite wide – i.e. including the most able, but covering something like the top quartile of the attainment range.

The author visited the school late in the school year (when most of the pupils would be 14 years old), to work with the group over two 50 minute periods, either side of the lunch break. There were 28 students present for the sessions: 9 girls and 19 boys. At this point in the year the group had completed the prescribed science curriculum for 11- to 14-year-olds, and time was made available for enrichment activities. The sessions consisted of a sequence of activities on 'explanations' in science, designed to build up to an activity where students would be asked to evaluate a set of 'explanations' as poor or good scientific explanations, and to justify this by reporting their criteria for the judgements. The general outline of the teaching sequence was:

- introduction to the 'teacher' (KST) and the theme of the sessions;
- suggest an explanation: a warm-up activity to remind pupils that producing satisfactory explanations is far from trivial, and to introduce the notion of an explanation being a response to a 'why' question;
- a teacher-led presentation on the theme of scientific explanations;
- explanations wanted: pupils were asked 'what are the questions you would most like to know the answers to?';
- sequencing explanations: selecting, sequencing and connecting components of explanations;
- evaluating explanations: selecting examples of poor and good scientific explanations, and justifying choices;
- a short questionnaire to find out what, if anything, the pupils enjoyed and/or found challenging about the work;
- in addition, two pairs of students (a pair of boys, a pair of girls), selected by the normal class teacher as able students who would be happy to talk, were interviewed.

In this chapter I will explain the nature of the lesson activities, and consider some examples of student responses. It is important to note that the 'teacher', being a visitor to the school, did not know the pupils, and did not know which of these top set learners were considered 'gifted'. However, a key feature of the approach used was to provide activities that had the potential to stretch the most able, whilst still allowing other pupils to fully engage and respond at their own levels. Although such 'differentiation by outcome' was pragmatically necessary in the particular context of these lessons, such an approach is also consistent with the views expressed elsewhere in this volume (e.g. see Chapters 1 and 2), i.e. that although it is important to ensure the most able learners are stretched, it is less desirable to apply labels that encourage us to limit our expectations about which students have the potential to demonstrate gifted traits in our classes.

Student responses to the teaching episode

Suggest an explanation

The first activity was intended to introduce the notion of an explanation being a response to a 'why' question. It was thought important that this activity should meet three criteria: be potentially challenging for the most able; be something that all the students could successfully engage with; and it should connect to student interests. A large bank of 'why' questions were prepared (fifty in total). Students were asked to work in pairs, and copies of the set of questions were distributed around the room so that students would be able to select a few questions that interested them.

Students became quite engaged in this activity, and it was allowed to run on whilst they remained on task and seemed to be enjoying the challenge. One of the most noticeable features of the set of responses was the extent to which answers were produced which were coherent, often extended, and matching scientific explanations. Although some of the questions should have been familiar from school science, this was still striking. That said, there were also a number of dubious suggestions, and many of the suggested explanations would be considered incomplete. However, the examples in Table 12.1 represent some of the more accomplished responses. Although it is clear that some of the examples involved reproducing previously taught material, they nonetheless suggest that these ideas have been learnt with sufficient understanding to allow pupils to construct creditworthy explanations.

When the pupils were asked at the end of the teaching episode which activities they found challenging, the most popular suggestion was this set of questions. Nine students suggested this as a challenging activity, and at least one of the students had identified something pretty fundamental about the nature of providing explanations: 'if you get an answer you can always ask why again and you can never explain it all'. In contrast, previous work has suggested that many students soon reach a point where they accept 'that's just how it is' (Watts and Taber 1996).

The pair of girls interviewed had appreciated the chance to select which of the questions they should attempt to answer, choosing biology examples which they judged easier. They still found the activity challenging, as they

Table 12.1 Examples of explanations provided by 13- to 14-year-olds

Question	Explanation
Why do we sweat?	*We sweat because* 'our body sometimes gets overly hot, whether it is from radiation from the sun or respiration in your muscles. Sweat is useful because it is mainly water; and water generally evaporates when it gets enough heat energy, which it will be able to 'steal' from the surrounding. The end result is that we lose heat energy thus cooling you down.'
Why does smoking damage health?	*Smoking damages health because* 'you are breathing tar, that lines your lungs and causes cancer. Nicotine is addictive, so you could keep taking this tar. It damages the cilia by the tar killing them off or clogging them up so they cannot move dirt and phlem [phlegm] up the throat. This is why smokers may get coughs and find it hard to breathe. The other harmful chemicals in cigarettes can cause cancer and other bodily disfunctions [dysfunctions].'
Why don't people lay eggs?	*People do not lay eggs because* 'our developing babies require more energy and the like provided, and if they developed externally then they would have limited supplies, whereas if the egg was inside the mother's body then the child would get virtually unlimited supplies through the placenta which is connected to the mother's blood stream.'
Why do only some planets have moons?	*Only some planets have moons because* 'when the big bang [sic] happened and the mass distributed but not evenly the larger masses of rock were drawn in by stars while some of the smaller masses got drawn in by the larger masses of rock because of their gravitational pull however some of the medium masses of rocks did not have a small mass of rock go near them or did not have enough gravitational pull to send the smaller rocks into orbit around them.'
Why do bees pollinate flowers?	Bees pollinate flowers because, 'well actually, bees don't deliberately pollinate flowers. The aim to get the nectar from the base of the flower so that they can turn it [to honey]. It is the flower plants who have adapted to make the bees pollinate them without knowing. The plants place the pollen so that when the bees are in the flower they take some pollen with them (it gets stuck to them). When the bees move to another flower it drops the pollen onto the female sex organ (stigma) and so a flower is pollinated. The flowers are simply using the bees as a way to reproduce.'
Why do birds have feathers?	Birds have feathers because 'they need the biggest surface area possible to push the air when they fly. Also they have feathers instead of fur because they are lighter with hollow bone in the centre. They are also aerodynamic. All of reasons help them to fly easier and faster.'
Why don't fish have arms?	Fish do not have arms because 'they don't need arms. The fish have adapted to have what they need, and they can move freely in the water. E.g. if a fish wanted food higher up, they can swim upwards and get it. Also they use fins instead as arms would drag and slow the fish down. The fins are used to propel the fish faster.'

had to 'go over' it, starting with 'a basic idea, but then you think further into it'. One of the boys interviewed described the activity as 'quite interesting because it definitely makes you think because . . . it's quite specific, so you're sort of making yourself think, with other knowledge'.

Presentation

The students were then given a presentation on the theme of scientific explanations. To get across the idea that scientific explanation can be quite complex, two examples were considered: the size of the known universe and natural selection. The different types of evidence that collectively support a Darwinian explanation of the evolution of modern life forms were reviewed (the 'explanation' to the question 'why do we believe life has evolved?'). The cosmic distance ladder was used as the second example – an explanation for how we have come to be able to put a value on the distance to the farthest detectable objects.

These two areas of scientific theory gave a glimpse of how scientific explanations can sometimes depend upon chains of logical connections (and so on a significant number of potentially incorrect assumptions), or may sometimes be based upon a weight of circumstantial evidence where definitive proof is not logically possible. These scientific 'stories' – one from the life sciences, one from the physical sciences – were thought to be suitable to interest the more able student – as well as giving an excuse to project images of dinosaurs and stars!

Explanations wanted

The students were then set a task to think about over their lunch break – 'what are the questions you would most like to know the answers to?' After the break the students were each given a sheet headed. 'Explanations wanted (The questions I'd most like to know the answers to)', and asked to suggest their own questions. Many of the suggestions related to biology (e.g. '*Why* do we have an appendix apart from to get appendicitis?'), especially human biology (e.g. '*Why* do men have nipples?'), or behavioural science (e.g. '*Why* are some things instinctive and others you have to learn?'). Although there was some interest in 'cosmic' questions (e.g. '*Why* have we found no other life in space?'), there were relatively few questions relating to the physical sciences (e.g. '*Why* do cornflakes go soggy?') among the group.

Quite a few of the questions should be answered at some point during school science (e.g. 'Why do we get bruises?', 'Why do humans take so long to grow up to adults compared to other animals?'), but there were also quite a few perceptive questions that were likely to remain a mystery in terms of the normal school curriculum (e.g. 'Why do humans have emotions?', 'Why do some people have perfect pitch?', 'Why do dogs wag their tails when they are happy?')

Elsewhere in this volume (in Chapter 9), Mike Watts and Helena Pedrosa de Jesus discuss the value of using students' questions in teaching the most able learners. Many of the questions elicited from this group of 14-year-olds would either form a useful starting point for science that is in the curriculum, or could provide the basis of interesting enrichment work.

Sequencing explanations

The next activity concerned sequencing potential components of explanations. This task was intended to build upon the earlier presentation where the complex (i.e. branching or daisy-chained) nature of explanations was considered. The activity was introduced on an overhead projector, using the question 'Why do solid substances melt when they are heated?' A set of statements, including some false ones, were moved around the projector glass to form a possible structure for a valid scientific explanation of the level expected in the school curriculum.

The students were then provided with a choice of two examples to work on in small groups. They were given information about the task:

> At the top of the sheet you will find a question. The statements on the sheet may help you construct an explanation to answer the question. However, you may not need all of the statements, and some may have been included to confuse you!

The students were also given a set of instructions to cut out the statements, rearrange them on a large sheet of paper, and then stick them down adding suitable connecting words ('because' etc.) and any additional information they wished to include.

The groups were given a free choice between a life science example ('Why do plants die if kept in the dark?'), and a physical science example ('Why is it important to use renewable power sources?'). These were expected to be questions that students would already have some ideas about, so the focus of the task was thinking about *how to structure* the explanation rather than working out what the answer could be. Both examples included some irrelevant or false statements, but these were included less to catch students out than to reduce any expectation that there was a single correct response comprising of a particular arrangement of all the statements.

Only one group completed the 'energy resource' option, producing an explanation that can be represented (with *italics* used to show words added by the students):

> It is important to use renewable power sources:
> *because* burning fossil fuels contributes to the greenhouse effect; *and* if the greenhouse effect becomes more intense then the average global temperature may increase.

because burning fossil fuels releases sulphur dioxide into the air; *and* sulphur dioxide is converted to sulphur trioxide in the air; *and* sulphur trioxide dissolves in water to make sulphuric acid.

because at the rate we are using fossils fuels we are likely to exhaust the supply within a century; *because* fossil fuels take millions of years to form.

This group were then able to sequence an explanation with three separate 'threads' or aspects – the greenhouse effect, the production of acid rain and the disparate timescales for the production and use of fossil fuels. Each of the threads is relevant and logically constructed.

Most groups chose to work on the question about plants, and responses of varying levels of complexity were produced. So the following example discarded most of the material provided, giving a simple, but logical explanation:

Plants die if kept in the dark:
because plants produce their food by photosynthesis; *and* photosynthesis requires energy; *and* plants use the sun's light as the energy source for photosynthesis.

Other groups tended to produce longer, and more involved explanations. These commonly included some flaws in the logic of the explanations, suggesting this task was genuinely challenging their thinking. The following example demonstrates a flaw found among the suggestions of several groups:

Plants die if kept in the dark:
because plants produce their food by photosynthesis; *and* photosynthesis requires energy; plants use the Sun's light as the energy source for photosynthesis; *therefore* plants contain a substance called chlorophyll which allows them to use the sun's light as a source of energy; *and* photosynthesis is a chemical process where carbon dioxide and water are reacted to form sugar (glucose) and oxygen.

In this example a good start is made of producing a logical chain, but the last two statements do not sit well in the sequence. This was quite typical of responses, in that the students seemed to be trying to include material that they saw as relevant, but had difficulty fitting it into the chain of explanation. Even when groups used the approach of having several threads of argument (as in the argument for renewable energy sources on pp. 164–5), they still found it difficult to formulate chains of argument. For example:

Plants die if kept in the dark:
because plants use the sun's light as the energy source for photosynthesis; *and* plants produce their food by photosynthesis; *because* photosynthesis

is a chemical process where carbon dioxide and water are reacted to form sugar (glucose) and oxygen; *and* photosynthesis requires energy *and* plants contain a substance called chlorophyll which allows them to use the sun's light as a source of energy; *because* photosynthesis requires energy.

This argument contains logical steps, but also material not directly relevant to the argument being made. A tentative suggestion is that these students had (rote) learnt that certain scientific facts were central to questions about this topic (the chemical reaction; the significance of chlorophyll) and felt the need to include these facts in a 'good' answer, even when it was not immediately clear how they fitted. Teaching argumentation in school science has only recently become the focus of teacher preparation (e.g. Erduran 2006), and is probably not currently an explicit focus of much science teaching.

When asked what they found challenging, five of the pupils cited the sequencing activity. Activities that involve cutting-and-sticking may still involve considerable cognitive demands – in this case 'deciding if something was relevant in the flow charts'. This may be worth bearing in mind as some pupils clearly enjoy these – as one student put it – 'kinetic activities'.

The interviewed girls again appreciated having some choice in the sequencing activity – 'it would be more difficult if you had done the one you didn't want to do, but if you do the one you want to do it's obviously because you might have some idea of what to do'. They clearly found the deliberate provision of redundant information made the task more complex, and added to the challenge – although this could be irksome:

> It was good, but it was a bit annoying having all the things that weren't relevant to it as well, cause you had to, *I suppose it was good really because you had to think about it,* which are relevant, but it was quite, annoying really, having to sort them out, and there were the ones that you knew were true, but they weren't relevant so you couldn't put those in as well [emphasis added].

The boys who were interviewed described this activity as 'pretty good, it was quite interactive as well'. They reported that, 'it makes you think, 'cause you're reading it and you're sorting it out yourself . . . you still had to think which ones were right and which ones weren't relevant, so yeah it did involve a bit of thinking'.

Evaluating explanations

The final task concerned 'critiquing explanations'. Students were provided with a set of thirty-five explanations, and asked to select examples of good or poor scientific explanations. The set was designed to include explanations of various degrees of complexity, including some with a range of flaws and weaknesses. Again working in groups, students were provided with two A3 sheets on which to glue their chosen examples. One sheet was headed 'poor scientific explanations' and had a series of boxes for students to complete the statement 'This is a poor explanation because . . . '. The other sheet, headed, 'good scientific explanations' had a single box to be completed: 'A good scientific explanation . . . .

The groups were asked to identify the characteristics they used to select good scientific explanations, and they were able to identify a number of pertinent criteria, e.g.:

> *A good scientific explanation* . . . is where the question is answered thoroughly. The answer doesn't repeat itself and it gives a detail[ed] description of the answer. The explanation explains the subject in detail, and makes it very clear so the reader can understand it easily.

> *A good scientific explanation* . . . doesn't ignore other possibilities. It is logical, and the answer is relevant. It doesn't leave any questions unanswered. It should not assume that things are connected.

> *A good scientific explanation* . . . does not go around in circles. It is clear and concise complies with recognised scientific ideas. It is essential, it is logical. It includes few complex words and sentences.

> *A good scientific explanation* . . . is rational and logical and has a solid grounding in accepted scientific theories.

The responses suggested that groups included logical argument, relevance to the questions, consistency with accepted scientific ideas, and clarity for the audience as relevant criteria. These were ideas that had been alluded to in the presentation, but it was still reassuring to see that students had taken up and could apply these points.

Perhaps of more interest was the selection of poor scientific explanations, as here there was the potential for applying criteria to identify when an explanation fell short. Weaknesses of some examples were readily identified:

> e.g. Bacteria cause disease because they are tiny single-celled living things.

> It doesn't explain *why* being a tiny single-celled living thing causes disease.

> The facts are correct but the explanation is unclear.

> There are lots of single-celled living things which don't cause disease – the statements are not connected.

Other examples were more readily analysed by some groups than others. For example one explanation offered was that: 'Acids are dangerous, and when using hydrochloric acid you should always wear safety spectacles. The stomach produces hydrochloric acid to digest food, so you should always wear safety spectacles when digesting food.' Whilst some groups selecting this as an example of a poor explanation were able to give appropriate reasons (e.g. 'they make the assumption that the acid is of the same strength. The acid is nowhere near the eyes', and 'When you are using acid externally you wear glasses, but when it is internal you should not'), other groups offered weaker justifications: 'Is not a sensible explanation. Does not make sense'. As with the sequencing task, critiquing explanations seemed to both engage the students' interest and provide a genuinely challenging activity for the range of abilities in this top set.

Four members of the group nominated this activity as challenging. The girls interviewed found that this activity 'was harder than the first ones', apparently because it involved two different types of criteria, relating to logical coherence and scientific veracity. One of the girls observed that something that had the form of a good explanation might be based on weak premises 'if you don't know that much about what you're talking about, then you might think it's a good explanation but it could just be like a simple version that you understand', and her companion observed that 'a good explanation doesn't have to be true'.

These girls felt they did not have the background to judge some of the explanations put before them, but this did not cause a problem as 'there were quite a lot of them, so you could choose, the ones you weren't sure you could just leave out, and there were enough to do it with the other ones as well'. One of the boys interviewed suggested that as 'there were more options, that made you think more'.

Overall response to the sequence of activities

At the end of the session, students were asked 'what (if anything) did you enjoy about the lessons?'. There were a wide variety of responses to this question, with some citing particular activities, while others suggested features of the sessions. Five students referred to how the sessions allowed them to use their own theories or work out their own answers, and one referred to the freedom to work independently. Three of the students thought the way the session was 'different' to a normal science lesson made it enjoyable, and three students specifically referred to the slides that had been shown (and another referred to the sessions being more 'visual'). Two students cited each of (1) the cutting-and-sticking activities; (2) the hands-on nature of the activities; and (3) the opportunity for free discussions.

The girls who were interviewed felt the sessions had been a good use of their time: as they 'got to choose', and the activities:

> were quite hands-on as well, doing it yourself, rather than kind of, like answering questions or something, especially like the last two activities we did, we had to think about it, and then do something, rather than just writing it.

The boys interviewed thought that the work on explanations 'was more interesting than normal science lessons'. They judged the difficulty of the work as 'just to the right level', a judgement apparently made with some metacognitive sophistication:

> [be]cause it sort of ranged a lot as well, it varied a lot, you know, so . . . you're learning different aspects of it, like, looking at different points of the subject, so you've got the whole thing as a whole overall, after doing all of the different ones, so you sort of put them all together and then you get the sort of main point of the subject . . . I think it helps to be able to see, so you can put it as different sides of the arguments, or different viewpoints, so that you can sort of work a way down the middle, work out what everything means if you put it all together.

Lessons from the lessons

Key aspects of the nature of science, such as the role and nature of explanation, need to be integrated into the teaching of science, as they are meaningless without scientific context. That said, the sequence of activities here (available on SEP 2004) could be built into schemes of work – providing lessons focused on 'explanation', building upon existing content knowledge, and so developing an appreciation of this feature of science, which can then be revisited and consolidated through reinforcement activities built into the teaching of subsequent topics.

There is always a limit to how much credence can be given to general points drawn from a case study of a single teaching episode, especially when evaluated and reported by the designer and teacher of the lessons. This is perhaps more so when the context is atypical: e.g. a visitor to school with the opportunity to work outside of a set scheme of work on a topic of choice. However, such cases can indicate potentially useful ideas and approaches to test out in other contexts.

Here I would like to focus on the role of choice in the success of these activities. Choice was deliberately built into this teaching episode at a number of points. The most obvious way in which choice was used was in terms of giving options of topic. So in the introductory activity students could select which phenomena they wished to explain from a bank of options. In the sequencing activity, two different science contexts were offered for the task. In the critiquing exercise, there was a wide selection of examples that the pupils could select from to use in their work. In part this functioned to allow pupils to select areas of science where their interest engaged them, as well as where they felt sufficiently secure in their subject knowledge to be able to succeed (something that was clearly important for the girls interviewed).

A second way in which choice was given was in terms of the way that elements were offered in the sequencing activity. Students were offered components of possible explanations, but the options included both 'distracters' and redundant information. This meant that the task became open-ended, allowing the possibility of a range of different 'correct' (if not necessarily 'full') answers. The opening activity just offered questions, with no clue as to the science knowledge to be used – potentially very open-ended (especially if explanations are judged in terms of being logical and building on science knowledge, rather than necessarily matching accepted science answers). The sequencing activity was more structured, offering all the main elements needed for an answer that would match curriculum science: yet it was not so structured to provide all-and-only-all the pieces of a set puzzle.

The types of 'choice' made available to students made the lessons more learner-centred (see Chapter 5), and gave them more of a feel of control over their work, rather than just being given a task to do. Choices made tasks more open-ended, *and* potentially more creative. For example, on the sequencing activity, some groups developed complex multi-thread arguments where others offered a single logical chain. When invited to offer explanations for phenomena, students were able to seek out relevant connections with their background knowledge, and draw upon anything that seemed pertinent.

Choice can provide a means of 'differentiation by outcome' – a way of setting a common task that allows all pupils to succeed at appropriate levels. All the 14-year-olds in these lessons were able to offer, sequence and critique explanations, but the range of outcomes was considerable. This type of choice allows each pupil to be challenged at a level where they can succeed, but without overtly labeling individuals (see Chapter 1). Some show considerable degrees of analysis, synthesis and judgement (see Chapter 6) – others less so.

This, of course, begs a question. The 'teacher' did not know these pupils, and so made no assumptions about what each individual could be expected to make of the work. In this context each learner (within their pairs and groups) was able to take on a level of challenge that was comfortable. Normally a teacher would have to judge their role in guiding learners' choices. As pupils seemed to enjoy the lessons it seems *unlikely* many were deliberately working well below their potential (cf. Csikszentmihalyi 1988). However, the approach relied on the pupils having enough metacognitive awareness and enough confidence in their abilities to regulate their own work. In this group there was certainly some evidence of metacognitive maturity – but this is not something that can always be taken as given, especially when many potentially gifted learners are known to habitually underachieve (e.g., see Chapter 3).

In conclusion, offering choice is recommended as a useful principle when planning lessons for the most able students. Choice *of topics* (where possible) engages learners, allowing them to link to interests and to demonstrate ability by selecting topics where secure background knowledge is available. Making even fairly structured activities as *open-ended* as possible allows creativity and gives opportunities for employing high-level cognition. Choice of *examples* can allow students of different levels of attainment, and with different strengths, to match the selected options to a level of demand that allows both progress in the task and enough challenge to facilitate useful learning.

However, offering gifted learners choice clearly implies delegating learners significant responsibilities – entrusting students to have the metacognitive awareness and motivation to regulate their learning. The use of such approaches assumes a learning environment where learners are accustomed to being trusted and exercising such judgement wisely.

Well-developed metacognition is often associated with the gifted (see Chapter 6), and clearly such trust may often be deserved, and rewarded (as in the case reported in this chapter). As always, the teacher needs to monitor and scaffold learning, and judge when learners are ready to take on more autonomy in their learning. There is potentially a virtuous circle here: offering choice both assumes and encourages metacognitive engagement. As the present case study shows, pupils seem to appreciate being given choices in their learning, and many will thrive on the challenge, and take opportunities to engage in high-level thinking about science.

Acknowledgements

Thanks are due to Dr Cathy Auffret for inviting me in to work with her students, and for setting up the sessions, and to the (then) Y9 students for their enthusiasm and engagement. The worksheets for the activities described here are available on a resource disseminated by the Science Enhancement Programme (SEP 2004).

Chapter 13

Practical work for the gifted in science

Alan West

If one thing characterises science as a school subject for many students it is the opportunity to do laboratory practical work. For many learners this is what makes science fun. It is tempting to think that practical work is more important for those who find the conceptual side of the subject intellectually demanding. And yet, scientific enquiry has the potential to challenge the most gifted learners, and allow them to demonstrate what they are really capable of. Unfortunately, the type of practical typically adopted in most school schemes of work falls well short of authentic scientific enquiry. In this chapter, Alan West describes the characteristics of practical work in successful enrichment programmes: characteristics that school science needs to adopt to really meet the needs of gifted young scientists.

This chapter will focus on the nature of practical work in science, in relation to the needs of the gifted, and will consider:

- the types and purposes of different types of practical work used in science teaching;
- student responses to practical work;
- the type of practical work that is most likely to engage, motivate, challenge and stretch gifted learners.

Many of the examples to which I refer will be drawn from my work as a practising science teacher; developer and organiser of a national award scheme for practical work in science (CREST – Creativity in Science and Technology); and developer and deliverer of university outreach to schools in science for gifted learners, including the National Academy for Gifted and Talented Youth (NAGTY) Summer Schools and the Higher Education Gateway programme. The chapter also draws upon interview material with gifted learners at school and college level who have been involved in various forms of intervention or enhancement activity, and data on attitude shifts arising through 'G&T' intervention in the form of laboratory based summer school activity.

Within this work we have referred to the term 'gifted learners' rather than use the 'gifted and talented' tag. However, in the context of practical work in science we should perhaps also give consideration to the *talented* dimension of the generic descriptor. While 'gifted' refers to students who are high academic achievers, 'talented' is frequently applied to those who have aptitude in the arts or sports, but equally it might be argued that there are students who have particular talents in the skills of practical science investigation, e.g. the good bench scientist capable of dealing with complex arrangements of apparatus and systematic processes. Some students will be gifted and talented:

> I'm not too bothered about the G&T label. You have to be gifted to be academic and talented to be more practical. There has to be a blend – you become talented through being gifted. Think of it through music – you can use your giftedness to make you talented.
>
> Student Jad age 18, November 2005

Practical work in science provides clear opportunities for students to demonstrate their creativity, particularly when this is linked to whole investigations. The Qualification and Curriculum Authority in England (QCA – see www.ncaction.org.uk/creativity) encourages schools to consider creativity in terms of four characteristics:

- imagination
- purpose
- originality
- value.

Practical work in science provides a window on a student's scientific ability that allows an individual's creativity to be spotted, particularly in an open-ended, problem-solving situation. Provision that allows a student to demonstrate creativity through problem-solving allows those who may not previously have been identified (or who possibly fall into the able under-achiever category) to be recognised through their practical capabilities as they may be seen to perform differently in the context of practical science *investigations*. Provision of appropriate practical science activities can provide key information about this sub cohort of gifted learners.

Five key dimensions for provision with gifted learners are (DfES 2002c):

- breadth – clustering together objectives for different areas and applying them in different contexts;
- depth – making objectives more demanding and in greater complexity or abstraction;

- acceleration – working at a faster pace;
- independence – allowing students to set their own tasks, extend their own ideas; working with minimal support and developing their own particular style of learning;
- reflection – encouraging students to make their understanding explicit and evaluate what they have learnt.

These key dimensions fit well with the organisation of some types of practical activity in science, particularly where students engage in whole investigations/ problem-solving.

In the early 1980s the Assessment of Performance Unit (APU) conducted research into the ways in which young people conducted scientific investigations. Part of the outcome of this work was a model for problem-solving investigations (see Figure 13.1), which subsequently became a template for much of what is now seen in the curriculum guidance for scientific enquiry (Sc1).

This iterative problem-solving model contains a number of key phases, which should form part of an investigation.

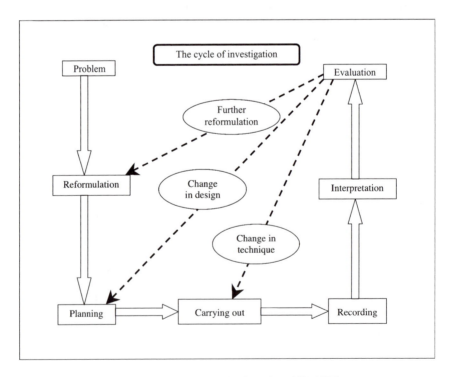

Figure 13.1 An iterative problem-solving model (based on APU 1989)

The problem

Identifying an appropriate problem is a critical factor for all students and their teachers. Identifying a problem in the first instance can be indicative of creativity and giftedness – seeing something in a different way that prompts a question for investigation.

A useful source of starting points for investigations are unusual phenomena that are demonstrated, described in the literature or experienced in some way by the students. So, for example, the fact that blue jeans fade is something that students are likely to have observed and may prompt questions about cause. If problems or observations of this type are made by the student and brought to the learning environment by them, they will be more motivated and more inclined to seek answers to the questions they have raised. The problem for teachers is the classroom management issue of dealing with such observations when they don't conform to planned progress through the subject. Problems become given rather than owned and therefore devalued particularly in the views of gifted learners. 'Too often problems given to us were trivial and did not really involve problem-solving at all. We were simple expected to regurgitate what we could have read about more quickly' (Student Martin, November 2005).

Reformulation

Reformulation involves taking the phenomenon identified as a problem and building around this a causal question that incorporates the variables that are to be investigated. This is the hypothesis that students over the decades have written at the start of their practical work, but usually without having ownership of the hypothesis. So, in the example of the cause of fading blue jeans students might hypothesise that this is due to the amount of washing; the type of washing powder used; exposure to sunlight etc. and suggest investigations to explore this. The reformulation step of the problem-solving process provides genuine opportunities for students to shape an investigation and establish some ownership for what will take place. Teachers need to be able to take the risk of allowing these students the freedom to do this if the work it to become a valid thinking skill activity for gifted learners. Being told what to do and what to investigate is clearly a cause of frustration for some gifted learners:

> There were more practicals in Year 9 and then in GCSE when there was just more course work. The topic you could choose yourself but maybe no variations; whatever the topics were, we all seemed to do the same thing in the same way. No clear progress was seen here and it made it quite dull.
>
> Student Florencia, November 2005

Planning

The planning stage of an investigation is primarily concerned with designing experimental activity around the variable being investigated. When allowed to plan in an open context students will generate greater ownership for the activity and derive motivation from this. Planning is a high level thinking skill and as such will be a key activity for gifted learners who have the ability to think through the implications of their activity and its relationship to the outcomes being sought. Planning also offers scope for gifted learners to demonstrate their creativity in terms of finding 'novel' (for them) ways of approaching an investigation. In the case of blue jeans this might translate into agreeing a 'fair test' protocol for comparing different washing powders or products.

Carrying out

Carrying out the investigation effectively means following the plan that has been made. The ability to do this in a consistent and reproducible way will require students to be talented in the practical context, i.e. they will have the ability and the dexterity to manipulate equipment, read instruments and to make appropriate observations within the dynamic of the laboratory or field context.

Recording

Organising who collects what and how many times things are observed or collected and the detail of what is written down is an extension of the planning process and part of the problem-solving cycle that involves high level thinking skills (see Chapter 6) and as such will be indicative of gifted learners.

Interpretation and evaluation

The interpretation phase of the cycle requires the investigator to relate the results to the experiment and to evaluate these in the context of the hypothesis and the experimental design. Such evaluation may cause further reformulation of the problem or highlight the need for a change in experimental design that will impact on the planning phase of the cycle. It might also be the case that interpretation and evaluation point to a need to change technique in carrying out the investigation. The latter stages of the cycle of investigation provide a valuable opportunity for gifted learners to demonstrate their high level thinking skills and also their creativity in terms of them overcoming what might be perceived to be failure in the early iterations of this cyclical process. Too frequently students in general are exposed to only segments of this cycle with little time or opportunity being available for iteration that might cause activity to be repeated and refined. The reasons for this are perhaps highlighted by the ways in which practical activities are used to support teaching and learning in science and these are reviewed below.

Exposing students to the whole cyclical investigation clearly provides an opportunity for them to demonstrate creativity and for this reason it was taken as a base line for activity within the CREST Awards programme. This encourages students to identify problems that might be addressed through scientific investigation or technological development. In QCA terms this is indicative of imagination and purpose. The reformulation of problems into something that can be tackled with the available resources gives rise to opportunities again for imagination but also originality and by following the cycle through to the point where the iterative process gives a result or product that can be valued-students gain an appreciation of the scientific process and are further motivated in their learning of science concepts. Within the CREST Awards programme, students are required to review the progress they have made in relation to the various phases of the cyclical investigation. Such self-assessment can provide teachers with an important indicator of both creativity and giftedness. Analytical investigations of this type still fall outside the experience of many students and the lack of such opportunity or the fact that students cannot readily understand the purpose for undertaking a segment of an investigation can be demotivating.

Readers will be aware of the different modes of science teaching but it is worth reflecting on these in terms of the relationship of practical science and the opportunity for gifted learners. Much of science instruction in the past, and to some extent the way in which a lot of teaching remains, is by the teacher transmitting knowledge to the students by standing in front of the class to introduce concepts and offer explanations. Such teaching may involve a variety of presentational techniques and may include:

- talk or a lecture in which new ideas are presented;
- practical demonstrations using equipment and reagents to demonstrate a particular phenomenon;
- demonstration lecture;
- enquiry and/or guided enquiry where students are introduce to a question and are then encouraged to hypothesise and plan;
- co-operative learning where learners negotiate a number of inter-dependent investigations;
- interventions by adults other than teachers;
- group presentations for students to feedback;
- literature review and collaborations through managed learning environ-ments (MLEs) where learners move beyond the bounds of a standard text. MLEs can also provide opportunities for expert intervention and mentoring; external 'experts' can extend the scope of investigations and collaborative working beyond the classroom or laboratory.

In preparing university outreach courses for gifted learners in the context of both short and long intervention periods, we have found it valuable to *blend* these approaches to introducing practical activity and sustaining the work once it is in place. We have adopted a common pattern across a number of courses of:

- background and range finding through demonstration lecture;
- problem analysis and question raising;
- team discussion to reformulate and plan possible investigations;
- time to carry out a meaningful investigation and establish a body of results data;
- interpretation and presentation of outcomes to peers and those who introduced the topic area;
- ongoing support and discussion through a closed community MLE.

It is valuable within this short overview to reflect on the comments of a small group of gifted learners who have been part of outreach intervention programmes delivered over the past five years. Although this is a small sample there are some interesting common features that emerge about practical work for these gifted learners.

> Science teaching . . . in school was not stimulating; we really didn't get taught very much that was stimulating. KS3 and GCSE was basic stuff; the chance to do project work and do my own research was a good motivation.

> Until Yr 10 we would dabble in interesting areas and we went quite fast but by Yr 11 we had to refocus our learning and just do what was on the curriculum and so we took 10 steps back and did things that we did in Yr 8 and this undermined the whole system.

> Practical work is massively important. Whilst theory is good, practical application is so important; practicals clarify many things. Newton's laws [1st, 2nd and 3rd laws of motion] is an excellent example of this and illustrates how they [scientists] determine these equations – where you are proving a concept through a demonstration. Anything happening in front of you is a proof of how it all works. It bridges the gaps between the text books and science to the real world.

> How could you learn if you don't have a practical? It's not enough just to read about it! Seeing it in practice and doing it yourself and you can alter and see what happens. Just watching you don't have that control.

> In secondary school we started more formal science. It was early on with the red cabbage experiment that I really started to latch on to science; it was fun and through good teaching and practical work, like the

experiments in biology, was stimulating. I enjoyed tests on your own body, so biology was more fun in the beginning. Flash bang chemistry – magnesium burning was fun. Copper sulphate, blue, and put zinc, and then the zinc turns to copper – and displacement reactions which were fun. Putting a scenario around the experiment like a murder investigation – who killed who – through a chemical test. There was a purpose to it all and you were doing real science. Without realising it, you have used knowledge to get to a solution. Practical work was good because lessons passed much quicker. I quite often found that lessons were going too slowly and theory in lessons was boring and tiresome.

What do we take from these personal statements? Students interviewed place a high level of importance on a *stimulating* science intervention or experience coupled with *owning* the science taking place within an investigation. For our gifted learners this was something that relieved the boredom of moving at the pace of other learners, allowed high level thinking activity to take place and provided stimulation and motivation.

Working with large numbers of gifted learners in the context of Summer School and Master Class activity it is clear to us that problem-solving approaches embodying students' own investigations provide an excellent vehicle for supporting the needs of these learners. Unfortunately it seems that generally this type of provision involves students being removed from the usual teaching environment and placed into some kind of specialist arena. Exposing gifted learners to experts who can answer their questions or support investigations that might lead to answers being generated is at the core of this extra provision. How much better to inject the reality dimension into normal classroom teaching, thereby providing uplift for all learners as well as those who are gifted (see 'Scientist in the hot seat' in Chapter 9).

Following a gifted learners' summer school for 11-year-olds passing into secondary school in Summer 2005, local authority providers commissioned a survey on *Pupil Attitudes to Self and School* (PASS). The PASS survey was taken by students attending the summer school at three points: on their first day, two weeks later at the end of the intervention, and then after a term back in school. The initial survey revealed that the students were generally confident in their own abilities, but were often negative about school and their teachers. The survey was analysed for the local authority, and fed back. According to the survey, the students:

don't appear to feel that school meets or supports those levels of competence and their preparedness to learn more than the school is capable of offering. So when they have negative attitudes about their feelings towards school it is because of the lack of enrichment opportunities and extension opportunities within the classroom and that moves across to being personalised with their teacher.

With primary age students this may be related to the limited science background of many primary teachers, but similar findings derived from some Y7 students who are taught science by subject specialists. When student responses from before and after the summer school were compared, it was found that the pupils,

> still felt confident about themselves and in many cases they felt more confident. . . . However, . . . where there were previous negatives on the first assessment many of those negatives increased by the second assessment they felt even more negative about what school might offer them than what their teachers do for them. So the intervention had a positive aspect in that it reinforces and reaffirms and maybe improves and increases positive attitudes about themselves as learners but it actually increased their negative attitudes about school ... the intervention was so successful that they compared it with what was lacking in school and what a programme like this can actually offer them as gifted learners.

Changes in the upper secondary science curriculum present teachers with a new specification for teaching and learning in England as of September 2006 (QCA 2005). This specification includes key statements like 'engage students in up-to-date and relevant science', 'how science works' and 'may favour particular learning styles'. What better way to give students an insight into the workings of science than to engage them in meaningful project based problem-solving practical work as part of the encouragement of 'a wider variety of teaching and learning styles'? This will be of motivational benefit to all learners, and especially gifted learners.

A new curriculum approach may provide opportunities to:

- seek input from Science and Engineering Ambassadors to introduce topics and to enrich through their direct experience;
- make use of volunteer schemes that place science undergraduates in school for a period of time;
- look at programmes like CREST which encourages context based problem-solving work around topics relevant to students;
- use problem-solving science to help identify gifted students through their practical problem-solving talents;
- explore the use of managed learning environments as a mechanism for enriching the learning context through additional resources and possibly e-mentoring;
- use MLEs to support collaborative learning within designated teams of gifted students and other learners;
- create opportunities for learners to present their work to one another and to an audience;

- use Higher Education Institutions (HEI) links to source ambassadors and to top up the experience of students by providing access to equipment and resources not found in school;
- ensure that teachers are part of this process and seen by students as scientists.

There are practical barriers to problem-solving work, particularly in challenging teaching environments, and so there should be renewed emphasis on training and professional development to support teachers managing the new curriculum opportunities for all learners. Otherwise issues around control and classroom management will continue to militate against many problem-solving practical activities which require control to be transferred to the learner and in turn may create further obstacles for gifted learners. However, the opportunity to infuse the types of activities currently only experienced in enrichment activities into the mainstream curriculum is certainly to be welcomed.

Chapter 14

Working together to provide enrichment for able science learners

Keith S. Taber and Fran Riga

*Earlier chapters have considered aspects of the nature of science –
modelling, scientific explanation, scientific enquiry, science in society – that
can inform science education for the gifted learner. In this chapter, Fran
Riga and I report how the nature of science was used as a key theme in an
after-school enrichment programme for 14- to 15-year-olds from a group
of schools. The chapter considers how such a context was able to offer
opportunities for students to demonstrate 'gifted' behaviours with like-
minded peers.*

This chapter discusses an after-school enrichment programme (ASCEND)
organised for secondary level students who were interested in, and considered
ready to be challenged in, science. The two features of the ASCEND project
which we will focus on are the use of the nature of science as a key organising
theme, and the way the programme brought together students from several
schools.

The ASCEND project

ASCEND, Able Scientists Collectively Experiencing New Demands, was a
project undertaken in partnership between the Faculty of Education at
Cambridge, the Federation of Secondary Schools in the city of Cambridge, and
the Science Enhancement Programme (which provided the funding that made
the project possible). ASCEND developed from the APECS (Able Pupils
Experiencing Challenging Science) project, which had been the focus for a
seminar series on 'Meeting the Needs of the Most Able in Science'. ASCEND
was an attempt to put into action some of the ideas that had been explored
in those seminars, in the context of a programme of enrichment.

After informal discussion with local schools, it was decided to work with
pupils in Y10 (i.e. 14- to 15-year-olds in the year before decisions were made
about college subjects and applications). The comprehensive schools in
Cambridge were invited to nominate students who would be interested in
attending after-school sessions, and who might benefit from being challenged

in their science learning. Four schools nominated students. Part of the logic of working with several schools was to ensure there would be a 'critical mass'. By definition most schools only have a small number of exceptionally able students in a year group (indeed one of the Cambridge schools declined to participate on the grounds that it had no suitable students), and ASCEND would allow these to meet and work with similar-minded individuals from other schools. One of the complaints commonly heard from high ability students is that 'friends who really understand us are few and far between' (NDE 1997: 55). The project was directed by the first author, a science education specialist, and organised in liaison with staff from the science departments in the four schools: Dr Cathy Auffret (Chesterton Community College), Eloise Froment (Parkside Community College), Peter Biggs (St Bede's Interdenominational School) and Susie Garlick (Netherhall School and Sixth Form College).

The programme was organised to run approximately fortnightly (during school terms) at a suitable time to allow students from the participating schools to walk, cycle or otherwise get to the Faculty of Education. The decision to hold the sessions in the University was a deliberate one: as well as being 'neutral' ground, this would be an adult environment, where the students could be treated as if conference or course delegates. To this end, the sessions were arranged such that they started with a thirty-minute window for a conference style registration during which delegates could take refreshments and socialise in the Faculty café (Taber and Riga 2006). The group then moved to teaching accommodation for a ninety-minute academic session.

The total number of delegates from the four schools was about thirty, although not all were able to attend all seven sessions. The sessions were staffed by a group of about a dozen teaching/research assistants: these were science education research students and trainee science teachers who had all volunteered to be involved in the project. Some teaching staff from the schools came and observed or joined in some activities. Each session started off with a short general introduction to the day's theme, given by the first author, followed by the delegates breaking up into groups, and usually spreading among several adjacent teaching rooms to work on the set tasks.

Planning the ASCEND approach

Two key themes for ASCEND were the nature of science, and metacognition. The nature of science was selected because

1   It was considered to be an area where standard school provision was often weak.
2   It offered a relevant theme which would not simply duplicate school studies.

3   It was considered to offer suitable opportunities for challenging the most able (see also Chapter 2).

In the curriculum context where ASCEND was situated, i.e. the English National Curriculum (NC), 'scientific enquiry' was established as one of the four main sections ('attainment targets', AT, in the official jargon) of the science curriculum. In principle, it made up an important part of the school science curriculum. However, the English NC has had a troubled history in this regard (Taber 2006a). Scientific enquiry ('Sc1') was intended to represent the processes by which scientists undertook enquiry into the natural world. However, in practice, it largely came to be based around an impoverished curriculum model of scientific investigations due to the way this aspect of curriculum was formally assessed at GCSE (school leaving examination at age 16) level (Kind and Taber 2005; Taber 2006b).

Other aspects of the nature of science were still supposed to be addressed through the teaching of the topics in Sc2–4: but this expectation initially took the form of a preamble to the statutory curriculum. When it was recognised that very little teaching about the nature of science took place in many classes, the curriculum was revised to give Sc1 two distinct threads, 'scientific investigations' and 'ideas and evidence'. Further it was made clear that explicit assessment of the 'ideas and evidence' thread would be included in national examinations (QCA 2002).

National monitoring exercises suggested that this was often a weak aspect of science teaching, with many teachers feeling underprepared and under-resourced for teaching about the nature of science (QCA undated).

Many teachers consider the NC curriculum too 'crowded' with material (the prescribed material for 11- to 14-years-olds is organised as 37 topics in the recommended scheme of work, see Kind and Taber 2005) to allow exploration of topics in depth (essential for stimulating the gifted), and there was a strong feeling that this type of curriculum gives students the view that science is just about learning a great many well-established ideas. However, it is more important that both future scientists, and the rest of the population (who need scientific literacy to support full participation in a technologically advanced democracy), develop scientific values and skills, and an appreciation of how knowledge comes to be judged reliable and so the basis for making decisions (e.g. Millar and Osborne 2000).

A great advantage of the nature of science as a focus for enrichment is that it is not intrinsically tied to any particular content. So even when students came from schools doing a good job introducing nature of science ideas, it was possible to explore the ideas further in contexts that did not repeat or pre-empt standard school work.

Moreover, there is good reason to believe that the nature of science offers learning opportunities that can challenge the most able. Gilbert (2002) had reviewed work on teaching science to the gifted and offered a number of

Table 14.1 Characteristics of gifted science learners – after Gilbert 2002

Characteristic	Characteristic indicator	Special focus
1. Readily learn novel ideas	Speed of adoption and use of vocabulary	History and philosophy of science, process of enquiry
2. Relate novel ideas to familiar ideas	Integration of novel and familiar ideas	Models in a historical sequence
3. Move beyond the information given, remaining within the context in which it has been learnt	Posing/answering 'what if' questions	Making predictions
4. Move ideas from the context in which they have been learnt to an unfamiliar context	Posing/answering 'transfer' questions	Moving between the sciences, relating to mathematics and technology
5. Use above to produce models	Parsimonious integration of ideas, preferably in visualisable form	Willingness to model novel phenomena/situations
6. Reflect on their own thinking and learning	Can attempt to explain how any of 1–5 was achieved	Forming overviews of sectors of a subject
7. Work within a group	Active role(s) adopted	Performance/perception of range of roles
8. Exercise leadership within a group	Persuades group over adoption of process or product	Marshalling of facts within argument structures

suggestions for the expected characteristics of gifted learners, and the types of learning foci that could match those characteristics (reproduced in Table 14.1).

Metacognition was introduced as a subsidiary theme, as it was considered that gifted learners would need well-developed metacognitive skills to work optimally. This was, in part, a recognition that effective students usually have already developed high levels of metacognition, and that exceptionally able learners are sometimes autodidacts who are able to largely teach themselves with little external input (see Chapter 6). One of the characterisitics to be *expected* of highly able students is that they show a high level of independence in their learning (Stepanek 1999).

This consideration was also a reflection on the role of differentiation in effective teaching. Even in top sets there is likely to be a considerable range of ability, and exceptionally able students would remain exceptional among their able but less exceptional peers. Effective teaching across wide ability ranges requires effective differentiation (through one means or another) by the teacher, and it is our view that for most forms of differentiation to be effective, learners have to be able to respond by taking some responsibility for regulating learning. This is likely to be especially so for the most able who are 'outliers' in the class population and may be assumed to be capable of high levels of independent learning. It was decided that ASCEND would be set up to assume, and test, the notion that more able students could indeed take responsibility for organising and monitoring their own progress on extended tasks. One of the common complaints reported from high ability students is that 'no one explains what being a high-ability learner is all about – it's kept a big secret' (NDE 1997: 55). It was decided to include an activity about learning and studying in one of the early sessions in the programme.

Organising the programme

A set of activities were designed for the ASCEND programme with a number of principles in mind. First, as discussed above, the main organising theme would be aspects of the nature of science, with a subsidiary focus on metacognition. Second, most of the activities would be based around small group work, partly because being able to take on roles within groups is believed to be one characteristic of gifted learners in science (Gilbert 2002). This also provided us with the ability to observe the students at work. The third key principle was that the work should be challenging, and so a minimum of guidance was provided in terms of exactly *how* to carry out activities. The delegates would be given tasks with overall aims, which they needed to plan and organise – and they also had to consider how they would evaluate their own achievements. In this way the 'default assumption', which was revisited during the project, was that when placed in a suitable, adult, learning environment, and offered responsibility for regulating their own learning, the delegates would be able to rise to the challenge.

In designing the activities, an attempt was made to provide contexts that would link with and support school learning, but without simply repeating or pre-empting work the delegates would meet in school science. The activities devised (described more fully in Taber, 2007) were based around the following themes:

- What is science? (How do we decide if some activity is or is not scientific?)
- Learning science (using information from psychology and brain science to identify good study habits, and modelling the science learner).
- Evaluating scientific explanations (criteria for a scientific explanation).
- Scientific laws (practical work: looking for patterns in data. This was linked to feedback cycles and exponential decay).
- Computer-based learning (an opportunity for delegates to work in a Faculty computer suite using materials designed to support independent study of physics at A level. This activity was the only one not organised in groups).
- Philosophies of science (considering historical vignettes of scientists in terms of competing models of the nature of science).
- Plant synthesis (developing a model of plant nutrition by synthesising ideas from biology, chemistry and physics/considering objections to genetic engineering in terms of evolutionary principles/knowledge).
- Scientific analogies (a card game encouraging players to find analogies between scientific concepts and everyday ideas and phenomena).
- Evaluating models (comparing two particle models, and two models of ionic bonding, in terms of how well they can explain phenomena/ properties).

The computer-based learning activity was not primarily related to the nature of science theme, but was an opportunity to work with some materials developed for independent learning of physics in the post-16 sector (see Kind and Taber 2005: 154). The 'learning science' activity was partly intended to inform the development of metacognition, but – in common with a number of other activities – also involved a modelling activity (see Chapter 7 for a consideration of the significance of modelling in science education).

What was learnt through ASCEND?

The space available here does not allow a detailed presentation of the rationale or nature of the different activities, nor an in-depth analysis of how students responded to the challenges. More detailed information is presented in Taber, 2007. The activities were documented, mainly through field notes taken by the teaching/research assistants, and by audio recordings of groups at work. This evidence has been analysed by the second author, and here we draw some general lessons from the successes and limitations of the programme.

Working and taking on roles in groups

At the start of each session, delegates were asked to organise themselves into groups, preferably with students from different schools. Generally, each group operated much like a team, working closely together, collaborating with each other, yet allowing one or two member(s) to guide while others were quite happy to follow. For example, one group, when asked to produce a poster of 'a Scientific Model of the Human Learner', decided to make a sketch of the brain, with every member contributing information, which they each wrote around the diagram.

In almost every group, activities were led by one (less often two) members of the group, who took it upon themselves to direct the group through the tasks. These 'leaders' tended to dominate discussions and appeared to enjoy expounding their ideas and theories, sometimes appearing to only be prepared to listen to others' opinions if these were *'intellectual'* enough. Moreover, other members of the group seemed to seek approval from the leader. Roles such as leader, reader, scribe, errand runner, timekeeper, etc. seemed to be assumed naturally without any visible signal or arrangement.

There were two instances, however, where the leader of a group was far more subdued. In these cases, the leaders quietly gave direction, keeping their groups on task throughout the session. When a group strayed off the set tasks, the leader would get them back on track by employing strategies such as redefining the topic in his/her own words, or, articulating the main idea under discussion. In one session, the 'leader' of one group reminded the members that they were '*not* trying to look at the quality of science but the quality of the *explanation* of the science', which then led on to a discussion about the relevance of explanations in science.

The students who assumed a leadership role, generally had the following characteristics in common:

- were vocal;
- took sudden, snap decisions;
- had a clear idea of *what* they wanted to do and *how* to do it;
- had a sound knowledge base from which to draw;
- tried to elicit support from others to confirm their ideas/opinions.

We also noticed that often a group might have one delegate who seemed to take on the role of (what is referred to in the internet age as) a lurker. A lot of the time the lurker appeared 'zoned-out'. They were initially silent (sometimes this lasted for up to half a session), and superficially seemed preoccupied with something else, or even bored and disinterested. However when they periodically engaged with the rest of the group it appeared they had been paying attention to what had been going on. Indeed, when they finally *did* speak/participate, they often had something very worthwhile to say. Their ideas were well formulated, and they often launched into arguments that sometimes superseded preceding discussions.

On the whole, delegates seemed to be thinking and working together within their groups (and sometimes between groups), sometimes thrashing out questions, problems and dilemmas, as though they *themselves* were scientists.

Ready assimilation of new learning

The resource materials used to support sessions were generally designed to have minimal direction, and often to provide unstructured and/or redundant (and in at least one case, excessive) information. Generally, students appeared to handle the volume of reading material with confidence: showing an ability to filter out which information would be most relevant. The ease and speed with which delegates seemed to be able to absorb and assimilate information from the materials provided was sometimes impressive. A boy in the session on *The Science of Learning* seemed perfectly comfortable oscillating from absorption in the stimulus materials, to contributing relevant snippets of new information to the group's discussions. Another boy described the Induction Model of Scientific Method after about 3 minutes into the session on *Philosophies of Science*, as follows: 'Model 1 is the one where we collect data and then collect more data, and more and more, until you can make a new law'.

The sessions included examples of new terminology, unlikely to have been met in school science. Assimilation of new knowledge was frequently demonstrated by delegates' attempts to rephrase information they had just acquired from the materials. In one group, a girl frequently asked her group members 'now how do we say that?', setting out to clearly paraphrase information before synthesising it into their activity. In a written task, a group had written 'neurones are responsible for Cognitive Processes (i.e. Thinking)', illustrating the need to paraphrase. There was also a tendency among some students to offer examples from their knowledge base, or from personal experience, to back up their reasoning or support their viewpoint. In the session on *Scientific Laws* students tried to recall knowledge from similar experiments performed at school in order to help them understand the experiments on negative feedback. In one interchange between a research assistant and a group, the former used the new term 'exponential decay', and later a boy from this group answered a question during the plenary at the end of the session, in which he correctly used the word 'exponential' to describe the shape of a curve – demonstrating that he had already incorporated this new concept into his vocabulary.

Planning and evaluating work

The materials generally provided minimal direction for how to undertake tasks. A common feature of the sessions was that the majority of students seemed so eager to get involved with the tasks that they often launched right into them with some excitement, without fully exploring the resource material provided. In most ASCEND sessions there was little evidence of careful planning of tasks before setting about doing them. Even when designing posters, delegates tended to plunge in, putting pen to paper (without drafting), and simply improvised as they went along.

A few students *did* take the time to read through the instructions, and were thus able to channel other group members. In some cases a member of a group might be quietly immersing themselves in the reading material seemingly 'in their own world', unaware of the discussions going on around them. However, on occasions, when a another group member stated something contrary to what was being read, they then corrected their colleagues by reading relevant passages aloud from the resource material, fuelling discussions on the topic. Some other students appeared to be able to skim read the materials, and very quickly absorb the information, which they then disseminated to the rest of the group at various points during the session.

In some ASCEND sessions, delegates did spend time at the beginning of the session in silent reading. One group during the session on *The Science of Learning* took a very organised approach. A girl took charge and divided the reading materials among the members, each taking a small pile to read. A period of quiet reading was followed by each member then contributing points (and quotes) for discussion from the papers they had read.

Two sessions focused on delegates' abilities to evaluate material (*scientific explanations* and *models*). One task required delegates to select two or three examples from a bank of questions, discuss answers, and then write suitable explanations. They then swapped explanations and critiqued each other's suggestions, either using the set of criteria supplied (which outlined both what makes good explanations in science, and what flaws to look out for when assessing explanations), or using their own criteria. Another task required students to produce a poster illustrating a model of plant nutrition. In this activity, delegates seemed to spontaneously edit, comment on and sometimes question each other's contributions.

Metacognition: awareness of learning processes, strengths and weaknesses

One of the early sessions of the project focused on *The Science of Learning*, where delegates were asked to use the resource materials supplied (a handout of information about aspects of learning, a set of stimulus figures, and reference books) to identify key points about learning that would be good advice to give students studying science. They were then required to produce a conference-type poster entitled 'a Scientific Model of the Human Learner', which incorporated key information about how scientists believe people learn. A girl described the learning process to other members of her group as follows: 'information . . . brain makes connections . . . brain begins to understand . . . therefore brain makes more connections to previously discovered ideas

. . . and begins to put them all together . . . brain understands'. A similar notion was voiced by a boy in another group who stated that 'the brain learns from prior experience'.

One of the learning practices observed during the sessions, which could be classified as a strength, was that students tended to stop periodically at various points in a task – especially when they ran into difficulties – and clearly summarise what they had done and what they knew up to that point. Students seemed to be aware that this process of *summarising* served as a platform from which to proceed to the next level of understanding of the concept under investigation.

On the whole delegates seemed to find it a weakness that often they could not offer quick answers and/or explanations to some of the problems they were investigating – sometimes seeming to get really annoyed by this. A girl in one group became so frustrated that she could not explain some everyday questions such as 'why do people have five toes on each foot?' that she announced: 'I've got a lot of questions, so will have to go on the internet to find out answers' – a remark which received universal consensus in her group. In another group a girl posed the question: 'How did people find answers to these questions?' to which a boy responded: 'somebody got it wrong then somebody got it right', perhaps demonstrating a notion of *how* science, as well as individual learning, progresses.

Appreciating the nature of modelling

An aspect of primary importance when considering the nature of science is the ability of scientists to develop models. A scientific model is also described as a representation of a phenomenon initially produced for a scientific purpose (Gilbert and Boulter 2000). During three sessions in the ASCEND programme, students were challenged to think about this particular aspect of the nature of science. The tasks they were set involved not only creating and developing models of their own to explain certain phenomena, but also evaluating/critiquing the extent to which certain models explained some selected phenomena.

A task students seemed to find particularly challenging was in the session on *evaluating models*, where they were required to consider two different ways of thinking about *particles* and had to judge each model by testing its usefulness in explaining what was happening in a number of different situations. The exercise gave students a taste of how difficult it is for scientists to try to explain a phenomenon, and how useful (and challenging) the development of a model can be. It also exposed delegates to the problems scientists experience when they grapple with forming sound explanations in terms of one particular model. The tasks required great patience and perseverance, and some students preferred to look for ways of simplifying the tasks and searching for generalisations. They tended to just go on to considering the next phenomenon or property when they got 'bogged down', rather than enter into in-depth discussions. They also tended to skip phenomena they knew little about – possibly because there were so many other items to choose from. Nevertheless, a couple of the groups *did* display a stubborn determination to resolve which model would be better at explaining a situation, and entered into fairly lengthy, detailed discussions.

Synthesis: making connections

Science is the attempt to understand and explain natural phenomena. In order to do this, scientists endeavour to process knowledge – a key element of which is making connections. Scientists make connections in a number of different ways, some of which are:

- through the process of *logical deduction;*
- by constructing either concrete or mental *models;*
- by devising and developing *theories;*
- by conjuring up *examples* based on prior knowledge or experience;
- by making *comparisons* – using metaphors and analogies – to help explain an event or observation.

In science, it is not, however, sufficient to make connections simply for the sake of making connections. They must lead to a conclusion, or some overarching goal – such as disentangling a problem or providing an explanation of the causes/effects of a phenomenon. Making connections is important in that it may lead to one's commitment to a particular belief, which, in the case of a student, might mean commitment to a scientifically accepted explanation, or alternatively, to a misconception.

During the ASCEND project, when students were presented with some sort of stimulus (e.g. an experiment or reading a handout), there was evidence (in virtually *every* task!) of students' thinking giving rise to a series of ideas, which most often incorporated examples drawn from familiar events or past experiences, and which helped them to make sense of the concept under scrutiny. So when explaining his concept of what makes something a *science* to his group, one boy drew on an example from building based on craft knowledge and engineering knowledge:

> it[science]'s much more of an organised thing . . . it's the difference between some person in Africa saying I can build my house out of these mud bricks, and an engineer saying I can build a skyscraper out of these steel girders *and* I know why it stands up.

One of the activities, the analogy game, actively encouraged students to form connections between scientific and more familiar ideas. Although some of the ideas presented were commonly used in science ('the nucleus is . . . like the brain because the nucleus controls what the cell does and the brain controls what we do'; 'a cell is like a brick . . . they're used to build up the body'), there were also more novel suggestions: 'a *molecule* is a complex arrangement of atoms and a *bible* is a complex arrangement of stories . . . and books and things'.

Working with complexity, ambiguity and uncertainty

Many tasks and activities used in the sessions were devised to challenge students by confronting them with situations which appeared complex and/or ambiguous, with students often facing solutions or explanations which were uncertain (cf. Chapter 6). When confronted with complexity, ambiguity and/or uncertainty, the strategies implemented by delegates were diverse. These responses included:

Accessing provided materials

Once delegates had identified the problem they were required to investigate and realised that they did not have a quick answer or explanation to offer, they began to skim through the reading material provided, then scanned for hints as to how to tackle the question.

Accessing prior knowledge and experience

Another strategy employed early in the process of resolving a problem, was to pool together any prior knowledge or personal experience they might have regarding the situation, and share this information with other group members. In one task, which involved categorising activities/occupations as 'science' or 'not science', one girl who seemed to have extensive knowledge about 'SETI', used her knowledge to overrule a boy in the group who suggested that it was more 'science fiction' than science. In another task (capacitor discharge experiment), a student who knew that voltage was directly proportional to current (although he admitted that they hadn't done it at school yet), shared this information with his group.

Defining/articulating the problem

Students sometimes resorted to defining, redefining, or articulating questions before proceeding to tackle the given task. For example, before attempting to answer the question 'why do we feel pain?', one group began by defining pain. To answer the question 'why do people age?', another group felt they first needed to tackle this by asking: 'age . . . in what sort of terms?', finally suggesting that aging occurs because it allows us to evolve faster.

Offering examples

One of the most frequent ways students seemed to try to make sense of complex or ambiguous situations was to attempt to give concrete examples. In one instance, a student gave the following example in an attempt to show that intuitive statements are not always true: 'it's intuitively true that the sun goes round the earth, however it is not so – they're making decisions based upon their . . . how they see it.'

Hypothesising

Students sometimes posed hypotheses or simply made predictions about what might happen. A fairly frequent way of addressing an issue was to use language such as 'suppose . . .', 'imagine . . .', or 'say . . .', e.g. 'say we send our photon to our mirror . . .' i.e. posing thought experiments. In another case, a boy from one group asked another boy in a group on the other side of the room, if he could describe his theory on why little rounded balls formed after NaCl was heated. The entire room fell silent and everyone listened to the boy expounding his theory, with questions asked at the end – it was much like a scene from a science conference.

Following logical processes

At times, delegates were inclined to think ideas through as a logical chain of events. In a practical exercise to explore the pattern in how water in two connected burettes reaches a common level, a student noticed that the water flowed fastest at the beginning, and then went on to explain that 'there's more water pressing down, which then makes this go up, but there's less water or force afterwards, so it goes down slower'. Similarly, a group taking temperature readings from hot water in a test tube noticed the temperature was dropping at an ever-slowing rate. They suggested that when 'the liquid is closer to room temperature it means it loses less heat' because there is less 'difference between its surroundings'. And a group working on the third (analogous) capacitor discharge experiment concluded:

> well if you think of it in terms of a circuit . . . the capacitor . . . is giving out current which is recorded by the ammeter but then more current flows back . . . but it's getting diminished each time because the capacitor's running out . . . so I suppose you could say it's positive-positive-negative [stages in a feedback cycle] because it's being depleted, so it's the negative feedback thing.

Conclusions from the ASCEND project

Clearly what we have be able to do here is little more than outline the nature of the programme, and offer some first thoughts as to what was going on in the sessions, and in particular in and between the minds of the delegates. Feedback from the young students was very positive (Taber and Riga 2006): they generally enjoyed and felt they benefited from taking part in the programme. We certainly would not claim to have developed the ideal enrichment experience for gifted learners. For one thing, we do not claim *all* the delegates would generally be considered 'gifted': rather some would more likely be judged as 'enthusiastic' high attaining students. This was not an issue for us for three reasons. The lack of any objective definition of gifted in science (and so confidence in how these judgements are able to be taken in schools), and the desire to attract a 'critical mass' of delegates, meant that we invited schools to send their keen students whom they considered would benefit from being challenged. More fundamentally, a strong belief that ability is not something firmly fixed (and that we do not have precise ways of measuring potential) encourages us to believe that some enthusiastic highly (but not currently exceptionally) achieving students may over time develop into exceptional scientists (see Chapter 1), and perhaps an experience such as ASCEND could act as a catalyst.

More significantly, our planning was based around two starting points: the notion of the nature of science as a suitable theme for the programme, and our interpretation of Gilbert's (2002) characterisation of what giftedness in science might mean. ASCEND provided us with the opportunity to test out how to operationalise these ideas, and the limited discussion of our data presented here only offers a flavour of how delegates responded to the challenges we set them. A closer look at our evidence is needed to see how the ASCEND activities need to be fine-tuned to provide the right balance between scaffolding and challenging learners (Taber and Riga 2006).

Nonetheless, we do feel able to offer some important (if hardly novel) conclusions. As expected, the nature of science provided suitable opportunities to set up challenging tasks, and the choice of mainly group-based activities did facilitate both discussion and opportunities for individuals to show intellectual leadership. Groups were often able to organise themselves over extended periods of time, working on tasks without clear instructions, making use of various resource materials that were sometimes not of immediately obvious relevance.

Perhaps even more importantly, at a time when school science has become characterised as often a grand tour of superficial visits to the 'key points' that examiners look for in a wide range of topics, there are still youngsters of both genders who are prepared to give up their own time to be stretched to think like scientists (rather than just learn curriculum science). These youngsters are able to appreciate that being challenged to think about scientific questions for themselves is a positive experience (Taber and Riga 2006).

Finally, we turn to one of the aspects of ASCEND that our sponsor, the Science Enhancement Programme, was especially interested in. ASCEND was a partnership project: the programme was designed and delivered at the

University, but was organised in association with local schools. By definition, any one school would have a limited number of 'gifted' science students, and even fewer interested enough to seek an enrichment programme. We believe part of the success of ASCEND comes from holding the sessions outside school, in an adult environment, with delegates from a number of schools. This allowed us to treat the delegates as young adults, with their own group identity, and they largely responded accordingly. The delegates enjoyed visiting the University, and enjoyed meeting like-minded individuals from other schools. Science is a collaborative activity, and we would like to think that ASCEND offers a model for how groups of schools might organise enrichment for those of their own students who would benefit from more challenge in science.

Chapter 15

Bringing learners and scientific expertise together

Matthew Newberry and John K. Gilbert

Chapter 7 reported some work from the Cams Hill Science Consortium (CHSC), an action research group facilitating teachers to support each other in the development of effective ways of teaching the most able – a model that has a great deal of potential. In this chapter, Matthew Newberry and John Gilbert review the development of CHSC, and offer insight into a range of the consortium's activities – both within typical teaching contexts, and through 'enrichment' activities such as a 'challenge' day for able learners. Some of the tools being developed within CHSC can be incorporated as planning/assessment instruments in any class, whilst offering particular support in evaluating challenge and progression for gifted students.

Meeting the needs of the most able in science

In can be argued that students who are 'gifted in science' have specific educational needs. These centre on being able to engage in an 'apprenticeship in thinking' (Rogoff 1990) with a scientist and/or teacher who is expert in a subject that is of direct interest to students. This association can to some extent be provided by access to materials produced by an expert e.g. through the internet. The subjects of direct interest to students are best addressed through the medium of problems to be solved or questions to be answered. It is equally important that such students develop the capacity to work with other students of like mind, if only to break down the sense of isolation that many feel. The activity presented here is offered as a case study of how these challenges can be addressed simultaneously. It was initiated by the Cams Hill Science Consortium (CHSC).

The context of collaboration: the Cams Hill Science Consortium

CHSC came about gradually. The relevance of models of and modelling to science education was initially advocated from a theoretical point of view

(Gilbert and Boulter 2000). This perception was subsequently found to be realistic at classroom level through a preliminary action research project conducted in association with the Hampshire Inspection and Advisory Service. At this time, many of the professional relationships that formed the basis of later work were established.

Since its establishment in 2001, the CHSC has gone through three phases so far:

Phase 1 (2001–3)

Established by Matthew Newberry (MN) and funded through Cams Hill School's Beacon Status, the project initially involved six science teachers from six different secondary schools working in partnership with MN and Professor John Gilbert (JKG). During this first phase teachers were supported to conduct case studies of action research, which focused upon developing models and modelling techniques and resources to improve student attainment in Key Stage 3 (KS3, i.e. ages 11–14 years) Science.

Phase 2 (2003–4)

Following the success of the six early projects, and the support of funding from Cams Hill School's newly acquired 'Leading Edge Partnership' status, the Consortium was expanded to have a total of thirteen teachers from twelve secondary schools across the region. The action research was planned for an 18-month cycle with teachers working in three localised cluster networks (South Hants, North Hants, East Sussex). Work continued at KS3 and was expanded into KS4 (14–16 years) and KS5 (16–18 years). In addition, the Cams Hill-Uplands Primary Consortium was established. This was a partnership between Cams Hill School and five primary schools, which was concerned with models and modelling across the whole curriculum (not just Science) for KS1 (5–7 years) and KS2 (7–11 years). The Consortium consisted of four network clusters supporting teachers with individual action research case studies. It was at this time that our work began to generate the five tools to support improving pedagogy and learning, which are explained later in the chapter.

Phase 3 (2004–6)

This has included work with 'INTECH', a hands-on science and technology visitor centre at Winchester (for details see www.intech-uk.com). Due to generous sponsorship the CHSC was able to expand again. There are now three primary (KS1, 2) groups each involving the science co-ordinators from five different primary schools working with MN, JKG and the local authority primary science education advisor. Each teacher is involved in conducting their own case study of action research focusing upon improving written explanations in science, KS1/2 or KS2/3 continuity, enhancing other teachers' understanding of progression within the science curriculum, and/or informal science education (through the INTECH connection). This work is funded by the AstraZeneca Science Teaching Trust. The three secondary groups continue, with funding from the Gatsby Technology Education Project. In short, the project now addresses issues affecting the progress of science students in a range of different schools covering all age ranges KS1- KS5.

As we have expanded, new teachers have been invited to join the work of the Consortium following personal recommendation by local authority science advisors and/or existing members of the group based upon their achievements in the classroom. We have a range of teachers at different stages in their careers spanning over thirty schools serving a variety of catchment areas. To support each teacher conducting their own case study of action research, each of the regional networks within the Consortium meets for at least one half-day once per school term, i.e. three times per year. In addition to this, teachers are supported through school consultancy visits by both MN and JKG as well as with proformas, resources and practical support to enable them to gather and analyse a portfolio of evidence of the impact(s) of their refined classroom interventions upon pupil engagement, learning and progression. As their projects mature, MN and JKG support individual teachers to cascade their work to other teachers in their schools by running a series of collaborative workshops and staff training. Once their work has been evaluated, the Consortium disseminate to wider regional and national audiences through our own and other teacher training conferences, through publications and via our own website www.thinkingframe.com.

The overall aims of the Consortium are to:

- develop creative approaches to raising standards in the teaching and learning of school science by the use of classroom action research;
- support improved progression in the learning of science by pupils across key stages by raising teachers' confidence in using scientific models and modelling techniques;
- investigate the opportunities for, and the effectiveness of, using models and modelling to raise standards of literacy in school science: in particular, to raise standards of pupils' understanding through the challenge of developing their own explanations;
- develop and evaluate the use of information and communication technology (ICT) resources to both raise standards of literacy in school science and to engage pupils in modelling activities;
- explore the role of models and modelling in the development of the skills of thinking/problem-solving and of scientific enquiry;
- develop networks of collaborative working based on action research among teachers, schools and local education authorities, initially in the south of England.

At the outsets of each of the three phases, the groups were introduced to the main ideas of models and modelling, these providing the intellectual framework within which the project rests (see Chapter 7). They were then provided with resources and materials which supported them working within a structured portfolio based approach, i.e. in systematically gathering evidence to analyse the impact of their action research upon teaching and learning within their schools. The processes adopted by the project conform to the general precepts of action research (Cohen *et al.* 2000), i.e.

- The intention is to improve science education in individual schools. Thus each teacher is entirely free to nominate the context in which and the purpose for which the work will take place.
- The spiral of cycles of planning, action, observing, and reflecting, is employed.
- The work is collaborative, not only within schools (at the initiative of the individual teacher) but also within and across groups (where meetings are conducted on the principles of supportive-criticism).
- The work involves the keeping of systematic personal records of what is done, why and how.
- Decision-taking is by individual teachers (with support from MN and JKG) and is based on the evidence that they have collected on the impact of specific issues on pupils' learning in their classes.
- The individual projects start on a small scale, but gradually expand in scope and the number of colleagues within a school that are involved. Allied projects in different schools also work in co-operation.
- Investigation of the contribution of models and modelling to the education of the pupils who are 'gifted and talented in science'.

So far, the project has produced five tools that are used, to different extents, across the individual projects (for further details see www.thinkingframe.com).

Key curriculum structuring models

I Models on placemats

The first tool is a consolidation of the view that the National Curriculum for Science rests on fundamental key curriculum structuring models. During KS1 and KS2 we have identified these models as Survival, Matter, Actions and Enquiry. As pupils progress to KS3 the models need refining and enhancing to become teaching models for the abstract concepts of Energy, Forces, Particles and Cells (Newberry *et al.* 2005). In addition to this, the range and sequence of skills associated with the variety of approaches to scientific enquiry need to be made explicit to the pupils. For each of these, a summary diagram (a 'placemat') has been produced that presents the model that is 'good enough' for use at the appropriate Key Stage (for an example, see Figure 7.1 in Chapter 7). These are being revised and sequenced by the Consortium to ensure challenge and progression through KS1, 2, 3 and 4. Gifted and talented pupils are being challenged to produce explanations of the science behind unfamiliar and/or everyday phenomena by applying the scientific principles and vocabulary summarised by the placemats within their written explanations. Teachers within the Consortium are developing pedagogic approaches to using the placemats approach interactively with pupils of differing abilities as well as developing a series of placemat resources to assist progression from KS1 through to KS3.

2 The 'levels mountain'

The 'levels mountain' (see Chapter 7, Figure 7.2) shows how the requirements for progression up successive 'levels of attainment' can be met in terms of models and modelling (Newberry *et al.* 2005). Again, this has been designed as a pedagogic tool to be used explicitly in the classroom with the pupils to share with them how they can improve the quality of their explanations of scientific phenomena. Our research has shown that this is best used as an interactive tool and it can motivate and engage pupils of all abilities. We have also shown that with a little practice pupils become very adept at levelling their own and their classmates' work and in so doing it helps teachers develop improved pedagogy within the science classroom.

3 The 'literacy ladder'

The 'literacy ladder' (see Figure 15.1) shows how skills of discussing and writing can be built up to support the attainment of higher 'levels of achievement'.

4 The 'Thinking Frame' approach

The 'Thinking Frame' approach is a set of resources and a methodology that weds the use of models in an attempt to solve a particular problem to an appropriate scaffolding designed to support discussion, debate and the sequence(s) of literacy skills needed to assist pupils to form their own detailed written explanations of a scientific phenomenon.

Below is an example of work produced by 'Rebecca', a highly able Year 7 pupil, during her teacher's first trial of the Thinking Frame approach with her particular class (Figure 15.2). This work was done in the second term of Year 7 and if compared against Rebecca's prior attainment at KS2 and her levels achieved in the CAT (cognitive abilities test) testing, it shows clear progression in science levels of achievement.

Pupil data 'Rebecca'		Cognitive abilities test scores		Key Stage 2 SATS data	
Calendar age	11.6	Verbal	120	English	5
NFER reading score	130 +	Quantitative	126	Maths	5
		Non-verbal	130	Science	5

After being introduced to the approach of the Thinking Frames, the class were encouraged to peer assess and reflect upon their achievements using the Thinking Frames approach. Through discussion they evaluated the approach (four stages of learning – 'Brainwave', 'See', 'Think/Sequence', 'Paragraph') as a method of assisting problem-solving in science by sequencing their scientific thinking and then offering a literacy scaffold to assist in the formation of a detailed written explanation.

The group were then encouraged to use the processes without the work-sheet resources to solve other problems in science. Applying the principles of the Thinking Frames approach Rebecca produced the following Level 7 explanation:

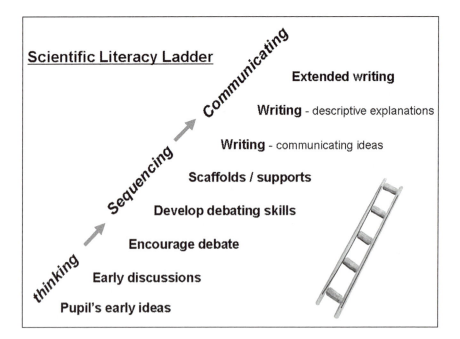

Figure 15.1 The literacy ladder

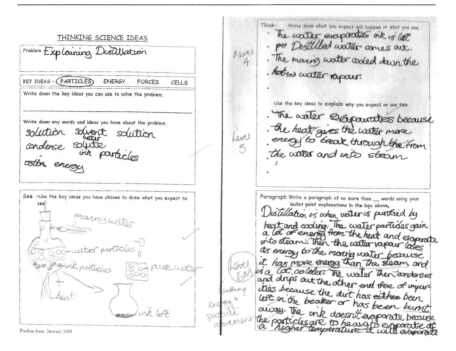

Figure 15.2 Rebecca's first use of the Thinking Frame

Why can we smell the perfume from a distance?

The particles in the perfume evaporate in the room temperature and start to spread out in the room because the heat has given the particles energy to rise into the air. The perfume particles move to places where there are less particles until they are evenly spread across the room and then they stop spreading out but are still moving. The particle spread out because they want to be evenly spaced.

Although this, like her first explanation, has some errors and could be improved, it does show elements of Level 7 thinking and demonstrates a clear improvement on her prior attainment. Rebecca, as a highly able pupil, was being challenged and supported by her teacher to engage with the Thinking Frames approach to form her own visualisation of models to explain an abstract phenomenon and then to form a written explanation. Rebecca's work is just one example within a series of case studies of action research conducted by the Cams Hill Science Consortium. These case studies cover action research into supporting and challenging pupils across KS1 to KS5 and have produced evidence to demonstrate that highly able pupils of all ages can be challenged and motivated by the Thinking Frames approach (see www.thinkingframe.com).

5 Gathering and analysing evidence of impact within the classroom

Measuring the impact of classroom interventions is not always something that teachers have experience of, or find easy to do. Through the course of designing and supporting a series of action research projects, we have designed a variety of auditing, monitoring and review processes in order to support and to assist teachers. One of the most effective is the evidence gathering templates that we have developed to encourage teachers to collate and gather evidence of the impact of their action research upon targeted individuals and groups of pupils. They work by supporting effective peer observation and encourage observation of lessons as a vehicle for assessing learning, not judging the quality of teaching. Teachers are finding these to be both an effective method of analysing the impact of their work and also a very useful vehicle for cascading best practice in teaching and learning to other teachers in their schools.

The individual projects being addressed have the following broad outlines:

- The development of 'teaching models' (Gilbert and Boulter 2000) to support progression up the mandated 'levels of attainment'. The themes being addressed include: respiration, refraction, photosynthesis, balanced/unbalanced forces.
- Moving from an understanding of qualitative forms of models to quantitative forms. This is being attempted for 'balanced equations/the mole/stoichiometry' and 'statistics in KS5 biology'.
- The use of the 'Thinking Frame' approach to improve specifically targeted cohorts of pupils including: underperforming pupils, gifted and talented, disengaged and difficult teaching groups. The approach has also been targeted to assist improvement in revision and exam preparation skills and so to improve pupil performance in public examinations.
- An exploration of the needs of the 'gifted and talented in science' and of ways to meet them.

It was in the particular context of the last of these aims that a 'Year 8 Able Pupil Science Challenge' was organised for 2 December 2005.

The 'Year 8 Able Pupil Science Challenge'

Although all the desirable attributes of 'science education of the gifted and talented' cannot be realised at the same time in an innovatory provision, a day-long activity was organised at INTECH, our 'Science and Technology Centre' collaborator. This event offered us a chance to:

- Invite groups of six pupils, identified as gifted and able in science by their schools, each group to work collaboratively on one aspect of a topic of contemporary social and scientific interest. That topic, chosen by the organiser of the Challenge (MN) was 'Understanding the potential offered by stem cell technology'. In their work, each group would be supported by two of their regular teachers.

- Involve pupils from schools that were members of CHSC, because the accompanying teachers, having expertise in action research, would be used to a high level of interaction with their pupils.
- Pilot an internet 'chat forum' for those pupils who were to attend the event. The intention here was to try to break down the sense of isolation that such pupils feel by allowing them to network with each other and the organisers before and after the event.
- Expose the pupils to contact with senior research academics on the day of the event. Professor Tom Fleming of the University of Southampton gave a detailed and informative lecture on the principles and potential of stem cell technology and some details of the work that is underway within his own department. JKG was available for consultation on issues to do with 'science communication' and acted as evaluator of the day.
- Enable the pupils to work in their groups uninterrupted (other than for refreshments!) for a day.
- Provide each group with guidance to relevant internet sources of specialist information.
- Place the pupil groups under a realistic time pressure, in that they had to produce three different outcomes for presentation to an invited audience (parents, governors of INTECH, pupils from other schools) by the end of the day.

Each group was provided with a laptop computer and CD on which was their activity brief, points to consider in their work, key supporting documents and the addresses of highly relevant websites. The five groups, with their titles and 'points to consider' were as follows:

1   Group 1. How can we get stem cells? What are they used for? Bognor Regis Community College;
2   Group 2. Arguments for and against stem cell research. The Hurst Community College;
3   Group 3. Stem cells and the law (at home and abroad). Cams High School;
4   Group 4. Stem cell research and cloning in the media. Priestlands School;
5   Group 5. Research into alternatives to using embryonic stem cells. Henry Beaufort School.

Each of the groups was provided with access to the internet, an opportunity to meet and interview the experts, some background materials and activities and resources to support making display materials. They were challenged to work first independently, then collaboratively within their groups and finally were given opportunities to collaborate with other groups and the facilitators and experts to support their work. The brief for each group was to research their specific areas of stem cell technology, and then to produce three forms of presentation about their work in time for an invited audience arriving in the afternoon:

- A webpage hosted on the INTECH website. To this end, specialist ICT staff were available all day for consultation. The groups were asked to design their page so as to ensure that visitors to the website were challenged to think and to learn.
- A 10–15 minute PowerPoint™ presentation explaining their work and findings to other participants and an invited audience. Each group was provided with a laptop computer to prepare their presentation. They had to script the several presenters of their show and to practice speaking with a microphone in the INTECH auditorium.
- An interactive display stand that included pictures and information from their findings. Support in preparing materials was available throughout the day.

Responses to the day

The need for such a day was recognised by Professor Fleming:

> I think it is really important that young, intelligent children should have the opportunity to learn about what is at the forefront of bio-medical research. We need these young people to have an avid interest in science and to be the new researchers of the future.

This recognition of need was also identified in feedback from the pupils and their parents:

> The day rocked, it was a great way of learning and it gives you independence and something to work towards. I wish school was like it . . . it felt like a business meeting, like they said, here's your task, here's the resources, there a meeting at these times, the public come in at this time, and we were just left to do our job, the bosses treated us like adults instead of kids.
>
> Pupil from Priestlands School

> I have really enjoyed getting together with different schools and being challenged. I would be interested in keeping in touch with the people from other schools using the forum.
>
> Pupil from Henry Beaufort School

Very good, please can you follow this up with other days on varying topics. Keep up the good work!

Mother of pupil from Cams Hill School

A very exciting and different opportunity for my daughter and her fellow pupils . . . I wish my Y11 son had had the chance to get involved in an event like this.

Mother of pupil from The Hurst Community College

Data was collected in three ways: by informal interviews conducted during the day (ten), by questionnaire at the end of the day (forty-two) and by a review of entries in the web based forum. Within the quotes that follows the following codes have been used:

TQ = Teacher quote from evaluation forms/written feedback
SQ = Student quote from evaluation forms/written feedback
IT = Quotes from recorded interviews of teachers
IS = Quotes from recorded interviews of students
VI = Quotes from recorded interviews of invited visitors to the afternoon presentations

The teachers, in response to the question 'what do you feel are the issues facing very able pupils and science in schools?', saw two sources of need. First, to overcome the restrictions of the curriculum and resources e.g:

TQ1. Opportunities to explore ideas in greater depth.
TQ2. Being able to develop their own areas on interest . . . [overcoming] the restriction of resources to carry about more elaborate investigative work.
TQ3. Not being stimulated enough by the curriculum, lack of time or equipment.
TQ4. Too much repetition, not enough independent learning. Few pupils of a similar ability to be worked with.

and, second, to avoid the anti-intellectual climate in some schools:

TQ5. Being bullied for being clever. Being proud of their ability. Having opportunities to develop within the school system.
TQ6. Bullying. Many feel that fitting in is a more necessary task than pushing themselves.
IT1. Sometimes the 'gifted and talented' kids can just get lost with all the behavioural issues. It is kids like these that could go on to become scientists and really help people. I think that they sometimes get overlooked.

The students were clear about why they had been selected to come e.g.:

IS1.   I'm quite good at science and that's why they chose me. I get one of the top marks.

although pragmatics played a part:

SQ1.   At school the teachers chose 8 pupils to do this challenge. The first 6 to get their forms in came.

However a somewhat broader perception was held, both by the pupils, e.g.:

IS2.   Apparently I'm good at science. I know that there are people who do better in their exams but I can talk about things and put my ideas across.

and by the teachers, e.g.:

IT1.   [The pupils] came from two top sets. We also wanted a mixture of boys and girls. As teachers we picked the ones that worked together well and also would be confident about speaking today.

IT2.   We looked at their scores and then we looked for the type of kid who would get something out of it. Then we looked at the tasks that they might have to do today. So we picked the ones that we knew would be quite good at talking and good at IT.

As would be expected, any day successfully labelled a 'challenge' would be found demanding by such pupils; in particular when questioned as to what particular areas that they found to be most challenging pupils replied:

SQ1.   Researching stem cells in the media.
SQ2.   Understanding the professor talking about stem cells.
SQ3.   Trying to complete the work in time.
SQ4.   Getting the presentations ready.
SQ5.   Speaking in front of everyone.

the latter views being supported by the teachers:

TQ4.   [Some pupils] needed input on presentation, but they were brilliant for Year 8.

which might have been helped by:

TQ6.   More preparation back at school before the day.

The pupils picked on a range of aspects to the day that they had enjoyed most. Some were focused on the content of what they had done, e.g.:

SQ2. Finding out about the uses of stem cells and listening to the professors.

SQ7. Finding out about stuff most teachers don't know much about.

Others were more concerned with how they had done the work, e.g.:

SQ3. Researching into the media.

SQ4. I enjoyed the method of learning – doing our own research and making presentations.

SQ5. I have enjoyed getting together with different schools and being challenged in groups.

SQ6. The adrenalin of doing the presentations and working in a team on something slightly challenging.

while some focused on the form of the output:

SQ8. I have enjoyed seeing everybody's work.

SQ9. The exhibitions, because they were interactive.

SQ10. Making the web page.

The teachers also had clear perceptions of the value of the day. In response to the question 'does this type of event address any of the issues (facing very able pupils and science)?', they wrote that:

TQ1. It will create enthusiasm among the able pupils who have been given a chance to explore their own views on these issues.

TQ2. Yes, a whole day of challenges is good. Informing them of new/future discoveries in science. To inspire them to help solve the big problems e.g. global warming.

TQ3. Challenging them both academically and socially. I hope the pupils will develop the relationships that have begun today.

Of particular interest were the remarks of the parents and of the governors of INTECH, who came to the presentations at the end of the day. They had views on the issues that pupils who are 'gifted and talented' in science face:

VI1. I feel science is not portrayed as an attractive or 'trendy' subject to follow as a career.

VI2. Flexibility in the curriculum to extend pupils' experience. Recruiting and retaining scientists into the teaching profession – teachers need a deep understanding of the subject to inspire and enthuse able scientists in the classroom.

VI3.   The moral and ethical issues involved in scientific research must be included (in the curriculum) for children to make up their own minds.

VI4.   The problem seems to be that the focus has shifted to raising the standards of the less able pupils while the more able are assumed to be able to look after themselves – and become bored.

VI5.   Having people with similar interests to share ideas and discuss topics with.

VI6.   Having teacher time to give encouragement and advice needed for pupils to fulfil their potential.

Activities such as this 'challenge day' were seen to have great potential to address these problems:

VI1.   It showed pupils how interesting and rewarding science can be.

V2I.   [It provided] flexibility in the curriculum and extended pupils' experience.

VI3.   [It was a way] of teachers learning how to inspire and motivate pupils.

VI4.   [The pupils] felt special and could mix with like-minded pupils, away from potential disruptions in the class.

Discussion

The literature suggests three general ways of addressing the curricular needs of the 'gifted and talented', by: *enrichment* (having them apply concepts that they have already been taught to novel content and contexts); *extension* (having them study the content of the current curriculum at greater depth than usual); and *acceleration* (having them meet the contents of the curriculum scheduled for later years) (Freeman 1998; O'Brian 1998). The Challenge was an *enrichment* only in so far that the pupils applied their (highly developed!) ICT skills to another context. However, they had met few if any of the scientific ideas involved beforehand, so it cannot be classed as an *extension*. It may therefore be seen as a type of *acceleration*, in that the theme of the day may be in the curriculum for post-16 studies if and when they get that far.

Using CHSC as the organisational background for the day seems to have worked for three reasons. First, as CHSC has *learning* as its primary focus, the teachers involved were especially alert to the nuances of meeting students' needs. Second, they had interactive question-and-answer skills that were more highly developed than usual, enabling them to use a Socratic rather than a didactic approach to working with the pupils. Third, having engaged in in-depth analysis of the National Curriculum for Science for England, they are well aware of the need to address modern science.

The structure of the day was successful. However, building on this experience will involve an address to a number of issues i.e.:

- Although it is possible to identify other interesting themes e.g. nanotechnology, global pandemics, global warming, the supply of expert scientists who are willing to come and address such an audience may be restricted.
- Working in groups was effective. However, for its efficiency to be raised, highly able pupils need to have more prior education/experience as to the allocation and discharge of roles in group work generally.
- Producing and making presentations was found very challenging by many pupils. Whilst their ICT skills seemed to be highly developed, many of them were very nervous at the prospect of speaking to an audience. More prior opportunities for 'public speaking' for highly able and gifted science students seem to be called for.
- The pupils selected to come were invited by their schools to do so mainly on the basis of their examination achievements and teacher assessment. Given that many gifted pupils are said to be underachieving (Freeman 1999), more sophisticated approaches to selection seem called for.
- The organisation of the activity itself and of extracting pupils from their schools proved very demanding. This type of event has proven to be highly valuable and highlights that schools need to increase the allocation of resources and time that they make available to support, challenge and motivate gifted and talented pupils.
- The pupils responded well to working on one theme for a whole day. However, a selective extension of this approach to timetable construction in schools would make it progressively more familiar for them.
- Because this was a 'one-off' activity, little if any preparation for it had taken place in schools. Nor, in most cases, was a follow-up activity planned by the schools. A requirement for both would lead to the Challenge having a greater long-term impact on the pupils involved. There was a wide variety of experience and professional expertise among the teachers attending the event, and some of the teachers were not confident to support and challenge their most able pupils in this context. This event highlighted a need for professional development opportunities and training to enable science teachers to learn about and share pedagogic approaches specifically targeted towards challenging gifted and talented pupils.

Chapter 16

An agenda for science education for gifted learners

Keith S. Taber

The authors of the preceding chapters have considerable experience in science teaching, supporting and developing science teachers, working with the gifted in school and out-of-school contexts, and carrying out research into aspects of teaching and learning science. Collectively these chapters offer considerable advice and insight into both the nature of giftedness in science and beyond, and into the kinds of good practice in science education that will support and challenge the most able learners. We have a good deal of understanding of what good science teaching and effective science learning activities might be. We have some very useful lists of indicators of giftedness, and some well-informed thinking about how these characteristics are best interpreted, demonstrated and developed in science. We know what gifted science education provision sometimes looks like (if often outside the normal curriculum), and we are fairly confident that we understand what teachers should be setting out to do in order to stretch the most able within the context of science lessons. I think this book does represent 'the state of the art' in terms of 'science education for gifted learners'.

The next steps

However, there is little room for complacency. It is also clear from the various contributions that:

- Official policy and guidance on identifying and providing for the gifted is often confused and impractical.
- Teachers often lack skills and training to recognise high potential (especially when co-existing with learning difficulties or disaffection).
- Institutional and curriculum contexts may often work against teachers following the best-current advice offered in this book.
- Research into exactly how gifted students can and do respond when teachers are able to implement the type of approaches recommended here, especially within the context of normal science classes, is needed.

We suspect that only a minority of teachers would be comfortable adopting the ideas here directly into their practice. Courses of initial teacher preparation (like the science curriculum they prepare new entrants to teach) are crowded, and there are many other priorities for professional development. Without their *own* learning being scaffolded (by courses, by opportunities to explore ideas in supportive institutional contexts, by constructive feedback and evaluation from trusted mentors) many science teachers may feel uneasy with some of the suggestions we make here (even those which seem to mirror curriculum and other developments): open-ended projects; making student questions central; providing choices of context, activity and modes of working; discussing issues with no scientific right answers; giving students more responsibility for their learning and its assessment; metacognitive modeling . . . .

In the UK, a new upper secondary level curriculum is just being introduced (for 14- to 16-year-olds): one that supposedly offers more flexibility, and potentially demands less learning of isolated material. This *should* free up teachers to follow more of the advice in this book. However, as Richard Coll points out (in Chapter 5) changes in curriculum are not in themselves enough to enable teachers to make desirable changes in practice. Teachers are still constrained by examination syllabuses that prepare students for high status school leaving examinations at 16. A review of the lower secondary science curriculum is expected to lead to similar curricular changes for 11- to 14-years-olds: but again teaching is currently channeled and constrained by the National Tests taken by 14-year-olds. A real test of any liberalisation of curriculum will be the nature of what is assessed. If the focus of assessment clearly encompasses higher-level cognition, demonstrating creativity, scientific intuition, effective argumentation, emotional and social intelligence, and so forth, then teachers will feel 'safer' in looking to challenge learners in the ways we recommend in this book. If the focus remains on reproducing the curriculum models and applying them to a range of standard examples and contexts, then a great opportunity will be lost.

Therefore, although I would wholeheartedly recommend the advice and guidance in this book to teachers, as representing the current state of knowledge, there is a lot more that we need to know if we are going to support teachers in carrying out our recommendations, and – in particular – judging whether they are offering an optimal level of challenge to the most able learners in science classes. It seems appropriate therefore to end the book, not with self-congratulations on a job well done, but rather with a look to what *more* is needed to better meet the special educational needs of the most able in science.

In particular, we need more focused research on effective science teaching for the gifted, but this needs to be research that effectively links to (explores, and informs) practice. Indeed we need a cyclic process, similar to that Alan

West discusses (in Chapter 13 in relation to student investigative work), to inform developments in science education for gifted learners. Ideally, such research would form the focus of well-funded, large-scale projects – carried out by experienced researchers sponsored by research councils and other august bodies. More commonly, research in science education depends upon the individual projects of masters and doctoral level students, and facilitating small-scale action research in individual classrooms and schools.

Yet even piecemeal research, carried out by lone graduate students and classroom teachers, has the potential to contribute as part of a coherent research programme. Indeed, there may even be a case for suggesting that we can do more to change teachers' classroom practice through a co-ordinated programme of small-scale action research.

An integrated model for researching practice

As earlier chapters have shown, there is already a considerable body of thinking to inform teaching science to the gifted – the 'conceptual frameworks' are already in place. What is lacking is a sufficient body of research into what this actually means, and potentially *can* mean, in various classroom contexts – to inform teacher education (initial and continuing), to inform curriculum development, and to inform education policies and wider practice.

In other words, we already have an agenda of ideas and principles that teachers can adopt. But we lack sufficient exemplification to show new and developing teachers what this can reasonably mean for their classroom teaching:

- research that would inform effective teacher education, by showing teachers *how to adopt and apply* these principles, and *how to evaluate* the outcomes;
- research of sufficient standing within the profession to allow the science education community, and those learned scientific bodies concerned about the future of science education, to confidently lobby for curriculum and assessment policies that support and facilitate the types of practices that challenge and develop our learners.

We need to be informed by more of the types of case studies of innovative and thoughtful practice that John Gilbert and Matthew Newberry report (Chapter 7 and 15) from the Cams Hill Science Consortium (CHSC). A context such as CHSC offers a comfort zone where teachers feel they do have permission to be innovative, and are supported by informed but constructive peer evaluation. This type of work demonstrates theory-in-action: what teachers can make of our recommendations in the context of real classes of real students whilst working in real schools. We need to know how teachers can be supported to implement best practice in discussing socio-cultural issues (Chapter 10), and context-base courses (Chapter 11); how *all* science teachers can develop classroom dialogue along the lines of the best practice Phil Scott identifies (Chapter 8); how full-time teachers with full-time teaching loads can adopt our ideas about student questioning, challenging students through the nature of science, implementing authentic investigations (Chapters 9, 13, 14), etc., within the constraints of institutions and curriculum requirements.

This needs to be an iterative process: if such research can bring about even modest changes – in teacher education and development; in curriculum and assessment procedures; in institutional structures and official policies and guidance – then these changes also need to be researched to push the improvement cycle forward.

An agenda for research and development

I would like to close this book then, with just some of the foci that might structure the programme of ongoing research that will move our agenda forward:

- really engaging students' interests as well as intellects through context-based courses;
- finding ways to provide engagement in topics in depth and over extended periods – both in practically based and other types of science project work;
- offering access to resources that support the development of scientific intuition;
- facilitating gifted students with learning difficulties to demonstrate potential through multi-modal teaching;
- adjusting the rhythm of types of classroom talk to differentiate for the most able learners;
- understanding the factors that lead to the best balance between working with similar gifted peers, and peer-tutoring in mixed groups to develop the most able;
- finding the optimal level of support when ceding responsibility for independence-in-learning and choice to gifted learners;
- challenging learners to reach their full potential without the kinds of labelling that can stigmatise, pressurise and exclude learners;
- adopting pedagogy to habitually demonstrate the process of modelling in action;
- adopting pedagogy to model scientific dialogue and argumentation;
- facilitating learning environments that are characterised as 'zones of low-conformity' and climates of enquiry that offer alternative solutions; tolerate and support constructive error; and encourage effective surprise – whilst offering a teaching environment that offers security for teachers;

- encouraging mastery goals, and self-regulated learning, within the constraints of a prescribed curriculum;
- understanding what emotionally intelligent science learning might be;
- investigating how the 'categories of disagreement' model may be best developed as a planning and differentiation tool for teaching about socio-scientific issues to challenge the most able;
- developing the 'gifts' of all our learners, regardless of gender, culture, multiple exceptionalities etc.

These are just some examples based upon the various recommendations and key ideas identified in this book. Each of these, and other areas, can be better illuminated by careful research within authentic (especially 'typical' class-room) teaching and learning contexts. Research in these areas will help us refine what we understand by best meeting the needs of the most able in science; help us appreciate what is possible in practice; help us better evaluate when learners are really being challenged, engaged and developed towards the realisation of their potential to enjoy and succeed in school science and beyond.

Bon voyage

In the first chapter, I set out to give an overview of the landscape that teachers might enter when looking to offer science education for gifted learners. In the chapters that followed, we described some of the scenery that the teacher venturing into that landscape might look out for. We certainly need more cartographers to map out the detail of the various regions. In the meantime, we invite teachers to consider the present volume as at least offering a compass to guide you into the territory. In places you may need to 'watch your step', but for the benefit of your gifted learners we hope you will start the journey. Perhaps you may even document and share the experiences of your travels. The main thing, though, is at least to set off, confident that you are moving in the right direction. We recommend that teachers do what they can to adopt the recommendations in this book. After all, we certainly believe that science teachers, like their gifted learners, respond well to being engaged in challenging work that they believe is relevant, interesting and worthwhile.

References

Abd-El-Khalick, F. and Lederman, N. (2000) 'Improving Science Teachers' Conceptions of the Nature of Science: a Critical Review of the Literature', *International Journal of Science Education*, 22, 665–702.

Adey, P. (1999) *The Science of Thinking, and Science For Thinking: A Description of Cognitive Acceleration through Science Education (CASE)*, Geneva: International Bureau of Education (UNESCO).

Adey, P. and Shayer, M. (1994) *Really Raising Standards: Cognitive Intervention and Academic Achievement*, London: Routledge.

AIP (2004) Einstein Image and Impact, American Institute of Physics, online at www.aip.org/history/einstein/, accessed May 2006.

Alexander, R. (2001) *Culture and Pedagogy: International Comparisons in Primary Education*. Oxford: Blackwell.

Alsop, S. (ed.) (2005a) *Beyond Cartesian Dualism: Encountering Affect in the Teaching and Learning of Science*, Dordrecht: Springer Kluwer Academic Publishers.

Alsop, S. (2005b) Motivational Beliefs and Classroom Contextual Factors: Exploring Affect in Accounts of Exemplary Practice. In S. Alsop, L. Bencze and E. Pedretti (eds) *Analysing Exemplary Science Teaching: Theoretical Lenses and a Spectrum of Possibilities for Practice*, Milton Keynes: Open University Press.

Alsop, S., Bencze, L. and Pedretti, E. (eds) (2005) *Analysing Exemplary Science Teaching: Theoretical Lenses and Spectrum of Possibilities for Practice*, Milton Keynes: Open University Press.

Alsop, S., Ibrahim, S. and Kurucz, C. (2006a) Anodyne Creations and Emergent Emotionality: a Digital Ethnographic Exploration of Emotional Contours in a Grade 7 and Grade 8 Laboratory and an Integrated Classroom. Paper presented at the National Association for Research in Science Teaching (NARST), San Francisco, April.

Alsop, S., Ibrahim, S. and Kurucz, C. (2006b) Crayons and Conical Flasks: Transitioning from the Mindscape of Emotionality to the Landscape of Rationality in Elementary Science Education. Paper presented at the Canadian Society for Studies in Education, York University, May.

Anderson, L. W. and Krathwohl, D. R. (2001) *A Taxonomy for Learning, Teaching and Assessing: A Revision of Bloom's Taxonomy of Educational Objectives*, New York: Longman.

Arlin, P. K. (1975) 'Cognitive Development in Adulthood: A Fifth Stage?', *Developmental Psychology*, 11 (5), 602–6.

APU (1988a) *Science at Age 11: A Review of APU Survey Findings 1980–84*, Assessment of Performance Unit, London: HMSO.

APU (1988b) *Science at Age 15: A Review of APU Survey Findings 1980–84*, Assessment of Performance Unit, London: HMSO.

APU (1989) *Science at Age 13: A Review of APU Survey Findings 1980–84*, Assessment of Performance Unit, London: HMSO.

Austin, D. (1995) *Gifted Education: A Resource Guide for Teachers*, Province of British Columbia: Ministry of Education.

Ausubel, D. P. (2000) *The Acquisition and Retention of Knowledge: A Cognitive View*, Dordrecht: Kluwer Academic Publishers.

Baldwin, A. Y., Vialle, W. and Clarke, C. (2000) Global Professionalism and Perceptions of Teachers of the Gifted. In K. A. Heller, F. J. Mönks, R. J. Sternberg and R. F. Subotnik (eds) *International Handbook of Research and Development of Giftedness and Talent* (2nd edn), Oxford: Elsevier Science, pp. 565–72.

Barker, M. (2003) Science Education and Environmental Education: What is their Relationship? In R. K. Coll (ed.) *STERpapers* Hamilton, New Zealand: Centre for Science and Technology Education Research, University of Waikato, pp. 53–67.

Bar-On, R. (1997) *Development of the Bar-On EQ-i: A Measure of Emotional Intelligence and Social Intelligence*, Toronto: Multi-Health Systems.

Baron-Cohen, S. (2003) 'Did Einstein and Newton Have Autism?' *New Scientist*, May, 2393.

Beasley, K. (1987) *The Emotional Quotient*, Wolverhampton: The British Mensa Society, May, pp. 25–36.

Beattie, D. S. (1986) *Report of Ministerial Working Party on Science and Technology*, Wellington, New Zealand: Ministry of Science and Technology.

Bell, B., Jones, A. and Carr, M. (1995) 'The Development of the Recent National New Zealand Science Curriculum', *Studies in Science Education*, 26, 73–105.

Bell, D. (2004) Commentary to *Standards and Quality 2002/03: The Annual Report of Her Majesty's Chief Inspector of Schools*, London: Office for Standards in Education.

Bennett, J. and Holman, J. S. (2002) Context-based Approaches to the Teaching of Chemistry: What Are They and What Are Their Effects? In J. Gilbert *et al.* (ed.) *Chemical Education Research-Based Practice*, Dordrecht: Kluwer Academic Publishers.

Bennett, J., Gräsel, C., Parchmann, I. and Waddington, D. (2005) 'Context-Based and Conventional Approaches to Teaching Chemistry: Comparing Teachers' Views', *International Journal of Science Education*, 27 (13), 1, 521–47.

Benson, E. (2003) 'Intelligent Intelligence Testing', *Monitor on Psychology*, 34 (2), 48, online at www.apa.org/monitor/feb03/intelligent.html.

Bevan-Brown, J. (1996) Special Abilities: A Māori Perspective. In D. McAlpine and R. Moltzen (eds), *Gifted and Talented: New Zealand Perspectives*, Palmerston North, New Zealand: ERDC Press, Massey University, pp. 91–110.

Bevan-Brown, J. (2004) Gifted and Talented Māori Learners. In D. McAlpine and R. Moltzen (eds), *Gifted and Talented: New Zealand Perspectives* (2nd edn), Palmerston North, New Zealand: ERDC Press, Massey University, pp. 171–97.

Biggs, J. (1988) 'The Role of Metacognition in Enhancing Learning', *Australian Journal of Education*, 32, 127–38.

Biggs, J. B. (1999) *Teaching for Quality Learning at University*. Buckingham: Open University Press.

Bloom, B. S. (1964) The Cognitive Domain. In L. H. Clark (1968) *Strategies and Tactics in Secondary School Teaching: A Book of Readings*, London: MacMillan, pp. 49–55.

Boaler, J. (1997) *Experiencing School Mathematics: Teaching Styles, Sex and Setting*, Buckingham: Open University Press.

Bodner, G. M. and McMillen, T. L. B. (1986). 'Cognitive Restructuring as an Early Stage in Problem Solving', *Journal of Research in Science Teaching*, 23 (8), 727–37.

Boler, M. (1999) *Feeling Power: Emotions and Education*, London, Routledge.

Brockman, J. (ed.) (2005) *Curious Minds: How a Child Becomes a Scientist*, London, Vintage Books.

Bruner, J. (1996) *The Culture of Education*. Cambridge, MA: Harvard University Press.

Bulman, L. (1985) *Teaching Language and Study Skills in Secondary Science*, London: Heinemann.

Burden, J., Holman, J., Hunt, A. and Millar, R. (2006a) *GCSE Additional Science*, Oxford: Oxford University Press.

Burden, J., Holman, J., Hunt, A. and Millar, R. (2006b) *GCSE Science Higher*, Oxford: Oxford University Press.

Burton, G., Holman, J., Pilling, G. and Waddington, D. (1994) *Salters Advanced Chemistry: Chemical Ideas, Storylines and Activity Pack*, Oxford: Heinemann.

Burton, G. Holman, J., Lazonby, J., Pilling, G. and Waddington, D. (2000) *Salters Advanced Chemistry Chemical Storylines* (2nd edn), Oxford: Heinemann.

Carson, R. (2002) *Silent Spring*, Boston, MA: Houghton Mifflin Company.

Cathcart, R. (1994) *They're Not Bringing my Brain Out*, Auckland, New Zealand: REAC.

Chin, C., Brown, D. E. and Bruce, B. C. (2002) 'Student-Generated Questions: A Meaningful Aspect of Learning in Science', *International Journal of Science Education*, 24 (5), 521–49.

Christopherson, J. T. (1997) The Growing Need for Visual Literacy at the University. Paper presented at the Visionquest: Journeys Towards Visual Literacy, 28th Annual Conference of the International Visual Literacy Association, Cheyenne, WY.

Clark, B. (1997) *Growing Up Gifted* (5th edn), Columbus, OH: Macmillan.

Clark, S. (2001) *Unlocking Formative Assessment: Practical Strategies for Enhancing Pupils' Learning in the Primary Classroom*, London: Hodder and Stoughton.

Coffield, F., Moseley, D., Hall, E. and Ecclestone, K. (2004) *Should we be Using Learning Styles? What Research has to Say to Practice*, London: Learning and Skills Research Centre.

Cohen, L., Manion, L., and Morrison, K. (2000) *Research Methods in Education* (5th edn), London: RoutledgeFalmer.

Colangelo, N. and Assouline, S. G. (2000) Counseling Gifted Students. In K. A. Heller, F. J. Mönks, R. J. Sternberg and R. F. Subotnik (eds) *International Handbook of Research and Development of Giftedness and Talent* (2nd edn), Oxford: Elsevier Science, pp. 595–608.

College of William and Mary (1997) *Acid, Acid Everywhere: A Problem-Based Unit*, Dubuque, IA: Kendall/Hunt.

Costa, J., Caldeira, H., Gallastegui, J. R. and Otero, J. (2000) 'An Analysis of Question Asking on Scientific Texts Explaining Natural Phenomena', *Journal of Research in Science Teaching*, 6 (37), 602–14.

Crick, B. (1998) *Education for Citizenship and the Teaching of Democracy in Schools*, London: Qualifications and Curriculum Authority.

Crocombe, G. T. (1991) Upgrading New Zealand's Competitive Advantage. In M. J. Enright, M. E. Porter, T. Caughey and NZTD Board (eds), *Porter Project: Porter Report*, Auckland: Oxford University Press.

Csikszentmihalyi, M. (1988) The Flow Experience and its Significance for Human Psychology. In M. Csikszentmihalyi and I. S. Csikszentmihalyi (eds) *Optimal Experience: Psychological Studies of Flow in Consciousness*, Cambridge: Cambridge University Press, pp. 15–35.

Dearden, R. F. (1981) 'Controversial Issues in the Curriculum', *Journal of Curriculum Studies* 13 (1), 37–44.

Delisle, J. (1984) *Gifted Children Speak Out*, New York: Walker and Company.

Dennett, D. C. (1991) *Consciousness Explained*, London: Penguin Books.

DfEE (1999) *Science: The National Curriculum for England*, London: Department for Education and Employment/Qualifications and Curriculum Authority.

DfES (2002a) Teaching Able, Gifted and Talented Pupils: Overview, online at www.standards.dfes.gov.uk/midbins/keystage3/, accessed 14 January 2004.

DfES (2002b) *Framework for Teaching Science: Years 7, 8 and 9*, Key Stage 3 National Strategy, London: Department for Education and Skills.

DfES (2002c) *Teaching Gifted and Talented Pupils, Module 1: Whole-School Training Module for Teachers of Gifted and Talented Pupils*, London: Department for Education and Skills.

DfES (2003) *Teaching Able, Gifted and Talented Pupils Module 4: Science for Gifted Pupils*, London: Department for Education and Skills.

DfES (2004a) *Excellence Cluster Guidance for Round 2 Statutory EAZs in Non-EiC Areas*, London: Department for Education and Skills.

DfES (2004b) *A National Conversation about Personalised Learning*, Nottingham: Department for Education and Skills.

DfES (2005) *Leading in Learning: Developing Thinking Skills at Key Stage 3 School Training Manual*, London: Department for Education and Skills.

Dillon, J. T. (1998) Theory and Practice of Student Questioning. In S. Karabenick (ed.) *Strategic Help Seeking – Implications for Learning and Teaching*, Mahwah, NJ: Lawrence Earlbaum Associates, pp. 195–218.

DoE (1972) *Children With Special Abilities: Suggestions for Teaching Gifted Children in Primary Schools*, Wellington, New Zealand: Department of Education.

Dudley-Marling, C. (2004) 'The Social Construction of Learning Disabilities', *Journal of Learning Disabilities*, 37 (6), Nov/Dec, 482–9.

Eccles, J. and Wigfield, A. (1995) 'In the Mind of the Actor: The Structure of Adolescents' Achievement, Task Values and Expectancy-Related Beliefs', *Personality and Social Psychology Bulletin*, 21, 215–2.

Edwards, D. and Mercer, N. (1987) *Common Knowledge: The Development of Understanding in the Classroom*, London: Routledge.

Erduran, S. (2006) 'Promoting Ideas, Evidence and Argument in Initial Science Teacher Training', *School Science Review*, June 2006, 87 (321), 45–50.

ERO (1998) *Working with Students with Special Abilities*, Wellington, New Zealand: Education Review Office.

Eyre, D. (1997) *Able Children in Ordinary Schools*, London: David Fulton.

Feather, N. T. (1989) 'Attitudes towards the High Achiever: The Fall of the Tall Poppy', *Australian Journal of Psychology*, 41 (3), 239–67.

Feldhusen, J. F. and Jarwan, F. A. (2000) Identification of Gifted and Talented Youth for Educational Programs. In K. A. Heller, F. J. Mönks, R. J. Sternberg and R. F. Subotnik (eds) *International Handbook of Research and Development of Giftedness and Talent* (2nd edn), Oxford: Elsevier Science, pp. 271–82.

Finster, D. C. (1989) 'Developmental Instruction: Part 1. Perry's Model of Intellectual Development', *Journal of Chemical Education*, 66 (8), 659–61.

Fisher, S. G. (1969) Working with Gifted Children in Science. In S. A. Bridges *Gifted Children and the Brentwood Experiment*, Bath: The Pitman Press, pp. 128–35.

Fletcher, K. P. (1995) International Chemistry Olympiad New Zealand Team Selection, Training and Evaluation. Paper presented at Teaching Gifted Students at Secondary Level First National Conference, Palmerston North, New Zealand, May.

France, B. (2001) Biotechnology Teaching Models: What is their Role in Technology Education? In R. K. Coll (ed.) *STERpapers*, Hamilton, New Zealand: Centre for Science and Technology Education Research, University of Waikato, pp. 34–52.

Frasier, M. (1997) 'Multiple Criteria: The Mandate and the Challenge', *Roeper Review*, 20 (2), A4–A7.

Freeman, J. (1995) 'Recent Studies of Giftedness', *The Journal of Child Psychology and Psychiatry*, 36 (4), 531–40.

Freeman, J. (1998) *Educating the Very Able: Current International Research*, Office for Standards in Education, London: The Stationery Office.

Freeman, J. (1999) 'Teaching Gifted Pupils', *Journal of Biological Education*, 34 (4), 185–90.

Freeman, J. (2001) *Gifted Children Grown Up*. London: David Fulton.

Gall, M. (1970) 'The Use of Questions in Teaching', *Review of Educational Research*, 40, 707–21.

Gallagher, J. J. (2000) Changing Paradigms for Gifted Education in the United States. In K. A. Heller, F. J. Mönks, R. J. Sternberg and R. F. Subotnik (eds), *International Handbook of Research and Development of Giftedness and Talent* (2nd edn), Oxford: Elsevier Science, pp. 681–94.

Galton, F. (1869) 'Hereditary Intelligence: An Enquiry into its Laws and Consequences', *MacMillan's Magazine*, 2, 157–66, online at http://galton.org/books/hereditary-genius/text/html/galton-1869-genius.html, accessed 5 January 2007.

Gardner, H. (1993) *Frames of Mind: The Theory of Multiple Intelligences* (2nd edn), London: Fontana.

Gardner, H. (1997) *Extraordinary Minds: Portraits of Exceptional Individuals and an Examination of our Extraordinariness*, New York: Basic Books.

Gentner, D. (1983) 'Structure-Mapping: a Theoretical Framework for Analogy', *Cognitive Science*, 7, 155–70.

Gentner, D. (1988) Analogical Inference and Analogical Access. In A. Prieditis (ed.), *Analogia*, London: Pitman, pp. 63–88.

George, D. (1992) *The Challenge of the Able Child*, London: David Fulton.

George, D. (1997) *The Challenge of the Able Child* (2nd edn), London: Fulton.

Georgiou, A. K. A. (2005) 'Thought Experiments in Physics Learning: On Intuition and Imagistic Simulation', unpublished M.Phil. thesis, University of Cambridge, Cambridge.

Gilbert, J. K. (2002) Characteristics of Gifted and Talented Pupils in Science, online at www.educ.cam.ac.uk/apecs/, accessed 7 May 2006.

Gilbert, J. K. (ed.) (2005a) *Visualization in Science Education*, Dordrecht: Springer.

Gilbert, J. K. (2005b) Visualization: A Metacognitive Skill in Science and Science Education. In J. K. Gilbert (ed.), *Visualization in Science Education*. Dordrecht: Springer.

Gilbert, J. K. (ed.) (2006) *Science Education in Schools: Issues, Evidence and Proposals*, London: Economic and Social Research Council and Association for Science Education.

Gilbert, J. K. and Boulter, C. J. (eds) (2000) *Developing Models in Science Education*, Dordrecht: Kluwer.

Gilbert, J. K., Boulter, C. J. and Elmer, R. (2000) Positioning Models in Science Education and in Design and Technology Education. In J. K. Gilbert and C. J. Boulter (eds), *Developing Models in Science Education*, Dordrecht: Kluwer, pp. 3–18.

Gilbert, J. K., Boulter, C. and Rutherford, M. (1998) 'Models in Explanations, Part 1: Horses for Courses', *International Journal of Science Education*, 20 (1), 83–97.

Gilbert, J. K., Taber, K. S. and Watts, M. (2001) Quality, Level, and Acceptability, of Explanation in Chemical Education. In A. F. Cachapuz (ed.) *2001, A Chemical Odyssey*, Proceedings of the 6th European Conference in Research in Chemical Education/2nd European Conference on Chemical Education, University de Aveiro, Portugal.

Goleman, D. (1996) *Emotional Intelligence*, London: Bloomsbury Publishing.

Goswami, U. (1992) *Analogical Reasoning in Children*, Hillsdale, NJ: Lawrence Erlbaum.

Gould, S. J. (1992) *The Mismeasure of Man*, London: Penguin (first published in 1981).

Graesser, A. C. and Person, N. K. (1994) 'Question Asking During Tutoring', *American Educational Research Journal*, 31 (1), 104–37.

Graesser, A. C., Person, N. K. and Huber, J. D. (1992) Mechanisms that Generate Questions. In T. Lauer, E. Peacock, and A. C. Graesser (eds), *Questions and Information Systems*, Hillsdale, NJ: Lawrence Erlbaum Associates, pp. 167–87.

Greeno, J. (1998) 'The Situativity of Knowing, Learning and Research', *American Psychologist*, 53 (1), 5–26.

Grevatt, A. (2005) *Key Stage 3 Science, 7 Level Assessed Tasks*, London: Badger Publishing.

Gross, M. U. M. (2004) *Exceptionally Gifted Children* (2nd edn), London: Routledge-Falmer.

Hallam, S. and Ireson, J. (2000) *Ability Grouping in Education*, London: Paul Chapman.

Harding, S. (1991) *Whose Science? Whose Knowledge? Thinking from Women's Lives*, Milton Keynes: Open University Press.

Harlen, W. (2006) Assessment for Learning and Assessment of Learning. In V. Wood-Robinson, *ASE Guide to Secondary Science Education*, Hatfield, Herts: Association for Science Education, pp. 173–80.

Harlen, W. and Malcolm, H. (1999) *Setting and Streaming: A Research Review* (revised edn), Edinburgh: The Scottish Council for Research in Education.

Hart, S., Dixon, A., Drummond, M. J. and McIntyre, D. (2004) *Learning Without Limits*, Maidenhead: Open University Press.

Hearnshaw, H. (1994) Psychology and Displays in GIS. In H. Hearnshaw and D. J. Unwin (eds), *Visualization in Geographic Information Systems*, Chichester: Wiley, pp. 193–211.

Heller, K. A. (1996) The Nature and Development of Giftedness: A Longitudinal Study. In A. J. Cropley, and D. Dehn (eds) *Fostering the Growth of High Ability: European Perspectives*, Norwood, NJ: Ablex Publishing, pp. 41–56.

Heller, K. A. and Schofield, N. J. (2000) International Trends and Topics of Research on Giftedness and Talent. In K. A. Heller, F. J. Mönks, R. J. Sternberg and R. F. Subotnik (eds) (2000) *International Handbook of Research and Development of Giftedness and Talent* (2nd edn), Oxford: Elsevier Science, pp. 123–40.

Hennessy, S. (1993) 'Situated Cognition and Cognitive Apprenticeship: Implications for Classroom Learning', *Studies in Science Education*, 22, 1–41.

Hesse, M. (1966) *Models and Analogies in Science*, London: Sheen and Ward.

Hill, C. G. N. (1977) Gifted is as Gifted Does. Paper presented to the Second Annual General Meeting of the New Zealand Association for Gifted Children, Auckland, New Zealand, September.

Hirst, P. H. (1972) Liberal Education and the Nature of Knowledge. In R. F. Dearden, P. H. Hirst and R. S. Peters, *Education and the Development of Reason*, London: Routledge and Kegan Paul, pp. 391–414.

Hirst, P. H. and Peters, R. S. (1970) *The Logic of Education*, London: Routledge and Kegan Paul.

Hobson, J. (2002) *Critical Thinking Workshop*, Perth, Western Australia: Murdoch University.

Holcomb, E. L. (1996) *Asking the Right Questions: Tools and Techniques for Teamwork*, Thousand Oaks: Corwin Press.

Howley, C., Howley, A. and Pendarvis, E. (1995) *Out of Our Minds: Anti-Intellectualism and Talent Development in American Schooling*, New York: Teacher's College Press.

Hume, A. (2003) The National Certificate of Educational Achievement and Formative-Summative Tensions: Are They Resolvable? In R. K. Coll (ed.), *STERpapers*, Hamilton, New Zealand: Centre for Science and Technology Education Research, University of Waikato, pp. 68–92.

Hume, A. (2006) 'Through the Looking Glass: An Investigation into the Nature of the Student-Experienced Curriculum for the National Certificate of Educational Achievement (NCEA) Science Achievement Standard 1.1: Carrying Out a Practical Investigation with Direction', unpublished Doctor of Education thesis, School of Education, University of Waikato, Hamilton, New Zealand.

Hume, A. and Coll, R. K. (2005) The Impact of a New Assessment Regime on Science Learning. Paper presented at the 34th Annual Conference of the Australasian Science Education Research Association, Hamilton, New Zealand, July.

Jenkins, E. and Nelson, N. (2005) 'Important but Not for Me: Students' Attitudes towards Secondary School Science in England', *Research in Science and Technological Education*, 23 (1), 41–57.

Johnstone, A. H. (1993) Introduction. In C. Wood and R. Sleet (eds), *Creative Problem Solving in Chemistry*, London: The Royal Society of Chemistry.

Johnstone, A. H. and Al-Naeme, F. F. (1991) 'Room for Scientific Thought', *International Journal of Science Education*, 13 (2), 187–92.

Justi, R. and Gilbert, J. K. (2002) 'Modelling, Teachers' Views on the Nature of Modelling, and Implications for the Education of Modelers', *International Journal of Science Education*, 24 (4), 369–87.

Keen, D. (2000) The Rainbow Connection: Giftedness in Multiethnic Settings, *Proceedings of the Now is the Future, the Gifted Student in Today's Secondary School Conference*, Auckland, 3–5 October.

Keen, D. (2001) Talent in the New Millennium. Research Study, 2001–2002, into gifted education in the Bay of Plenty, Otago and Southland Regions of New Zealand Report on Year One of the Programme, November 2001. Paper presented at the AARE Conference Crossing Borders: New Frontiers for Educational Research, Fremantle, Australia, 2–6 December.

Keller, E. F. (1983) *A Feeling for the Organism: The Life and Work of Barbara McClintock*, New York: W. H. Freeman.

Kellmer-Pringle, M. (1970) *Able Misfits: the Educational and Behavioural Difficulties of Intelligent Children*, London: Longman.

KS3NS (2003a) *Science for Gifted Pupils, Module 4: Science for Gifted Pupils*, Key Stage 3 National Strategy, London: Department for Education and Skills, online at www.standards.dfes.gov.uk/keystage3/respub/agt, accessed 22 August 2006.

KS3NS (2003b) *Strengthening Teaching and Learning of Energy in Key Stage 3 Science 2003*, Key Stage 3 National Strategy, London: Department for Education and Skills.

Kind, V. (2004) *Contemporary Chemistry for Schools and Colleges*, London: Royal Society of Chemistry.

Kind, V. and Taber, K. S (2005) *Science: Teaching School Subjects 11–19*, London: Routledge.

Kloss, R. J. (1988) 'Toward Asking the Right Questions: The Beautiful, the Pretty, and the Big Messy Ones', *Clearing House*, 61 (6), 245–8.

Kramer, D. A. (1983) 'Post-Formal Operations? A Need for Further Conceptualization', *Human Development*, 26, 1983, 91–105.

Krathwohl, D. R. (2002) 'A Revision of Bloom's Taxonomy: An Overview', *Theory Into Practice*, Autumn, online at www.findarticles.com, accessed 24 February 2004.

Lakoff, G. and Johnson, M. (1980) *Metaphors We Live By*, Chicago: University of Chicago Press.

Lange, D. (1988) *Tomorrow's School's: The Reform of Education Administration in New Zealand*, Wellington, New Zealand: Government Printer.

Lee-Corbin, H. and Denicolo, P (1998) *Recognising and Supporting Able Pupils in Primary Schools*, London: David Fulton.

Levinson, R. and Turner, S. (2001) *Valuable Lessons*, London: The Wellcome Trust.

McAlpine, D. (1996a) Who are the Gifted and Talented? Conceptions and Definitions. In D. McAlpine and R. Moltzen (eds), *Gifted and Talented: New Zealand Perspectives*, Palmerston North, New Zealand: ERDC Press, Massey University, pp. 23–41.

McAlpine, D. (1996b) The Identification of Children with Special Abilities. In D. McAlpine and R. Moltzen (eds), *Gifted and Talented: New Zealand Perspectives*, Palmerston North, New Zealand: ERDC Press, Massey University, pp. 23–41.

McAlpine, D. (2004) What Do We Mean by Gifted and Talented? Concepts and Definitions. In D. McAlpine and R. Moltzen (eds) *Gifted and Talented: New Zealand Perspectives* (2nd edn), Palmerston North, New Zealand: ERDC Press, Massey University, pp. 93–132.

McAlpine, D. and R. Moltzen (eds) (1996) *Gifted and Talented: New Zealand Perspectives*, Palmerston North, New Zealand: ERDC Press, Massey University.

McGee, C. (1997) *Teachers and Curriculum-Decision-Making*, Palmerston North, New Zealand: Dunmore.

McGill, I. and Brockbank, A. (2004) *The Action Learning Handbook*, London: RoutledgeFalmer.

McGuinness, C. (1999) *From Thinking Skills to Thinking Classrooms*, DfEE Brief 115, online at www.sustainablethinkingclassrooms.qub.ac.uk/DFEE_Brief_115.pdf, accessed 10 August 2006.

McLaughlin, T. (2003) Teaching Controversial Issues in Citizenship Education. In A. Lockyer, B. Crick and J. Annette, *Education for Democratic Citizenship: Issues of Theory and Practice*, Aldershot: Ashgate, pp.149–60.

Macleod, R. (2004) Educational Provision: Secondary Schools. In D. McAlpine and R. Moltzen (eds), *Gifted and Talented: New Zealand Perspectives* (2nd edn), Palmerston North, New Zealand: ERDC Press, Massey University, pp. 239–62.

Maiorana, V. P. (1992) *Critical Thinking Across the Curriculum: Building the Analytical Classroom*. Bloomington, IN: ERIC Clearinghouse on Reading and Communication Skills.

Mallick, J. and Watts, D. M. (in preparation) A Critical Action Research Approach to Drug Education for Parents and Young People.

Maltby, F. (1984) *Gifted Children and Teachers in the Primary School 5–12*, Lewes, East Sussex: The Falmer Press.

Marchbad-Ad, G. and Sokolove, P. (2000) 'Can Undergraduate Biology Students Learn to Ask Higher Level Questions?', *Journal of Research in Science Teaching*, 37 (8), 854–70.

Marland, E. (1987) *Gifted and Talented Children: A Bibliography of the New Zealand Documentation*, Wellington, New Zealand: New Zealand Council for Educational Research.

Marris, M. (1984) Gifted Children: A Family Matter. Paper presented to the Eight Annual General Meeting of the New Zealand Association for Gifted Children, Auckland, New Zealand, October.

Marton, F., Fensham, P. and Chailkin, S. (1994) 'A Nobel's Eye View of Scientific Intuition: Discussions with the Nobel Prize-Winners in Physics, Chemistry, Medicine (1970–1986)', *International Journal of Science Education*, 16 (4), 457–73.

Matthews, B. (2006) *Engaging Education: Developing Emotional Literacy, Equity and Co-Education*, Milton Keynes: Open University Press.

Matthews, M. (1994) *Science Teaching: The Role of History and Philosophy of Science*, New York: Routledge.

Matthews, M. R. (1995) *Challenging New Zealand Science Education*, Palmerston North, New Zealand: Dunmore.

Mbajiorgu, N. and Reid, N. (2006) *Report of a Literature Search: Factors Influencing Curriculum Development in Chemistry*, Glasgow: Centre for Science Education, University of Glasgow.

Millar, R. (2003) Teaching about Energy. In *Strengthening Teaching and Learning of Energy in Key Stage 3 Science*, additional support pack, Key Stage 3 National Strategy, London: Department for Education and Skills, pp.101–19.

Millar, R. and Osborne, J. (2000) *Beyond 2000: Science Education for the Future* London: School of Education, King's College London.

Milne, L. (2004a) Put Your Finger on Your Nose if You Are Proud of Your Technology! Technology in the New Entrant Classroom. In R. K. Coll (ed.), *STERpapers*, Hamilton, New Zealand: Centre for Science and Technology Education Research, University of Waikato, pp. 95–109.

Milne, L. (2004b) Where Have All the Fish Gone? In R. K. Coll (ed.), *STERpapers*, Hamilton, New Zealand: Centre for Science and Technology Education Research, University of Waikato, pp. 111–27.

Mitchell, D. and Mitchell, S. (1985) *Out of the Shadows: A Chronicle of Significant Events in the Development of Schooling for Exceptional Children and Young Persons in New Zealand 1850–1983*, Wellington, New Zealand: Department of Education.

Mitchell, D. R. and Drewery, W. J. (1985) *Exceptional Children and Young People in New Zealand: A Bibliography of Material Published between 1972–1983*, Hamilton, New Zealand: University of Waikato.

Mitchell, D. and Singh, N. (1987) *Exceptional Children in New Zealand*, Palmerston North, New Zealand: Dunmore.

Mitchell, D., McGee, C., Moltzen, R. and Oliver, D. (1993) *Hear Our Voices: Final Report of Monitoring Tomorrow's Schools Research Project*, Wellington, New Zealand: Ministry of Education.

MoE (1993a) *National Education Guidelines*, Ministry of Education, Wellington, New Zealand: Government Printer.

MoE (1993b) *Science in the National Curriculum*, Ministry of Education, Wellington, New Zealand: Learning Media.

MoE (1993c) *The New Zealand Curriculum Framework*, Ministry of Education, Wellington, New Zealand: Government Printer.

MoE (1996a) *Biology in the New Zealand Curriculum*, Ministry of Education, Wellington, New Zealand: Learning Media.

MoE (1996b) *Chemistry in the New Zealand Curriculum*, Ministry of Education, Wellington, New Zealand: Learning Media.

MoE (1996c) *Physics in the New Zealand Curriculum*, Ministry of Education, Wellington, New Zealand: Learning Media.

MoE (1996d) *Technology in the New Zealand Curriculum*, Ministry of Education, Wellington, New Zealand: Learning Media.

MoE (2000) *Gifted and Talented Students: Meeting Their Needs in New Zealand Schools*, Ministry of Education, Wellington, New Zealand: Learning Media.

MoE (2002) *Curriculum Stocktake Report to Minister of Education*, September 2002. Wellington, New Zealand: Ministry of Education.

MoE (2003) *Learning for Tomorrow's World Programme for International Student Assessment*, New Zealand summary report, Wellington, New Zealand: Ministry of Education.

MoE (2004a) *Mathematics and Science Achievement in New Zealand. First Results from the Trends in Mathematics and Science Study 2002–2003 (TIMSS) for Year 5 Students*, Wellington, New Zealand: Ministry of Education.

MoE (2004b) *Mathematics and Science Achievement in New Zealand. First Results from the Trends in Mathematics and Science Study 2002–2003 (TIMSS) for Year 9 Students*. Wellington, New Zealand: Wellington, New Zealand: Ministry of Education.

Moltzen, R. (1992a) 'Gifted Education Post-Picot: Have the Issues Changed?' *Gifted Children – Their Future: Our Challenge*, 17 (2), 3–10.

Moltzen, R. (1992b) The Impact of Changes in Educational Administration in New Zealand on Gifted and Talented Children. In M. McCann and S. Bailey (eds),

Proceedings of the Fourth National Conference for Education of Gifted and Talented Children, Melbourne, September 1992, pp. 174–80.

Moltzen, R. (1995) Students with Special Abilities. In D. Fraser, R. Moltzen and K. Ryba (eds), *Learners with Special Needs in Aoteoroa/New Zealand,* Palmerston North, New Zealand: Dunmore, pp. 267–306.

Moltzen, R. (1996a) Characteristics of Gifted Children. In D. McAlpine and R. Moltzen (eds), *Gifted and Talented: New Zealand Perspectives,* Palmerston North, New Zealand: ERDC Press, Massey University, pp. 43–61.

Moltzen, R. (1996b) Historical Perspectives. In D. McAlpine and R. Moltzen (eds), *Gifted and Talented: New Zealand Perspectives,* Palmerston North, New Zealand: ERDC Press, Massey University, pp. 43–61.

Moltzen, R. (1996c) Maximising the Potential of the Gifted Child in the Regular Classroom: A Professional Development Issue. In J. Chand, R. Li and J. Sprintes (eds), *Proceedings of the Eleventh World Conference of Gifted and Talented Children,* Hong Kong: University of Hong Kong.

Moltzen, R. (1998) *Taking Gifted Education into the Future,* Auckland: New Zealand Association for Gifted Children.

Moltzen, R. (2000a) 'Gifted Education in New Zealand towards 2000: Surviving or Thriving?' *Gifted Children – Their Future: Our Challenge,* 18 (1), 5–10.

Moltzen, R. (2000b) Students with Special Abilities. In D. Fraser, R. Moltzen and K. Ryba (eds), *Learners with Special Needs in Aotearoa New Zealand* (2nd edn), Palmerston North, New Zealand: Dunmore, pp. 333–76.

Moltzen, R. (2004) Historical Perspectives. In D. McAlpine and R. Moltzen (eds), *Gifted and Talented: New Zealand Perspectives,* Palmerston North, New Zealand: ERDC Press, Massey University, pp. 1–21.

Moltzen, R. and Easter, A. (2000) *Gifted Education. Module 1, Definitions of Giftedness: Professional Development for Selected Waikato Schools,* Hamilton, New Zealand: School of Education, University of Waikato.

Moltzen, R., Mitchell, D. and Middleton, S. (1992) *Children with Special Needs,* Hamilton, New Zealand: University of Waikato.

Moltzen, R., Riley, T. and McAlpine, D. (2001a) 'Gifted Education Under Construction: A Blueprint for New Zealand', *APEX The New Zealand Journal of Gifted Education,* 13 (1), 5–15.

Moltzen, R., Riley, T. and McAlpine, D. (2001b) 'Guiding Our Gifted and Talented Students: One Nation's Story', *Gifted and Talented International,* 16 (1), 57–68.

Montgomery, D. (ed.) (2000) *Able Underachievers,* London: Whurr Publishers.

Montgomery, D. (2003a) 'Handwriting Difficulties in the Gifted and Talented', *Handwriting Today,* 2, Summer 2003, online at www.warwick.ac.uk/gifted/research/.

Montgomery, D. (ed.) (2003b) *Gifted and Talented Children with Special Educational Needs,* London: NACE/Fulton.

Moon, S. E. (2004) *Social/Emotional Issues, Underachievment and Counseling of Gifted and Talented Students,* Thousand Oaks, CA: Corwin Press.

Moore, J. and Gilbert, J. K. (1998) *Improving Standards in Hampshire and Southampton Schools for Pupils in KS3: Interim Report for 1997/8,* Fleet, Hants: Hampshire Inspection and Advisory Service.

Morelock, M. and Feldman, D. H. (2000) Prodigies, Savants and Williams Syndrome: Windows into Talent and Cognition. In K. A. Heller, F. J. Monks, R. J. Sternberg, and R. F. Subotnik (eds), *International Handbook of Research and Development of Giftedness and Talent*, Oxford: Elsevier Science, pp. 227–241.

Mortimer, E. and Scott, P. (2003) *Meaning Making in Secondary Science Classrooms*, Maidenhead: Open University Press.

Moseley, D., Baumfield, V., Higgins, S., Lin, K., Miller, J., Newton, D., Robson, J. Elliott, J. and Gregson, M. (2004) *Thinking Skill Frameworks for Post-16 Learners: an Evaluation*, Guildford: Learning and Skills Research Centre.

Murray, I. and Reiss, M. J. (2005) 'The Student Review of the Science Curriculum', *School Science Review*, 87 (318), 83–93.

NAS (1996) *National Science Education Standards*, National Academy of Sciences: Washington DC.

NDE (1997) Promising Curriculum and Instructional Practices for High-Ability Learners Manual, Nebraska Department of Education, online at www.nde.state. ne.us.

Newberry, M., Gilbert, J. and Hardcastle, D. (2005) 'Visualising Progression through the Science Curiculum in order to Raise Standards', *School Science Review*, 86 (316), 87–96.

NFER (2006) Non-Verbal Reasoning, National Foundation for Educational Research, www.nfer-nelson.co.uk/catalogue, accessed 27 March 2006.

Nieswandt, M. (2005) Attitudes to Science: A Review of the Field. In S. Alsop (ed.), *Beyond Cartesian Dualism: Encountering Affect in the Teaching and Learning of Science*, Dordrecht: Kluwer Academic Publishers, pp. 41–52

Nobel (2005) Interviews with Laureates in Chemistry, online at www.nobelprize.org accessed 27 March 2006.

O'Brian, P. (1998) *Teaching Scientifically Able Pupils in the Secondary School*, Oxford: National Association for Able Children in Education.

Ogborn, J. and Whitehouse, M. (2000) *Advancing Physics AS*, London: Institute of Physics.

O'Halloran, K. H., McIvor, D. G., Robinson, W. R. and Parkyn, G. W. (1955) *The Education of the Child with Superior Intelligence: Final Report*, Wellington, New Zealand: Department of Education.

OME (2004) *The Individual Education Plan (IEP)*, Toronto: Ontario Ministry of Education.

Osborne, J. and Collins, S. (2000) *Pupils' and Parents' Views of the School Science Curriculum*, London: Wellcome Trust and King's College.

Osborne, J., Simon, S. and Collins, S. (2003) 'Attitudes towards Science: a Review of the Literature and its Implications', *International Journal of Science Education*, 25 (9), 1049–79.

Pais, A. (1982) *'Subtle is the Lord. . .': The Science and the Life of Albert Einstein*, Oxford: Oxford University Press.

Paul, R. W. (1993) *Critical Thinking – What Every Person Needs to Survive in a Rapidly Changing World* (3rd edn) J. Willsen and A. J. A. Binker (eds), Santa Rosa, CA: Foundation for Critical Thinking.

Paul, R. W. and Elder, L. (2006) *Critical Thinking: Tools for Taking Charge of Your Learning and Your Life* (2nd edn), Upper Saddle River, NJ: Pearson/Prentice Hall.

Pearsall, J. (ed.) (1999) *The Concise Oxford Dictionary*, Oxford: Oxford University Press.

Pearson, G. (1999) *Strategy in Action: Strategic Understanding and Practice*, Harlow: Pearson Education.

Pedrosa de Jesus, M. H. (1991) 'An Investigation of Pupils' Questions in Science Teaching', unpublished Ph.D. thesis, University of East Anglia.

Pedrosa de Jesus, M. H., Almeida, P. and Watts, D. M. (2004) 'Questioning Styles and Students' Learning: Four Case Studies', *Educational Psychology*, 24 (4), 531–48.

Pedrosa de Jesus, H., Almeida, P. and Watts, D. M. (2005) 'Orchestrating Learning and Teaching in Inter-Disciplinary Chemistry', *Canadian Journal for Science, Technology and Mathematics Education*, 1 (5), 71–84.

Pendarvis, E. and Howley, A. (1995) Effects of Poverty, Sexism and Racism on Intellect. In C. Howley, A. Howley and E. Pendarvis, *Out of Our Minds: Anti-Intellectualism and Talent Development in American Schooling*, New York: Teacher's College Press.

Piaget, J. (1972) *The Principles of Genetic Epistemology*, London: Routledge and Kegan Paul (first published in French, 1970).

Pickens, K., Reid, N., McAlpine, D., Marland, E. (1992) *Gifted and Talented Children: A Bibliography of the New Zealand Documentation 1992 Update*, Wellington, New Zealand: New Zealand Council for Educational Research.

Picot, B. (1988) *Administering for Excellence: Effective Administration in Education*, Wellington, New Zealand: Taskforce to Review Education Administration.

Pizzini, E. L. and Shepardson, D. P. (1991) 'Student Questioning in the Presence of the Teacher during Problem Solving in Science', *School Science and Mathematics*, 91 (8), 348–52.

Pribyl, J. R. and Bodner, G. M. (1987) 'Spatial Ability and its Role in Organic Chemistry; A Study of Four Organic Courses', *Journal of Research in Science Teaching*, 24 (3), 229–40.

Pyryt, M. C. (2000) Talent Development in Science and Technology. In K. A. Heller, F. J. Mönks, R. J. Sternberg and R. F. Subotnik (eds) *International Handbook of Research and Development of Giftedness and Talent* (2nd edn), Oxford: Elsevier Science, pp. 427–37.

QCA (2002) *Changes to Assessment 2003: Guidance for Teachers of KS3 Science*, London: Qualifications and Curriculum Authority.

QCA (2003) *Key Stage 3 Sample Scheme*, London: Qualifications and Curriculum Authority.

QCA (2005) *Science: Changes to the Curriculum from 2006 for Key Stage 4*, London: Qualifications and Curriculum Authority.

QCA (2006) Identifying Gifted Pupils, online at www.nc.uk.net/gt/science/index.htm, accessed 22 March 2006.

QCA (undated) *Summary of the Key Findings from the 2001–2002 National Curriculum (NC) and Post-16 Science Monitoring Exercise*, London: Qualification and Curriculum Authority.

Ratcliffe, M., Harris, R. and McWhirter, J. (2004) 'Teaching Ethical Aspects of Science – Is Cross-Curricular Collaboration the Answer?', *School Science Review*, 86 (315), 39–44.

Reid, N. A. (2004) Evaluation of Programmes. In D. McAlpine and R. Moltzen (eds) *Gifted and Talented: New Zealand Perspectives* (2nd edn), Palmerston North, New Zealand: ERDC Press, Massey University, pp. 425–39.

Reisberg, D. (1997) *Cognition*, New York: Norton.

Renzulli, J. S. (2004) A General Theory for the Development of Creative Productivity through the Pursuit of Ideal Acts of Learning. In VanTassel-Baska, J. (ed.) *Curriculum for Gifted and Talented Students*, Thousand Oaks, CA: Corwin Press, pp. 65–91.

Renzulli, J. M. and Reis, S. M. (2000) The Schoolwide Enrichment Model. In K. A. Heller, F. J. Mönks, R. J. Sternberg and R. F. Subotnik (eds), *International Handbook of Research and Development of Giftedness and Talent* (2nd edn), Oxford: Elsevier Science, pp. 367–81.

Rhee Bonney, C., Kempler, T. M., Pintrich, P. R., Zusho, A. and Coppola, B. P. (2005) Student Learning in Science Classrooms: What Role Does Motivation Play? In S. Alsop (ed.) *Beyond Cartesian Dualism: Encountering Affect in the Teaching and Learning of Science*, Dordrecht: Springer, pp. 83–97.

Riley, T. (2004) Curriculum Models: The Framework for Gifted and Talented Education. In D. McAlpine and R. Moltzen (eds), *Gifted and Talented: New Zealand Perspectives* (2nd edn), Palmerston North, New Zealand: ERDC Press, Massey University, pp. 309–43.

Riley, T., Bevan-Brown, J., Bicknell, B., Carroll-Lind, J. and Kearney, A. (2004) *The Extent, Nature and Effectiveness of Planned Approaches in New Zealand Schools for Providing for Gifted and Talented Students*, Wellington, New Zealand: Ministry of Education.

Rogoff, B. (1990) *Apprenticeship in Thinking: Cognitive Development in Social Context*, New York: Oxford University Press.

Rosenthal, R. and Jacobson, L. (1970) Teachers' Expectations. In L. Hudson (ed.) *The Ecology of Human Intelligence*, Harmondsworth: Penguin, pp. 177–81.

Rosiek, J. (2003) 'Emotional Scaffolding: An Exploration of Teacher Knowledge at the Intersection of Student Emotion and the Subject Matter', *Journal of Teacher Education*, 54 (5), 399–412.

RSNZ (2005) CREST (Creativity in Science and Technology), Royal Society of New Zealand, online at www.rsnz.org/education/crest/, accessed 31 January 2005.

Rutherford, F. and Ahlgren, A. (1990) *Science for All Americans*, New York: Oxford University Press.

Rutland, M. (2005) 'Teaching for Creativity in Secondary School Technology', unpublished Ph.D. thesis, Roehampton University.

Sacks, O. (1995) *An Anthropologist on Mars*, London: Picador.

Schreiner, C. and Sjøberg, S. (2004) *Sowing the Seeds of ROSE: Background, Rationale, Questionnaire Development and Data Collection for ROSE (The Relevance of Science Education) – a Comparative Study of Students' Views of Science and Science Education*, Acta Didactica 4/2004, Oslo: Department of Teacher Education and School Development, University of Oslo.

Schultz, R. (2002) 'Understanding Giftedness and Underachievement: At the Edge of Possibility', *Gifted Child Quarterly*, 46 (3), 193-207.

Schunk, D. (1989) 'Self-Efficacy and Achievement Indicators', *Educational Psychology Research*, 57, 149–74.

Scott, P., Mortimer, E. and Aguiar, O. (2006) 'The Tension between Authoritative and Dialogic Discourse: a Fundamental Characteristic of Meaning Making Interactions in High School Science Lessons', *Science Education*, 90 (4), 605–31.

SEP (2004) *Teaching Ideas and Evidence in Science at Key Stage 3*, London: Science Enhancement Programme.

Sharron, H. (1987) *Changing Children's Minds*, London: Souvenir Press.

Shayer, M. and Adey, P. (1981) *Towards a Science of Science Teaching: Cognitive Development and Curriculum Demand*, Oxford: Heinemann Educational Books.

Shore, B. M. and Dover, A. C. (2004) Metacognition, Intelligence and Giftedness. In R. J. Sternberg, *Definitions and Conceptions of Giftedness*, Thousand Oaks, CA: Corwin Press, pp. 39–45.

Shuker, R. (1990). 'Two Cheers for Tomorrow's Schools: An Analysis of Recent Developments in New Zealand School System', *SITES*, 20, 69–79.

Shulman, L. (1987) 'Knowledge and Teaching: Foundations of the New Reforms', *Harvard Educational Review*, 57 (1), 1–22.

Silverman, L. K. (1986) What Happens to the Gifted Girl? In C. J. Maker (ed.), *Current Issues in Gifted Education, Vol. 1: Defensible Programs for the Gifted*, Rockville, MD: Aspen.

Silverman, L. K. (1989) 'Invisible Gifts, Invisible Handicaps', *Roeper Review*, 22 (1), 37–42.

Simon, S. A. and Jones, A. T. (1992) *Open Work in Science: A Review of Existing Practice*, London: Centre for Educational Studies, King's College, University of London.

Sjoberg, S. (2002) *Science for the Children?*, University of Oslo: Department of Teacher Education and School Development.

Slack, K. (2003) 'Whose Aspirations Are They Anyway?', *International Journal of Inclusive Education*, 7 (4), 325–35.

Stepanek, J. (1999) *Meeting the Needs of Gifted Students: Differentiating Mathematics and Science Instruction*, Portland, OR: Northwest Regional Educational Laboratory.

Sternberg, R. J. (1993) The Concept of 'Giftedness': A Pentagonal Implicit Theory. In *The Origins and Development of High Ability*, CIBA Foundation Symposia Series, Chichester: John Wiley and Sons, pp. 5–21.

Sternberg, R. J. (2001) 'Giftedness as Developing Expertise: A Theory of the Interface between High Abilities and Achieved Excellence', *High Ability Studies*, 12 (2), 159–79.

Sternberg, R. J., Forsythe, G. B., Hedlund, J., Horvath, J. A., Wagner, R. K., Williams, W. M., Snook, S. A. and Grigorenko, E. L. (2000) *Practical Intelligence in Everyday Life*, Cambridge: Cambridge University Press.

Strand, S. (2003) *Getting the Best from CAT: A Practical Guide for Secondary Schools*, London: nferNelson.

Sutherland, P. (1992) *Cognitive Development Today: Piaget and His Critics*, London: Paul Chapman Publishing.

Susskind, E. (1969) The Role of Question Asking in the Elementary School Classroom. In F. Kaplan and S. B. Sarason (eds), *The Psycho-Educational Clinic*, New Haven, CT: Yale University Press, pp. 132–50.

Taber, K. S. (2001) Teacher – Teach Thyself, and Then Teach Others by Your Example: Some 'Simple Truths' about Teaching and Learning, online at www.leeds.ac.uk/educol/documents/00001812.htm.

Taber, K. S. (2002) *Chemical Misconceptions – Prevention, Diagnosis and Cure, Volume 1: Theoretical Background*, London: Royal Society of Chemistry.

Taber, K. S. (2006a) 'Teaching about Ideas and Evidence in Science – towards a Genuinely Broad and Balanced "Science for All"', *School Science Review*, June 2006, 87 (321), 26–8.

Taber, K. S. (2006b) 'Towards a Curricular Model of the Nature of Science', *Science and Education*, published online first.

Taber, K. S. (2007) *Enriching School Science for the Gifted Learner*, London: Science Enhancement Programme.

Taber, K. S., de Trafford, T. and Quail, T. (2006) 'Conceptual Resources for Constructing the Concepts of Electricity: the Role of Models, Analogies and Imagination', *Physics Education*, 41, 155–60.

Taber, K. S. and Riga, F. (2006) 'Lessons from the ASCEND Project: Able Pupils' Responses to an Enrichment Programme Exploring the Nature of Science', *School Science Review*, June 2006, 87 (321), 97–106.

Taylor, I., Barker, M. and Jones, A. (2003) 'Promoting Mental Model Building in Astronomy', *International Journal of Science Education*, 25 (10), 1205–25.

Terraiser, J. C. (1985) Dyssynchrony – Uneven Development. In J. Freedman (ed.), *The Psychology of Gifted Children*, New York: Wiley, pp. 265–74.

Thompson, K.G. (1984) *The Gifted and Talented: Provisions and Programmes*, Auckland: New Zealand Association for Gifted Children.

Tolan, S. (1996) Is it a Cheetah?, online at www.stephanietolan.com/is_it_a_cheetah.htm, accessed May 2006.

Tomlinson, C. A. (2005) 'Quality Curriculum and Instruction for Highly Able Students', *Theory into Practice*, 44 (2), 160–6.

Treagust, D. F., Harrison, A. G., and Venville, G. (1998) 'Teaching Science Effectively with Analogies: An Approach for Pre-Service and In-Service Teacher Education', *Journal of Science Teacher Education*, 9 (1), 85–101.

TTA (2002) *Qualifying to Teach Handbook of Guidance*, London: Teacher Training Agency.

Tuckey, H. and Selvaratnam, M. (1993) 'Studies Involving Three-Dimensional Visualisation Skills in Chemistry', *Studies in Science Education*, 21, 99–121.

Tufte, E. R. (2001) *The Visual Display of Quantitative Information* (2nd edn), Cheshire, CT: Graphics Press.

UKTS (2003) *UKTS Newsletter: Thalassaemia Matters*, 94, UK Thalassaemia Society, online at www.ukts.org/pages/newsletter.htm, accessed 31 August 2006.

UYSEG (2000) *Salters Horners Advanced Physics AS Student Book*, University of York Science Education Group, Oxford: Heinemann.

UYSEG (2001) *Salters GCSE Science Year 10 Student Book*, University of York Science Education Group, Oxford: Heinemann.

UYSEG (2005) *Salters-Nuffield Advanced Biology AS Student Book*, University of York Science Education Group, Oxford: Heinemann.

VanTassel-Baska, J. (1986) 'Effective Curriculum and Instructional Models for Talented Students', *Gifted Child Quarterly*, 30, 164–9.

VanTassel-Baska, J. (1998) Planning Science Programs for High-Ability Learners, ERIC EC Digest #E546, ERIC Clearinghouse on Disabilities and Gifted Education November 1998, online at http://eric.hoagiesgifted.org, accessed 8 September 2006.

VanTassel-Baska, J. (2003) Implementing Innovative Curricular and Instructional Practices in Classrooms and Schools. In J. VanTassel-Baska and C. Little (eds) *Content-Based Curriculum for High-Ability Learners*, Waco, TX: Prufrock Press, pp. 355–75.

Vygotsky, L. S. (1962) *Thought and Language*, Cambridge, MA: MIT Press.

Vygotsky, L. S. (1988) *Thought and Language* (3rd edn), London: MIT Press.

Vygotsky, L. S. (1978) *Mind in Society: The Development of Higher Psychological Processes*, Cambridge, MA: Harvard University Press.

Wallace, B. (2000) *Teaching the Very Able Child,* London: NACE/Fulton.

Walters, P. (1991) *Why Help the Gifted?* Auckland: New Zealand Association for Gifted Children.

Watts, D. M. (2004a) 'The Orchestration of Teaching and Learning Methods in Science Education', *Canadian Journal for Science Mathematics and Technology Education,* 3 (4), 25–39.

Watts, D. M. (2004b) Technological Access towards Social Inclusion: Some Developments in Science Education in the UK. Paper presented to the UNESCO International Seminar 'Quality Science for All', Brasilia, Brazil, 29 Nov–1 Dec.

Watts, D. M. and Alsop, S. J. (1997) 'A Feeling for Learning: Modeling Affective Learning in School Science', *The Curriculum Journal,* 8 (3), 351–6.

Watts, D. M., Alsop S. J., Gould, G. F. and Walsh, A. (1997) 'Prompting Teachers' Constructive Reflection: Pupils' Questions as Critical Incidents', *International Journal of Science Education,* 19 (9), 1 025–37.

Watts, D. M., Gould, G. and Alsop, S. (1997) 'Questions of Understanding: Categorising Pupils' Questions in Science', *School Science Review,* 78 (286), 57–63.

Watts, M. and Taber, K. S. (1996) 'An Explanatory Gestalt of Essence: Students' Conceptions of the "Natural" in Physical Phenomena', *International Journal of Science Education,* 18 (8), 939–54.

Wellington, J. and Osborne, J. (2001) *Language and Literacy in Science Education,* Buckingham: Open University Press.

Wells, G. (1999) Putting a Tool to Different Uses: A Re-evaluation of the IRF Sequence. In G. Wells *Dialogic Enquiry: Towards a Sociocultural Practice and Theory of Education,* Cambridge: Cambridge University Press.

White, L. (2000) 'Underachievement of Gifted Girls: Causes and Solutions, *Gifted Education International,* 14, 125–32.

Winner, E. (2002) *Gifted Children: Myths and Realities,* New York, Basic Books.

Winstanley, C. (2004) *Too Clever by Half: a Fair Deal for Gifted Children,* Stoke-on-Trent: Trentham Books.

Ziegler, A. and Heller, K. A.(2000) Changing Conceptions on Giftedness and Talent. Conceptions of Giftedness from a Meta-Theoretical Perspective. In K. A. Heller, F. J. Mönks, R. J. Sternberg and R. F. Subotnik (eds), *International Handbook of Research and Development of Giftedness and Talent* (2nd edn) Oxford: Elsevier Science, pp. 3–22.

Ziegler, A. and Raul, T. (2000) 'Myth and Reality: a Review of Empirical Studies on Giftedness', *High Ability Studies,* 11(2), 113–36.

Index